THE LOUISVILLE SLUGGER® ULTIMATE BOOK OF HITTING

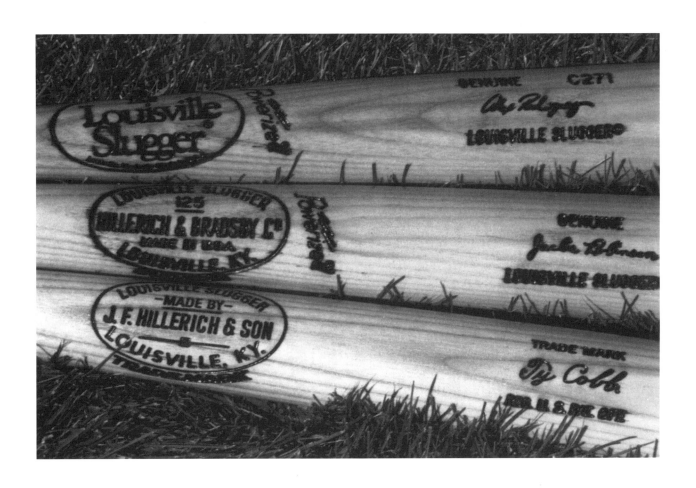

THE LOUISVILLE SLUGGER® ULTIMATE BOOK OF HITTING

John J. Monteleone
and
Mark Gola

Photography by Michael Plunkett

A MOUNTAIN LION BOOK

An Owl Book
Henry Holt and Company
New York

Henry Holt and Company, Inc.
Publishers since 1866
115 West 18th Street
New York, New York 10011

Henry Holt® is a registered trademark
of Henry Holt and Company, Inc.
Louisville Slugger® is a registered trademark of
Hillerich & Bradsby Co., Louisville, NY

Library of Congress Cataloging-in-Publication Data
Monteleone, John J.
    The Louisville slugger ultimate book of hitting / John Monteleone
and Mark Gola. — 1st ed.
        p. cm.
    Includes index
    ISBN 0-8050-4413-2 (alk. paper)
    1. Batting (Baseball) I. Gola, Mark. II. Title
GV869.M66 1997
796.357'26—dc21

                                                                96-46283

Henry Holt books are available for special promotions
and premiums. For details contact: Director, Special Markets.

First edition—1997

Printed in the United States of America
All First editions are printed on acid-free paper.

To two great dads, Andrew Monteleone, who once said as he watched and listened to the sounds of batting practice reverberate in Yankee Stadium, "Some people say the sweetest sounds in the world come from the strings of a Stradivarius, but for me, it's the sound of horsehide meeting ash," and Edward F. Gola, a true educator, for his guidance and wisdom both on and off the baseball diamond.

Contents

Acknowledgments

This book was conceived, developed, and produced by Mountain Lion, Inc., a book producer that specializes in instructional and general reference books in the sports category. A book producer brings together and relies on the special skills of many people. The following contributed to producing *The Louisville Slugger® Ultimate Book of Hitting* and to all of them we say, "Thanks."

—Mark Gola, researcher and writer, who collaborated on writing the text, conducted the many interviews of major league baseball players and coaches, and edited the photographs; and D. W. Crisfield, who assisted Mark.

—Michael Plunkett, photographer, who took all the high-speed, stop-action, and step-by-step instructional photographs.

—David Sobel, senior editor for Owl Books, who shepherded the project and made valuable suggestions for improving the text; Jonathan Landreth, assistant editor, who pinchhit for David when he was away scuba diving in some tropical clime; and Lucy Albanese, director of design at Henry Holt and Company, who supervised the design of the book and coordinated its manufacturing.

—Jean Atcheson, who copyedited the book; and Deborah Patton, indexer.

—Bill Williams and George Manning of Hillerich & Bradsby Co., who gave invaluable editorial assistance and enthusiastic support.

—Max Crandall, who designed the pages to make them easily accessible to the reader and Margaret Trejo of Trejo Production, who painstakingly built the pages of the book according to Max's vision.

—Joan Mohan of Mountain Lion, who typed the manuscript, and Randy Voorhees of Mountain Lion, who contributed the hitting records and batting facts found at the end of each chapter.

—Also: James "Andy" Anderson, curator, photography archives, Ekstrom Library, University of Louisville; Joanna Brunno, AP Wide World Photos; Ellen Pollack, Library of Congress; Bob Hertzel, sportswriter; Bob Broeg, sportswriter; John Blake, Texas Rangers; Jim Tredinich, Pittsburgh Pirates; Jim Schultz, Atlanta Braves; Dick Bresciani and B. J. Baker, Boston Red Sox; Heather Tilles, John Maroon, and Tim Bishop, Baltimore Orioles; Larry Shenk, Philadelphia Phillies; Dave Gallagher, former California Angel; Sonny Pittaro, Rider University baseball coach; Ron Polk, Mississippi State baseball coach; Gary Ward, Oklahoma State baseball coach; Tom Petroff, former Detroit Tigers minor league coordinator; Stan Davis, Hopewell Valley Regional High School baseball coach; Dr. Paul Bereman; Jeff Timperman; Jon Ireland; Alex McKnight; Michael Nocar; Kyle Donnelly, and Paulette Gola.

Foreword:
Little Things Rack Up Big Hits

I've always preached that doing all the little things in baseball will make you a better player at any level. Hitting is no exception. I pay attention to all the details that will make me a better hitter.

During January in the off-season, I will hit 50 balls a day off a batting tee—I concentrate on maintaining correct batting mechanics. Hitting off a batting tee is the best way to perfect your swing, the surest path to developing a consistent form and to learning to hit to all fields. In February, I will take regular batting practice, but hit all the pitches the other way, that is, to left field. I won't practice turning on a ball—that is pulling a ball to the right side—until I reach spring training in March. These are little things, but they keep my hitting mechanics solid and prevent me from falling into bad swing habits during the off-season and pre-season.

When I practice batting before a game, I don't just go into the batter's box and flail at each pitch. I work on a game approach. I imagine game situations—that is, runners in scoring positions—and practice hitting the pitches where they will advance or score the runner. When I simulate moving a runner from second base to third base, I'll pull a pitch to the right side. Next, I'll imagine a runner on third and try to score him with a fly ball or grounder to the right side. I will also concentrate on hitting several pitches to the opposite field and up the middle. This keeps my mechanics solid—no pulling out, no topped ground balls to the right side. Again, these are little things, but they pay off. And practicing them gives me the confidence to perform them in a game situation.

If I'm in a slump and I'm not hitting the ball sharply where it's pitched, I try to hit a line drive toward the shortstop. One little thing on which to concentrate, but focusing on this one thing clears my mind of other swing thoughts that might confuse me, and gets me back on track at the plate.

Bat preparation is another detail that I don't overlook. For example, I like the grips of my bat enhanced with a mix of pine tar and rosin. This ensures a tacky grip that will keep the bat from flying out of my hands.

A Louisville Slugger® C-263 model is my personal choice—the bat of my former Padres teammate Steve Garvey. One day in 1986 I picked up Garvey's bat by mistake, thinking it was mine, and it felt good. I liked it so much that I asked Louisville Slugger's designers if they could make me a dozen.

Again, it was a little detail, but Garvey's bat was 34 inches and 32 ounces. I liked the model and style—medium barrel and medium handle with good overall balance—but I needed one that was shorter and lighter. I knew my swing. To be able to inside-out the ball to left field, handle the inside pitch without getting jammed, I needed a bat I could handle and control completely. So I asked Louisville Slugger to make a C-263 model bat 32½ inches, 31 ounces. They did, and it's been my regular bat ever since.

Little things, but they lead to confidence and consistency. Those qualities are the payback from selecting the right bat. When you find a bat you trust, one you're really comfortable with, then you can concentrate totally on seeing and reacting to the ball.

Louisville Slugger was the first bat company to offer me a contract. So I'm pleased to be a part of *The Louisville Slugger® Ultimate Book of Hitting,* because it lays out all the those little things—and more—that I've been talking about. If you read it, study it, and then put to use the ideas it presents, I'm sure you will start hanging out frozen ropes with regularity.

A big league hitter needs not only to have a game plan but also a game face. He's making his living at the plate. In amateur ball, putting too much pressure on yourself while you're learning can be counterproductive. So keep the fun in your game. Keep it simple—see the ball, take a rip . . . connect.

One last little thing: Don't forget to touch all the bases during your home-run trot!

Tony Gwynn

Preface

A wise man once said, "Life is a journey, not a destination." And so for this writer, this book is but another step in a journey to discover and share with others the basic fundamentals of batting. As a professional minor league baseball player three decades ago, I experienced flawed batting instruction dispensed by well-meaning but ill-informed teachers. I saw first hand that the people who should know—that is, professional baseball's batting instructors—really knew and understood very little about the art and science of hitting. Not only that but they also had no definitive resource to consult. Not until 1970, when Ted Williams's classic book, *The Science of Hitting* was published, did anyone attempt to systematically document the principles of hitting.

The reality of the situation was that most batting information was passed down orally, often around the batting cages as players shared their anecdotal, always incomplete truths. And because of professional baseball's traditional aversion to formalized study, players trying to improve their batting skills ended up hoarding fool's gold along with 24-karat nuggets. The elusive tenets and batting secrets traded and passed among coaches and players (from all levels of the game) went uncrystallized, undocumented, unreported, and generally unpublished.

Through the years I have endeavored, whenever possible, to assist in bringing forth the knowledge of what happens when a batter swings at a pitched baseball. In 1980, I produced Charley Lau's *The Art of Hitting .300*. Lau was a great observer, a serious student of the swing, who studied hours and hours of videotape in order to develop his ideas. In 1989, I helped three-time American League batting champion Tony Oliva bring his book, *Hitting Like a Champ*, to market. In 1994, I assisted Rob Ellis and Mike Schmidt in developing their book, *The Mike Schmidt Study*, one of the most intelligent and cohesive discussions of hitting yet produced.

So *The Louisville Slugger® Ultimate Book of Hitting* is merely another step in this writer's learning and telling about the best ways to hit a baseball. The overriding goal has always been to meld together seemingly contradictory and conflicting theories or models of hitting such as the Ted Williams *rotational* model versus the Charley Lau *weight shift* model. Williams may argue vehemently that he never hit a ball utilizing any of Charley Lau's weight shift principles, but, of course, it just ain't so. (I've seen photographs of Ted's classic swing—ball soaring, back foot flying off the ground, weight planted totally on the front foot à la Lau *weight shift*.) And we all remember George Brett, Lau's most famous disciple, *rotating* on a Goose Gossage heater and rocketing it into the upper right field stands at Yankee Stadium.

The point here, however, is not to take sides, nor to bash one hitting guru and praise another, nor to overlook any contribution to the collection of hitting knowledge. Because if we are ever to *get it right*—to understand the art and science of hitting—there needs to be room for all. Just as Williams got a lot of hitting principles right, so did Lau. And so did many others along the way.

Because *The Louisville Slugger® Ultimate Book of Hitting* gathers and fits together the many pieces of the hitting puzzle (regardless of who initially discovered or correctly explained a hitting principle), it may not satisfy the reader looking for a new theory. But it will please the reader whose need is for a comprehensive and systematic presentation of hitting's basic principles along with easy-to-follow, step-by-step instruction.

In addition, our treatment presents batting insights from a resource largely heretofore untapped—the *Famous Sluggers Yearbooks* published by Hillerich & Bradsby Company from 1923 through 1978. These yearbooks, filled with hitting tips, batting practices, and personal experiences of baseball's greatest hitters, including Ty Cobb, Babe Ruth, Tris Speaker, Lou Gehrig, Joe DiMaggio, Harry Walker, Lefty O'Doul, Ted Williams, Stan Musial, Mickey Mantle, Al Kaline, Harmon Killebrew, Rod Carew, and Pete Rose, demonstrate that—even before videotape and stop-action photography were used to study hitting—players were able to put together bits of the hitting mosaic.

The following pages contain our synthesis of the thoughts of baseball's greatest hitters and batting coaches. Readers will learn the basics of hitting, such as getting started; taking a proper grip and stance; learning the strike zone and hitting zone; improving one's vision; defining one's role in the offense; dealing with the dreaded batting slump, and more. *The Louisville Slugger® Ultimate Book of Hitting* provides a succinct yet comprehensive discussion of the art and science of hitting a baseball, which unstintingly sustains its reputation in the world of sports as the single most difficult thing to do.

John J. Monteleone
November, 1996

Introduction

This book is for anyone who wants to learn about the art and science of hitting. It is divided so that by reading and studying the first three chapters and the special section for beginners, "Getting Started," the reader will discover the basics—the grip, stance, and swing—of hitting a baseball.

The remainder of the book deals with more advanced batting skills, such as vision, defining your role as a hitter, varying your approach to situations, and learning the strike zone and your personal hitting zone; the mental aspects of hitting, including dealing with slumps; and how to practice and train.

Sections of this book dealing with basic swing mechanics should be read, thought about, tried and practiced, and then reread. By returning to the text and photographs for further study, readers will begin to cultivate and eventually ingrain the motor skills necesary for mastering the art of hitting. And they will learn to discard bad hitting habits.

A special section, *The Physics of Hitting a Baseball*, discusses, among other issues of matter and motion, the effect that bat selection can have on batting performance. This discussion includes wood versus aluminum models, lighter versus heavier, and longer versus shorter. Just as high-speed photography has confirmed much of what old-timers reported through trial and error and their kinesthetic "feel" about the mechanics of the swing, scientific inquiry and testing have confirmed those bat performance characteristics that players have discovered through actual experience.

For example, players since the end of the "Dead Ball Era" (1919) have reported—and subsequent testing has confirmed—that bats with greater weight or mass produce longer hits. As Babe Ruth himself said, "In my first three years as a fielder [1920–22] I used bats 36 inches long and anywhere from 40 to 54 ounces in weight." The Babe's 54-ounce "beasts" produced 148 four-bagger "beauties" for his new team, the New York Yankees. *The Louisville Slugger® Ultimate Book of Hitting* includes its unique discussion of the physics of hitting a baseball because it is the authors' intention not only to describe the physical limits of performance but also to put into context the extraordinary feats of the game's great sluggers.

Readers are cautioned that not every individual who takes up the art of hitting will have a classic stance or pre-swing routine. Aspiring players may exhibit certain idiosyncratic movements, such as wrapping the barrel of the bat around the head or flapping a front elbow (like Hall of Famer Joe Morgan) while waiting for the pitch. As long as these distinct characteristics do not interfere with the basic stance and swing principles that govern a model swing, then there's no need to change them. Stan Musial peeked at the pitcher from a crouched stance. Joe DiMaggio batted from a wide stance with a short stride. Kirby Puckett kicked his front leg prior to launching his swing. Cal Ripken lays his bat on his rear shoulder before moving his hands and bat upward to the launch position. Despite these differing pre-swing characteristics—all deviations from the norm or model shown in this book—each of these players eventually launched the swing utilizing sound, basic swing mechanics. Coaches and parents coaching their children should concentrate on watching and correcting this aspect of the swing, not the pre-swing movements that serve to keep a batter comfortable and relaxed.

We cannot stress enough the importance of practicing correctly and practicing often. If you have purchased this book, then you must be interested in learning how to hit. You've taken the first step—learning the basics. But it is only a first step. Aspiring hitters must practice, practice, and practice some more. Thomas Edison once remarked that he attrributed his success to one percent inspiration and 99 percent perspiration. The formula for excelling at hitting a baseball is no different.

"ALL I WANT TO DO IS GIVE
THAT THING A RIDE . . . ANYWHERE."
— Babe Ruth

THE ULTIMATE CHALLENGE

1

"Hitting is the most difficult thing to do in sports."

— *Ted Williams*

In 1941, an impressionable, 23-year-old Red Sox player named Ted Williams took the baseball world by storm. In just his third major league season, he had batted .406 and was well on his way to a brilliant career that would grant him a spot in baseball's Hall of Fame. During that 1941 season, he made his goal clear. "All I want out of life," he said, "is that when I walk down the street folks will say, 'There goes the greatest hitter that ever lived.'"

Did he achieve it? Many would argue that he did. Others might throw out names like Ty Cobb, Hank Aaron, Lou Gehrig, or Pete Rose. Hitting a baseball is a such a complex and complicated skill that the debates can go on forever. Is a high home run total really better than a high average? What about number of hits? And, most importantly, who has the best method of hitting the ball?

Unfortunately, there is no right answer to that last question. There's no magic combination of stance, grip, stride, and swing that can turn a young hitter into a superstar. Every hitter has his own theory, and even some of the most outrageous ones work. Ty Cobb had a spread grip. Joe DiMaggio had a wide stance. Joe Morgan flapped his elbow. Kirby Puckett lifts his knee up. All of these players have quirks that go against conventional wisdom, yet all have been phenomenally successful. The secret of your success will be finding a style that works for you.

A short, compact swing has earned Tony Gwynn seven National League batting titles.

2

A lot of people say hitting a golf ball is the toughest thing to do, but a golf ball is stationary. I still can't hit one real well but at least you don't have to worry about a curve or slider.

— *Phil Rizzuto*

That's not to say that you should immediately go out and develop a funky swing. You have to start with a fundamentally sound base. Every single one of those hitters was building on some basic skills. If you're looking to improve as a hitter, you first need to make sure your fundamentals are correct. Only then can you tinker with that solid base to discover what sort of options and embellishments are most effective for you.

In this book the basics, and the theories behind them, will all be discussed. You will learn the difference between a weight shift and a rotational swing, when to use one instead of the other, and which is more appropriate for your hitting style and physical make up. The preferred grips and stances and how each of them affects your swing will be covered, as well as the launching position, the swing itself, and the follow-through. In addition to the physical aspects of the swing, the book will tell you how to learn the strike zone and find your hitting zone, how to discern the type, speed, and location of the pitch coming at you, and many other mental aspects of the game. Situational hitting, slumps, and practice techniques round out the book.

Comprehensive though it is, this book is still just a jumping-off point. Because it is so hard to be successful at the plate you must be dedicated to improving your skills. It takes knowledge, practice, and more practice—and even then, you're only going to succeed 30 percent of the time.

Hitting is certainly the most difficult thing I ever tried to do. That's one of the reasons I tried to play baseball. I enjoyed the challenge of hitting a baseball coming at you at 90 plus miles per hour with a round bat.

— *Michael Jordan*

So why is hitting a baseball so difficult? To begin with, there's no flat surface. You're hitting a round ball with a round bat. The opportunities for a mishit are quite large. You need a great deal of hand-eye coordination, balance, timing, and quickness before you can even think about the details. And while making contact with the ball is probably the most significant aspect of hitting, you also need to get your upper and lower body timed with your swing in such a way as to generate maximum power. When you finally throw in the decision-making process of when to swing and when not to, the question is basically answered.

But still there's more. You also have to consider the time factor. The entire process of hitting takes place in only four tenths of a second. And what about the fact that baseball is the only sport that allows the defense to have the ball first? You can't set it up on a tee like a golf ball or have a nicely placed leading pass as you do in soccer. Instead, the ball is thrown at you by a player whose sole aim is to deceive you. Even if you do manage to make contact, there are nine guys stationed out in the field who are doing their very best to field your hit. It's clear to see why the job of a hitter is by no means an easy one.

But that's what makes hitting great. By definition, every competitive athlete enjoys a challenge and there's none better than hitting a baseball. Once a player plants his feet in the batter's box, he has accepted the greatest individual challenge in all of sports.

Though baseball is a team sport, you're on your own in the box. There are no assists in hitting. Even though your entire team is depending on your success at the plate, what you accomplish or fail to accomplish sits squarely on your shoulders—another feature that separates baseball from other team sports. Even a quarterback in football, who is as much on display as a hitter is, can blame his blockers or receivers for a poor outing.

Fortunately, the standards of success in hitting are much lower than those of any other sport, or any other aspect of life for that matter. A .300 batting average is the mark of a good hitter. That means that seven times out of the ten that this good hitter is at the plate, he's going to make an out. A basketball player shooting 30 percent would be on the bench. So would a quarterback who only hit his receiver 30 percent of the time. A student in school wouldn't even come close to passing a class with such a percentage. It just proves how difficult hitting can be.

Yet although hitting is a process that can never be perfected, it can always be improved. No wonder it's been an obsession with players, coaches, and fans for more than a century and practiced and studied more than any other act in the history of sports. There's always the chance that someone will discover the ultimate way to hit. But even if the success rate stays at the lowly .300, there is nothing sweeter than that 30 percent of the time when you find the ball with the meat of the bat and connect for a hit.

You have a guy on the mound who might have four pitches working, eight other guys wearing gloves and very small lanes to hit the ball through. Fail seven out of ten times and you're a success. The standard is that the odds are stacked against you.

— *Wade Boggs*

Bernie Williams possesses all the tools a team in today's modern game looks for in a hitter. He can hit for power, average, has good running speed, and also hits from both sides of the plate.

Many major league switch-hitters have hit home runs from both sides of the plate in one game. During the 1995 season San Diego Padre slugger Ken Caminiti turned the trick 3 times in one week!

Hitting is the summation of internal forces. It's everything. It's not just the hands or wrists. You have to get the whole body into it.

— Jim Lefebvre, former major league player and manager

■ During the 1989 season Wade Boggs collected more than 200 hits for the seventh consecutive time—a major league record.

■ Roger Maris set the major league record for most home runs in a season with 61 during the 1961 season. Remarkably, not a single one of Maris' round-trippers was a grand slam. Lou Gehrig holds the all-time record for career grand slams with 23.

■ The 1996 Baltimore Orioles set the all-time team record for most home runs in a season with 257. The previous record had been held by the 1961 New York Yankees (240). The Orioles top home run producer was Brady Anderson with 50.

■ During his incredible career, Stan "the Man" Musial amassed a total of 3,630 hits, the fourth highest total of all-time, behind only Pete Rose, Ty Cobb and Hank Aaron. Musial collected 1,815 hits at home and 1,815 hits on the road. Now that's consistency.

■ During the 1987 season New York Yankee Don Mattingly hit six grand slams and hit a home run in eight consecutive games, tying a major league record.

■ In 1987 Oakland Athletic Mark McGwire set the major league rookie record for home runs in a season by smashing 49 dingers.

■ During a 1986 game, Minnesota Twins shortstop Greg Gagne hit two inside-the-park home runs. Most players don't hit one "inside-the-parker" in a career.

■ During a 1966 game, Alanta Braves *pitcher* Tony Cloninger hits two grand slams and a sacrifice fly to total nine RBI. Let's see a DH do that.

THE GRIP
AND STANCE

"*Don't stand a certain way or use a specific bat to imitate someone else. Find what feels comfortable to you and work with it.*"
— *David Justice*

It's fairly safe to say that if Andy Warhol had tried to paint like Michelangelo he would have failed utterly. And if Jerry Garcia tried to be Elvis Presley it would be a disaster. In most of life, you need to find your own style to be successful. That goes for hitting a baseball, too.

Before a batter introduces bat to ball, he has to find his "style" of hitting—specifically, a stance and grip that work for him, not what works for a major leaguer. Just because Carl Yastrzemski had incredible success holding the bat high doesn't mean he should be copied by someone who feels more comfortable holding it low. And the Jeff Bagwell crouch may only work for Jeff Bagwell.

Back in the late 1800s and early 1900s, batting stances were much more uniform, largely because it was the "Dead Ball Era." The Dead Ball Era got its name from the use of a less lively ball, which was kept in play throughout the game. Hitting for power and pulling the ball were as yet unheard of, so most players held their hands low with their feet close together, looking just to make contact. Many hitters, such as the great Ty Cobb, choked up—held the bat several inches from the end of the knob—high on the bat and separated their hands for better bat control. They sprayed the ball around the field, hit for high average, and were not concerned about getting their entire body into the swing.

That's hardly the case today. There are power hitters, spray hitters, dead-pull hitters, opposite-field hitters, players who hit selectively for average, and players who hit everything in or near the strike zone. And they all look different stepping up to the plate. This is not to say that each batter must have a radically new stance and grip that no one has ever seen before. A player's style in the batter's box is really no more than what is comfortable and what plays to his strengths.

BAT SELECTION

Before you can work on your grip or your swing, you have to choose your weapon. Finding a bat that accommodates your size, strength, and hitting style is vital to your success in the batter's box. Do you want a thin handle? A fat barrel? Aluminum or wood?

The first step in hitting is to find the right bat. Get one that feels good in your hands, with the weight right for your kind of swinging. If you're a full swinger, experiment with a lighter bat. If you're a short-swinger, test a heavier one.

— *Mickey Mantle*

I use a 34½ inch bat that's either 32 or 33 ounces. If I'm facing a pitcher who throws hard, I'll use a lighter bat. If it's a guy who throws a lot of off-speed junk like a knuckleballer, I think it's better to use a bat that's a little heavier.

— *Ellis Burks*

Ellis Burks chose the right bat on this swing, as he watches one sail over the left-field fence.

Bats have changed, along with hitting styles, throughout baseball history. Gone are the long, heavy hickory bats used in the eras of Ruth and Cobb. They've been replaced by shorter, lighter, and thinner bats, enabling hitters of the modern era to generate more bat speed while stealing more time to look at a pitcher's offering before deciding whether to swing or not. Ash is now the ideal wood for crafting baseball bats because it has just the right amount of strength, resiliency and weight that a batter needs to hit the ball with authority.

Major league rules allow the barrel of the bat to be a maximum of 2¾ inches in diameter, but most are made thinner than that in an effort to keep the weight of the bat down. Players generally feel they gain more overall if they give up a little size to get more bat speed. If the bat is "lugged" through the strike zone, it will not send the ball as far as if it were "whipped" through the hitting zone. Some hitters also like the thinner barrel because wood becomes stronger the more it's shaved down.

The place hitters or spray hitters are the ones who generally like the thicker barrel. The don't rely on bat speed to hit the ball to the opposite field, and the thicker barrel has a slightly enlarged "sweet spot," which produces more consistent solid contact. Ty Cobb used a 34½-inch, 40-ounce bat with a thick handle to slap the ball past infielders with great accuracy. On the other hand, Tony Gwynn arms himself with a 32-inch, 29-ounce bat to work his magic. One of the biggest bats in the Major Leagues today is a 35-inch, 36-ounce model used by switch-hitting outfielder Bobby Bonilla.

Today, aluminum bats have become the choice of amateur hitters. Metal bats, though not allowed in the major leagues, have a couple of considerable advantages over their wooden counterparts.

Bats made of aluminum tubing break far less frequently and can last for years without being replaced. Compare that to the wooden bat statistics. The average major leaguer goes through six dozen bats per season! Metal bats' other advantage is their flexibility in terms of design. Light bats can now have a large barrel.

Aluminum bats have been the target of criticism by many professional players and baseball purists. Because studies have shown that balls fly farther and faster off metal bats, even when they're not hit with the meat of the bat,

---

THE BATS OF THE BIG BATTERS

Rod Carew
34½-inch, 32-ounce
Louisville Slugger

Ty Cobb
34½-inch, 40-ounce
Louisville Slugger

Mickey Mantle
35-inch, 32-ounce
Louisville Slugger

Babe Ruth
36-inch, 42-ounce
Louisville Slugger

Ted Williams
35-inch, 33-ounce
Louisville Slugger

I use a big bat simply because it feels comfortable, and the ball jumps off of it. I've tried using lighter bats, but I get around on the ball too fast. I stick with the same size bat from both sides of the plate no matter who is throwing.

— *Bobby Bonilla*

Bobby Bonilla connects with his 35-inch, 36-ounce Louisville Slugger.

It Takes All Kinds

Power hitters are capable of hitting the ball over the fence throughout the park. Spray hitters also hit the ball to all fields (right, center, and left), but their specialty is line drives, not the towering fly balls of the power hitters. Spray hitters usually hit for high average.

Dead-pull hitters put most of their batted balls in play on the same side as their stance at the plate. Opposite-field hitters drive the ball to the opposite side of the field.

For example, a left-handed batter who hits to the third-base side of the diamond would be an opposite-field hitter.

the critics fear that hitters who use aluminum bats will fail to develop good fundamentals. Once they enter the professional ranks where they're forced to use wood, such players will find themselves struggling at the plate.

Todd Walker has had personal experience of the shift in his smooth transition from being a three-time All-American at Louisiana State University to a first-round draft pick of the Minnesota Twins and currently a major league infielder. He argues that too much is made out of the controversy over hitting with metal or wood. According to Walker, hitters should simply concentrate on hitting the ball solidly.

"I think that if you put the fat part of the bat on the ball, it will get out there no matter what you use," he says. "I haven't seen a very big difference between wood and metal in the distance, the ball will travel. It's just that you've got to hit the ball with the meat of the bat to get that distance if you're using wood. The ball will get through the infield a little quicker with aluminum, but that shouldn't have any bearing on your swing."

Basically, do what feels right for you and the rest should fall into place. All players, whether they're power hitters or singles hitters, professional or amateur, should find themselves a bat that feels comfortable to swing.

> Until Babe Ruth arrived, Cincinnati Red Edd Roush used the heaviest Louisville Slugger®—a 48-ouncer.

THE GRIP

Like the stance and bat selection, the grip, too, is a personal thing, but there are some basic guidelines you can follow. Your top hand is always your dominant hand, which means that right-handed hitters have their right hand on top and left-handed hitters have their left hand on top. When you pick up the bat, lay the handle at the junction of your fingers and palm in your top hand (Figure 3), if anything, slightly more toward the side of the fingers. Close the grip by rolling your fingers on top of the handle and bringing your thumb up to your top finger. Repeat this with the bottom hand, slightly more toward the palm this time (Figure 4), keeping little or no space between the two hands. Ideally, the second knuckles of the top hand should be between the second and third knuckles of the bottom hand (Figure 5). If your knuckles are aligned (Figure 7), you're holding the bat too far down in the palms of your hands.

Holding the bat too far down in the palms inhibits your flexibility. It makes it more difficult for you to "snap" or roll your wrists over. Your swing will be "all arms" and you'll lose bat speed. And let's not forget the pain factor. If you hold the bat in the palm of your hand and get jammed by a pitch, you're likely to end up with a bone bruise at the base of your thumb, a nagging injury that could bother you all season.

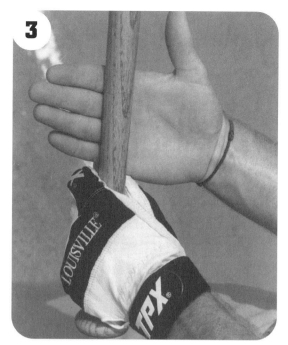

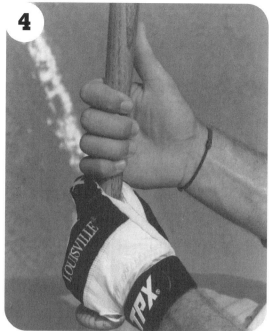

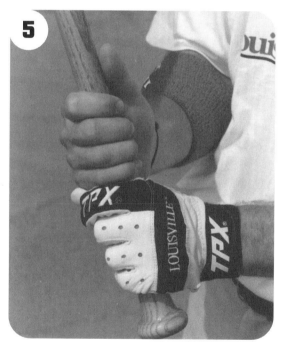

Figures 3 and 4: The bat should be held more in the fingers than your palms. Get a firm grip, but not too tight, almost as if you were holding a pencil. Figure 5: The second knuckles of the top hand should lay somewhere between the second and third knuckles of the bottom hand.

The first thing I ask a young hitter is to grip the bat and then swing it. Nine times out of ten, the problem is right there. Most youngsters think you grip the bat with your hands. You don't! You grip it with your fingers.

— *Stan Musial*

Of course, holding the bat too high in the fingers can cause problems, too. The bat is less secure in your hands, so your hits will be weaker. With all of that said, however, you still need to be comfortable. If you try this grip for a while and it feels awkward and you're not producing, you probably need to make some adjustments. But make your tinkering minor. The slightest change might make plenty of difference.

When working with your grip, it may help to understand how the hands function together. Both hands work as a unit when you hit the ball, but each has its own job to do. The top hand pushes and snaps the bat through the hitting zone. It's the hand that generates bat speed, and its movements are controlled by the fingers, wrists, and arms. Rolling the wrist over is a function of the top hand.

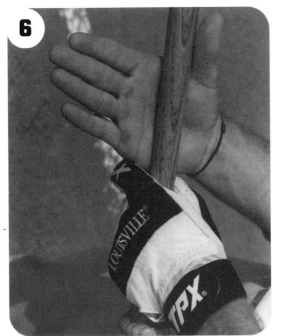 

The bottom hand is a guide to your swing, pulling rather than pushing the bat through the hitting zone. More of the major muscles in your arms and upper body are utilized through the lower hand, creating the power. This is why many switch hitters hit from their "natural" side of the plate for better average and hit from the opposite side for more power.

CHOKING UP

Hitters hold the bat in different places, but the most common is down at the end near the knob. Mickey Mantle even took it a step further and actually had his pinkie finger wrapped under the knob of the bat. That said, it is often effective to move the hands *up* the bat, or in other words, choke up.

Younger hitters can gain a lot by choking up. Choking up gives you a little more bat control by shortening your swing. Better bat control creates a better contact hitter. Some young players may hesitate to choke up, fearing it might imply that they are weaker hitters. All they need to do is take a look at Barry Bonds. Throughout his career, Bonds has choked up an inch or two on the bat, yet he hits more than 30 home runs a year. He gives up some length on the bat in order to generate better bat speed, which in turn creates more power. And the all-time hit leader, Pete Rose, used to choke up on the bat to make more consistent contact and gain better bat control.

There are certain situations, too, that might call for a little choking up. If you have two strikes on you and are behind in the count, it's a good idea to choke up and swing at any pitch in the strike zone. There also may be a time in the game when you may have to move a runner by hitting the ball to the right side of the infield. Choke up on the bat to give yourself better command of your bat and increase your chances of hitting the ball where you want it to go.

Early in my career, when I wasn't quite as strong, I used a bigger bat and choked up four or five inches. This gave a larger barrel, but I was still able to maintain good bat control. It enabled me to stay away from hitting fly balls and to hit more line drives.

— *Mickey Morandini*

Figure 8: All-Star second baseman Mickey Morandini hits second in the lineup for the Philadelphia Phillies and chokes up on the bat to gain better bat control. Figure 9: Dante Bichette, who led the National League in hits, home runs, and RBIs in 1995, grips and re-grips the bat as he awaits the pitch. Bichette does this as a relaxation technique to keep his hands from getting too tense.

NO TENSION

Once you've found your grip, relax. As the late great hitting instructor Charley Lau used to say, "Tension is the enemy." Tension will significantly decrease your ability to maneuver the bat with success. It will decrease your power, your speed, and your control. A lot of young hitters think that the tighter they hold the bat and the more intense they are, the more muscle they'll get into their swing. Not true by a long shot.

The bat should be held almost as if you were holding a pencil. You have a good grip on it while you're writing, but if someone were to come up behind you, they would be able to grab it out of your hands because you're not squeezing it tightly. When you swing, the hands will contract reflexively, and then the muscles will tighten. The key is to remain as loose as possible until you start your swing.

> The most important thing about finding your grip is to remove tension. Anything you can do to take tension away helps, because tension destroys a hitter.
>
> *— Charley Lau*

THE STANCE

Trying to find the poster boy for the perfect stance is like trying to determine the greatest running back of all time. An old-timer might claim former Cleveland Brown Jim Brown as the best while a young fan might claim it's the Detroit Lions' Barry Sanders. There are a hundred different opinions and a thousand ways to analyze the question.

How can you choose the perfect stance when so many players have had success with radically different styles? Stan Musial kept his feet very close together while Joe DiMaggio used an extremely wide stance. John Kruk held his hands high while Jay Buhner holds his hands down by his belt buckle. The key is finding what works for you.

A pitch arrives at the plate in less than half a second. There is no time to see the pitch and step to hit it. You must think "step and hit (swing)." Step, find the ball, adjust for its position in the strike zone, and swing.

There is an exception, however, when you have to guess which pitch and what location. For example, if you anticipate a curveball on the outside portion of the plate, you can step to hit. But watch out if you've guessed wrong. You may get jammed, or even hit, by a fastball, not the curveball you were expecting.

— *Charley Lau*

Think of a marvelous meal set on a beautiful colored tablecloth made of fine linen, with shining silver and sparkling crystal. Then imagine rushing through this meal at breakneck speed, not enjoying the food or the setting.

You wouldn't believe how many ballplayers fire through their at-bats at the same speed. Instead of taking their time, setting up in the box, enjoying the meal, they rush right through an at-bat as if they were eating in a fast-food restaurant. *Your stance is the foundation of your swing. Take your time.*

— *Rod Carew*

While it is hard for a coach (or a book) to get specific about what is right for a particular batter, there are some basic principles you can use to lay the foundation of your stance. The first of these is the athletic position.

Many sports use the athletic position. A basketball player is in it when he plays man-to-man defense. Volleyball and tennis players use it as they wait for serves. A defensive back in football uses it when he's getting ready to cover a receiver.

The feet are about shoulder width apart. There's a slight bend in the knees, and the upper body is leaning forward a bit. The weight of the body should be on the balls of the feet. This should create maximum balance and maximum ability to spring into action.

Once you understand the athletic position, you need to adjust it slightly for the sport of baseball. When you're batting, your weight should not be equally distributed. Although you still want some weight on the balls of your feet, you

Chipper Jones exhibits a classic stance. His upper body is centered with his hands held back. His lower body has a solid base with his weight slightly shifted on his back leg.

want to shift most—but not all—of it onto your back leg while you're waiting for the pitcher's delivery. In order to generate power, your weight should be moving from back to front. However, you must have some, however slight, backward movement "to load your backside" *before* making a move to the front leg.

START SQUARE AND GO FROM THERE

You're where you want to be in the box, but now you have to figure out if your stance should be square or closed or open. The most frequently used stance by hitters at all levels of play is the square stance. Your feet are about shoulder width apart and in direct line with each other and with the pitcher.

The square stance has both strengths and weaknesses. On the plus side, it allows you to get to a wide variety of pitches. You can step from square to open to better handle an inside pitch, step from square to closed to get at an outside pitch more easily, and step square to square to bang the ball "back through the box." Keep in mind, though, that this "stepping to hit" is an advanced technique and is usually done when a batter is looking for a pitch in a certain location. Most of the time, you will "step and hit," which means stepping consistently in one spot and adjusting your swing to the pitch location as soon as the ball is released.

A young hitter should start out using the square stance. You should be able to draw a straight line from the top of your feet directly out to the pitcher. In Figure 13, the hitter is taking his stride from "square to square." Although it's a very small stride, he steps directly back at the pticher and keeps the front toe closed.

A Caution

The square stance sometimes leads inexperienced hitters to step from square to open (called "stepping into the bucket") more often than is needed. If you do this, you lose the strength of your lower body as well as plate coverage on outside pitches. There can be many reasons for stepping into the bucket. For one, it's human nature to step back or away (into the bucket) when an object is thrown hard in your direction. Second, you may step in the bucket to help get the barrel of the bat out in front on inside pitches.

Luckily, you can overcome this bad habit. You can train yourself to get beyond the fear and you can reposition your feet—move farther away from the plate—to help in hitting the inside pitch.

THE CLOSED STANCE

In the closed stance, your front foot is lined up closer to the plate than your back foot (Figure 14). This closes your body to the pitcher and should be used if you seem to have difficulty hitting the outside strike. The closed stance gives you better coverage of the middle and outside parts of the plate.

With a closed stance, you will probably end up hitting up the middle or to the opposite field, because the front foot is forward, forcing your shoulder to stay closed longer. In addition, you'll be able to adjust better to an off-speed pitch because you're delaying your swing and will be able to see the ball longer.

The drawback to the closed stance is that the fastball on the inside part of the plate is going to be harder to catch up to—that is, get the bat barrel out in front to meet the ball. It's more difficult to get your hips open and your hands through the zone in time when you're given a fast inside pitch, because your hands have to travel farther in delivering the barrel of the bat to meet the ball. Closed-stance hitters often get into the habit of "pulling" the bat through the zone with the bottom hand rather than firing the bat through with the top hand. When the bottom hand leads the bat, the barrel of the bat will be late

Figure 14: The closed stance puts the hitter in good position to drive the ball up the middle and to the opposite field.

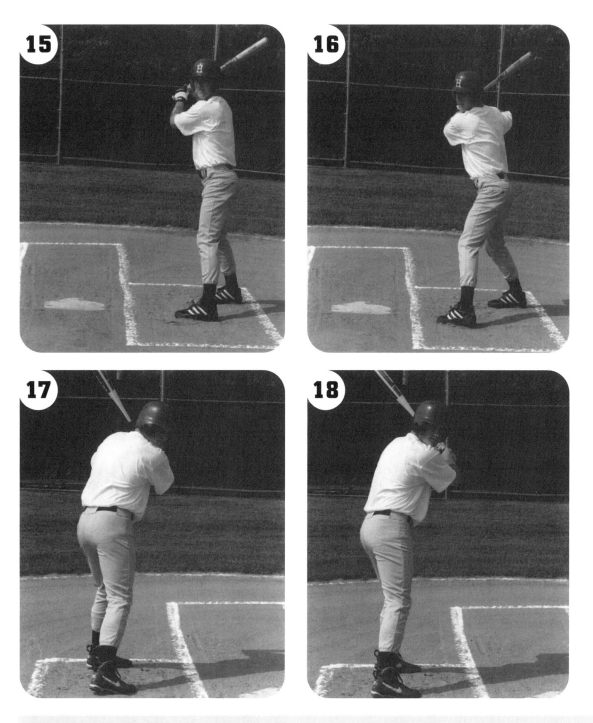

Figure 14: The closed stance puts the hitter in good position to drive the ball up the middle and to the opposite field. Figures 15 and 16: When the hitter steps from closed to closed, he'll have trouble handling pitches on the inside part of the plate. Figures 17 and 18: Notice in Figure 17 that the hitter is only using one eye to see the pitch. Be sure to turn your head to face the pitcher with both eyes (Figure 18). Using both eyes may double your chances of getting a hit.

in reaching the ball over or in front of the plate, which results in the batter getting jammed (hitting the ball too close to the hands).

If you're going to use the closed stance, you need to make sure you turn your head fully toward the pitcher, rather than letting it turn away as you close your shoulder from the pitcher. It's hard enough to see a fast ball with two eyes, so just imagine how you're limiting yourself if only one eye is viewing the pitch.

The open stance allows the hitter to get the hips through the hitting zone sooner. Some hitters use this stance when they're facing a pitcher who throws hard.

I don't think there's a whole lot in a stance. A guy can stand on his head at the plate as long as his hands are in the launch position right before he swings. If a certain stance feels comfortable, use it. If you're having trouble, try something else.

— *Dante Bichette*

THE OPEN STANCE

The open stance is the opposite of the closed stance. In this, it is the rear foot that is closer to the plate. The open stance has a lot of versatility. Both spray hitters, like Brett Butler, and sluggers, like Jose Canseco, use the open stance to their advantage.

The most obvious reason for adopting the open stance (shown in Figure 19) is when you're having trouble with the inside pitch. By moving your front foot away from the plate, you give your lower and upper body a head start if the pitcher throws the ball over the inside part of the plate. That makes it much easier to turn wide open on the pitch to get the barrel of the bat on the ball.

Power hitter Ryan Klesko uses an open stance; because of his great strength, he hits home runs to all parts of the ball park.

The open stance will also turn your head toward the pitcher more, which ensures that you'll be watching the pitch with both eyes.

The drawback to the open stance is that pitches over the outside part of the plate will be hard to reach, yet will be called strikes if you let them go by. Because of this an open-stance hitter should learn always to stride toward the plate, thus bringing his stance to a slightly open or square position when launching the swing. Stepping away from the plate, a practice common with batters learning to hit with an open stance, causes your shoulders and head to "pull off" the ball, which, of course, won't result in very good hitting.

TO ADJUST OR NOT TO ADJUST

Some hitters, like Pete Rose and Wade Boggs, think that once you find a successful stance—whether it's open, square, closed, crouched, or high—you should never change it. Why mess with a good thing?

Other hitters, like Rod Carew and Don Mattingly, changed their stance all the time, sometimes in the middle of an at-bat.

Carew used what he called the "flex stance," which enabled him to change between the three stances (square, open, and closed) depending on the pitcher, the situation, or the way he was being pitched to. Carew studied his opponents, observing what the pitcher threw, when he threw it, and into what area of the strike zone he would throw certain pitches. This information dictated which stance he would use.

Rod Carew noted a similar philosophy in Don Mattingly:

Don Mattingly has been able to make adjustments in his hitting approach from at-bat to at-bat during a ball game. Late in the 1985 season, the Angels purchased John Candelaria, a hard-throwing left-handed pitcher who had been a 20-game winner for the Pirates in the National League. His first game for us was against the Yankees (and Mattingly). Whenever you are seeing a pitcher for the first time, the pitcher has the advantage. To make things more difficult, Candelaria has a three-quarter side-arm delivery, which is intimidating to left-handed hitters (such as Mattingly).

During the game in the middle innings when Mattingly came to the plate for the second time against Candy, I noticed he had altered his stance from the previous at-bat. He had closed his right shoulder substantially, that is, showed more of his back to the pitcher. Don walked during that at-bat. So, as he stood on first, he told me he had found out that during his first at-bat he had a tendency to want to release his upper body too soon against the left-handed side-arm offerings of Candelaria. He decided during his next at-bat he would close his upper body. This, he felt, would force him to keep his front shoulder in longer and would delay his mechanics—the movements of his swing. This adjustment especially helped him against Candy's breaking pitches (curveball and slider).

Despite the opposing philosophies of Boggs, Bichette, Carew, and Mattingly, there is no right or wrong answer as to whether you should adjust your stance. Obviously, if you're not successful at the plate, something needs

Honus Wagner, the Flying Dutchman, was the first major league baseball player to give permission to use his autograph on Louisville Slugger® bats. He signed an endorsement contract on September 1, 1905.

to be done, but first you should analyze what is happening at each at-bat. Is there a pattern? Are you always popping the ball up? If so, maybe you should raise your hands in your stance. Are you hitting the ball off the handle? Well, then maybe you should back off the plate. Ask a teammate or a coach what they think you're doing wrong at the plate. Once you find your weakness, you can determine whether it can be improved by a change in your stance.

Just remember, the stance is one of the few things you can dictate at your at-bat. You're stuck with the pitcher, the out situation, the pitch count, the pitch selection, and the positioning of the defense, but the stance is up to you. Figure out if you like changing it depending on the situation, or if you like the consistency of always having the same starting point.

THE BOX

Your first decision comes the minute you step up to the plate. With the batter's box measuring six feet by four feet, you're looking at a lot of dirt for your feet. Baseball only requires that you stay within the lines. After that, it's up to you. Do you stand right at or even with the plate? Do you move toward the pitcher? Back toward the catcher? Do you move away from the plate or crowd it?

To make this decision, you need to analyze your abilities and look at your physical size and strength. Full plate coverage should be of primary importance. When your arms are extended in your swing, the barrel—and only the

Where you stand in the box will dictate whether or not you have full plate coverage. Notice in Figure 21, the hitter is too far from the plate. His bat doesn't cover the outside part of the plate even with his arms fully extended. It's also possible to have too much plate coverage as shown in Figure 22. The hitter should take his stance so that the barrel of the bat covers the entire plate area when his arms are extended, as shown in Figure 23.

barrel—of the bat should cover the entire plate. If you're standing too far away from the plate and the bat doesn't quite reach the far side, you'll not only have a lot of outside strikes called on you, but you'll also be unable to lay the solid part of the bat on those strikes. If you're standing too close and the barrel is over the far side of the plate, you'll wind up hitting a lot of balls off the handle. That's ineffective and painful.

Once you're comfortable with your plate coverage, you can make adjustments depending on problems you are having. If you have a long swing, you may have more trouble handling an inside pitch, so you can back off a little. And a player who is having trouble getting good wood on outside strikes would inch a little closer.

So now you're positioned horizontally in the box, but you need to figure out the other direction. The center is a good place to start. Some players start there and never move.

Other batters base their front-to-back positioning on the type of pitcher they're facing. When a pitcher has a hard fastball that you are having trouble catching up with, you may want to move to the back of the box to give yourself an extra fraction of a second to get the bat around. And against a breaking-ball pitcher, you may want to move up to intercept the ball earlier in its downward/sideward break.

If you're going to move around in the box, though, you might have to deal with a changing strike zone. A breaking ball at elbow level might be called a ball if you're standing even with the plate, but it might be called a strike if you've moved up and it dips into the strike zone over the plate after it passes you.

THE LAUNCHING POSITION

No matter how or where your stance is set, you need to start with your hands in a comfortable position that will allow you to move them quickly into the launching position.

The launching position is where the bat and hands need to be just before you start to generate your swing. All good hitters do this. Whether they use an open or a closed stance or stand near or far from the plate, they eventually get into the launching position. In the launching position, your hands should be at about shoulder height, just to the rear of your back shoulder and in front of and in toward your body (see Figures 24 and 25). The bat angle is about 45 degrees from the ground.

As you step into the batter's box, your first job is to get yourself set, so that you can make a smooth transition to the launching position. Most coaches and hitting instructors will tell you to start with your hands as close as possible to the launching position. This will allow you to get into position without a lot of movement. If you have to drop, raise, or pull your hands a great distance, it could really throw off your timing. This advice is not carved in stone, however. If you think something else might work better for you, try it. Many players have an alternative that feels much more natural to them.

Major league outfielders Juan Gonzalez and Dave Justice hold their hands high; so did Hall of Famer Carl Yastrzemski. Yastrzemski held his hands high and vertical, but he had extraordinarily strong arms and fast hands that enabled him to get his bat down and through the zone. Later in his career, as

The situation would dictate my positioning in the batter's box. I'd take my stance, then as the pitcher got into his windup, I'd back up six inches or move forward six inches. This would depend on what his best pitch was and how he pitched me in previous at-bats. It's important to pay attention to what, when, and where he's throwing during the game when you're in the dugout. You have to be a student.

— *Steve Garvey*

My stance and where I hold the bat before the pitch is something that feels comfortable to me. As the pitch comes in I get my hands into the launch position, but holding the bat down with my feet close together is all part of my trigger action. It's something I tried and that I've had a lot of success with. It doesn't mean I would try to suggest that everyone takes that approach, but it's something that has worked for me.

— *Mickey Tettleton*

Figures 24 and 25: Ken Caminiti crouches down and holds his bat low, but just before he swings, he's set in the launch position. Figures 26 and 27: Jay Buhner uses a slightly open stance and stands straight up at the plate. As the pitch is delivered, he moves his hands and legs into the correct positions. Buhner often displays great power to the opposite field.

his reactions slowed, he was forced to bring his hands down and shorten the distance to the launching position.

Mickey Tettleton and Jay Buhner both hold their hands low, then raise them to the launching position. Ken Griffey, Jr., holds his bat back beyond his back shoulder, while Mark McGwire keeps his hands in front, almost in line with his front shoulder. Wade Boggs holds the bat away from his body, as does power hitter Albert Belle. All of these hitters have different starting points, but they get similar results when they swing the bat

JUST DO IT

Get in the box and simply do what feels right. It's only after you have established the hitting approach that feels most comfortable for you and your style of hitting that you can try out different ideas or make slight adjustments. No matter what your grip and stance look like, if they get you into the launching position in time to swing and meet the ball, they've done their job. If you look at Figures 24 through 27, you'll see two different styles ending up with exactly the same result. That's your goal.

In 1988, Oakland Athletic Jose Canseco became the first player in baseball history to hit 40 or more home runs and steal 40 or more bases in the same season.

"If you play for ten years in the major leagues and have 7,000 at bats and 2,000 hits you have had a pretty fair career but you've gone 0-for-5000."

— *Reggie Jackson*

- Ray Jansen really knew how to enter and leave in style. Playing for the St. Louis Browns on September 30, 1910, Jansen got five hits in five at-bats in his only major league game for a lifetime batting average of 1.000.

- When Harmon Killebrew hit his 500th career home run in 1971 the home plate umpire was Bill Kunkel. Killebrew had more to thank Kunkel for than calling a good game behind the plate. In 1961, as a pitcher for the Kansas City Athletics, Kunkel had allowed three home runs to the Minnesota Twins' Killebrew.

- On September 15, 1938, Paul "Big Poison" Waner and his brother Lloyd "Little Poison" Waner of the Pittsburgh Pirates became the only brothers to hit back-to-back homers, accomplishing the feat against New York Giants pitcher Cliff Melton.

- Pitcher Joe Niekro played major league baseball for 22 years. During that time he hit exactly one home run, and that was against his brother Phil, a pitcher for the Atlanta Braves.

- After hitting his 100th career home run, outfielder Jimmy Piersall ran around the bases backwards.

- Ozzie Guillen played in 159 games in 1986 and drew only 12 bases on balls.

- Pitcher Hoyt Wilhelm hit a home run in his first major league at-bat. Wilhelm went on to enjoy a 21-year career but he never hit another home run.

- In a September, 1987 nine-inning game the Toronto Blue Jays hit an amazing 10 home runs, an average of more than one homer per inning. This still stands as the all-time record for most home runs by a team in a nine-inning game.

PULLING THE TRIGGER

3

"It don't mean a thing if you ain't got that swing."

— *Tony Oliva*

Learning a consistent swing was the most difficult aspect. I noticed that the players who succeeded always had simple and consistent swings. It didn't matter what the pitch, count or score was—they just found a comfortable swing and stayed with it.

— Michael Jordan

I copied [Shoeless Joe] Jackson's style because I thought he was the greatest hitter I had ever seen, the greatest natural hitter I ever saw. He's the guy who made me a hitter. I copied his swing. I couldn't copy Ty Cobb's hand action because Ty was looking more for base hits than for power. Jackson stood with his feet fairly wide apart, his right foot shoved forward (toward the plate) and the left foot back of the right. This gave him a good turn (coil) to start with. I kept my feet close together. I could get more leverage that way. But I was more easily caught off-balance by a left-hander. I had more trouble with left-handers than Joe had. He never had much trouble with anyone who threw a ball.

— Babe Ruth

You hear it all the time from commentators when they're calling a big ballgame on television: "Swing and a base hit to centerfield!" or "Swing and there's a long drive deep to left field!" or "Swing and a miss! He struck him out." The excitement begins when the bat whips across the plate, whether it's strike three, a slap to the opposite field, or a huge cut that sends the ball soaring toward the fence.

Some players have such great swings that you could sit and watch them go after pitches all day, even when they swing and miss. The short and powerful stroke of Jose Canseco, the smooth and fluent whip of Ken Griffey, Jr., and the graceful cut of Will Clark are some of the swings that mesmerize and captivate the fans. Joe DiMaggio was said to have one of the most powerful strokes the game has ever seen, yet it appeared effortless. Babe Ruth took a thunderous cut at the ball, which he said he patterned after "Shoeless" Joe Jackson's swing. Much like a smashing left hook from a boxer, the swing is a forceful, physical act whose job is to punish the incoming object. Some hitters do it with style and grace, some with brute strength and power, while others just do whatever they have to do to put the bat on the ball. Whatever the case may be, the bat is the hitter's weapon, the ball is the enemy, and his swing is the ammunition with which he can defeat the pitcher.

No matter what the stroke looks like, though, there is a certain commonality in the swings of all successful hitters. Simply stated, they stride, they swing, they follow through—and in most cases, they have rhythm.

RHYTHM AND MOVEMENT

Just as a tennis player rocks back and forth as he's waiting for his opponent to serve to him, the baseball player can benefit from a little rhythmical movement. Being in motion, rather than standing flat-footed, makes for a smoother transition.

It used to be that hitting instructors taught their students to remain as still as possible in the batter's box. Today, it's very common for them to recommend that hitters waiting for the pitch should have some motion.

Several major league hitters, past and present, have used various movements of different parts of their body to preface their swing. New York

Joe DiMaggio combined power and grace in his swing to belt 361 home runs and compile a lifetime .325 batting average. The "Yankee Clipper" was a tough out, striking out only 369 times in 6,821 at bats during his 13-year Hall of Fame career.

2

Barry Bonds' trigger action is generated by a hitch right before his swing. Bonds has great bat speed which allows him to drop his hands, and move them up before he strides.

Yankees first baseman Tino Martinez taps his front foot up and down while the pitcher is in his windup. Hall of Fame third baseman Mike Schmidt would wiggle his hips in the box to get movement. Joe Morgan flapped his elbow while he awaited the pitch.

Dusty Baker, manager of the San Francisco Giants, is such a strong believer in rhythm and movement that he had speakers installed in the Giants' batting cage so that they could listen to music when they took batting practice. Baker suggests to his players that they get a song in their mind when they go up for an at-bat during a game.

Creating rhythm and movement in the stance will help you in a number of ways. It relaxes you and reduces tension. It gets your body in motion, which makes any kind of weight shift a smoother transition. A slight movement will also keep you balanced and on the balls of your feet.

Charley Lau explains it this way: "The whole idea of rhythm and weight shift is so simple. If you've ever pounded a stake into the ground with a sledgehammer, taken an axe to a log or tree trunk, or cut a piece of wood with a handsaw, you've used exactly the same principles. Think of the rhythm you develop when you use a handsaw and the way you shift your weight forward and back, forward and back.

"Or think of the way you bring a sledgehammer or ax over your head, down to the target, pause a second, and then bring the tool arcing back up, over and down again. The rhythm and the alternating shifts of weight let you put your whole body into the task, maximizing the effect of each blow.

"Which is exactly the same thing you want to do when you hit a baseball. The problem is that, unlike swinging an ax or driving a stake, hitting a baseball is not a continuous, ongoing process. It is, or at least it appears to be, a single, explosive swing taken from an-all-but stationary position."

Of course, too much movement can be more of a problem than no movement at all. If your head moves up and down or too far laterally, the eyes will have trouble focusing on a high velocity pitch. Also if your pre-swing movement puts you in a poor position to launch yourself, you'll have trouble.

I believe in movement. You cannot do anything from a dead standstill. All the good hitters I've seen move. You have to have rhythm. The worst thing a hitter can have is tension. When tension sets in, you're in trouble.

— *Dusty Baker*

I think the movement is the thing that really keeps me ready. Some guys stand real still in the box, and then the ball's coming and they try and do everything at once. I have a slight rock for timing. Then when I'm ready, I end up back. That's just for me. I think everybody's different, but I think all hitters have some kind of timing mechanism that works for them. I think if you have a little movement, it's relaxing.

— *Ryne Sandberg*

Will Clark turns his front knee just before he strides. This cocks his hips and keeps his power on his back side until he is ready to commit to his swing.

RECOIL

With your body relaxed and balanced in some type of rhythm movement, you're prepared to begin the backward motion, placing the weight of your body on the back leg. To do this, you need a recoil of your front knee. In other words, the front knee should turn slightly inward. This will transfer your weight to your rear leg and sort of cock your hips into position (Figure 3).

Some players, like Brady Anderson, Ruben Sierra, or Paul O'Neill, will actually raise their front foot and bring the entire leg back, rather like a pitcher in his windup. Others will use a slight recoil to avoid too much movement. Whatever recoil you use, this is the movement that signals your body that it's time to get into the launching position. After this, hitting should be all reaction.

The high leg kick works as a trigger to keep my weight back first, and then it gets everything into my swing. Some think it sometimes induces the hitter to overstride, but if your weight is back and you have balance, I don't think a leg kick will cause over-striding. The longer you carry your weight on your back leg, the longer you can dictate when you want to go to the ball.

— Paul O'Neill

Ruben Sierra has a high front leg kick, much like a pitcher uses in his windup. This keeps his weight back as long as possible. After identifying the pitch, he strides forward and drops his raised foot.

THE STRIDE

After you've set your body in the lock-and-load position, you're ready to make your first forward movement toward the ball. This is the stride. Striding with the front foot widens your base and gives the lower half of your body more leverage to put power into your swing.

Although the stride is crucial to a good swing, don't misinterpret the term to mean an exaggerated movement of the front leg. Overstriding can be disastrous.

The stride should be a very minimal and soft movement of your front foot. Depending on your height, it can be as little as four inches but rarely more than twelve inches. The stride should be a very "quiet" movement. Picture yourself checking to see if the ice on a pond is thick enough to skate on. You wouldn't step on it with your whole weight or you might plunge through. You'd test it with a light tap first. That's the step you're taking in the batter's box.

When you stride, you should try to keep your toe closed (see Figure 7). While this is impossible to maintain once your hips and upper body rotate, concentrating on it during the stride will keep you from opening up too soon.

You also want to make sure that your stride is directly back toward the pitcher. If you step out, you're opening up your stance, and if you step in, you're closing your stance and you'll get jammed more easily. If you step toward the pitcher, then you have more options when you need to adjust your upper body to the pitch. Some hitters are under the misconception that you

I found out very early—and it still is true—that a man who definitely overstrides can't hit. And I know of no cure for it. I've talked to Mr. [John] McGraw, Connie Mack, and I challenge anyone to definitely cure it.

Lots of things you can cure, but overstriding is a brain lesson—it's a timing process of the mind that the man cannot judge clearly, and he steps too far. He's a home-run hitter on certain pitches. But when the pitcher starts changing speed and throwing balls that deflect from a straight line—when those combinations come upon him—he's finished. DiMaggio brings his foot up and puts it right down in the same place. Sisler strides six inches. I don't know of any great hitters who aren't short striders.

— Branch Rickey

Figures 5 through 7: Tony Gwynn's stride is very soft; it employs a minimal movement of the front foot. Notice the short distance he steps forward, and how he keeps the front toe closed.

8

T y Cobb and others used to say the direction of the stride depended on where the pitch was—inside pitch, you'd bail out a little; outside, you'd move in toward the plate. This is wrong because it's impossible. It takes less than .40 seconds for the ball to reach the batter. You [the batter] have already made your stride before you know where the ball will be or what it will be.

— *Ted Williams*

A s you make your stride, something else should happen naturally. Your arms, hands and the bat should move in the opposite direction. Remember: stride forward, bat backward.

— *PeeWee Reese*

N ever rush your swing. To get as much power as possible the bat must gather speed as it meets the ball. Hurrying your swing and uncocking the wrists too quickly cuts off the important wrist power.

— *Joe DiMaggio*

should try to step to the pitch, but there simply isn't enough time to see the ball and then adjust your step. Your front foot should already be planted by the time you recognize the pitch type and its location.

During the stride, your foot is not the only body part that's moving. At the same time as the foot is stepping forward, your hands should be heading backward. When the lead foot plants, your bat should be cocked in the launching position.

Even though you're striding forward, you still want to keep your weight back on the ball of your rear foot, and your head as still as possible, eyes focusing on the pitch.

The stride is the trigger that puts the rest of your body in motion. When your front foot comes down and plants, your hips begin to rotate and the hands start to come through. That's why, no matter how small the step may be, it's so important to perfect your stride.

THE SWING

You've taken your stride and you're in your launching position. Finally, it's time to swing. So how do you do it? Fortunately, the swing can be broken down into smaller components, which may help.

Your first (minimal) movement should be to pull the bat forward and down-ward. Moving your hands in this direction starts to bring the bat down into the hitting zone. In other words, point the knob of the bat at the ball. Your bottom hand should be the lead hand, and your top hand should be relaxed and tension-free.

Now your hips and lower body begin to rotate. As this happens, your upper body will slightly lower itself down into the pitch. This lowering is natural; it does not mean you drop your back shoulder. Dropping the back shoulder as you swing causes severe uppercutting, resulting in strikeouts, infield pop-ups, fly balls, and pretty much everything undesirable. Every swing already has a natural loop to it, so adding an uppercut would put the path of your swing at too much of an upward angle.

Figures 9 through 11: Paul O'Neill first pulls the bat down and forward. In Figure 11, he's pointing the knob of the bat at the ball. It's not until after this point that the top hand takes over the swing.

As your body starts to rotate, the top hand takes charge and snaps the bat through the hitting zone. When the bat finally makes contact with the ball, your hands should be in the "palm up, palm down" position. This means the palm of your top hand is facing up toward the sky, and the palm of your bottom hand faces down to the ground. Your head should be locked, and eyes looking down at the point of contact.

As soon as you've made contact, roll your wrists over. Even though the ball has already been hit, this is extremely important. If you don't do this, you will lose bat speed and power. And the timing of this wrist rolling has to be perfect. If you roll the wrists too late, then it's as if you never rolled them at all. If you roll them too early, you'll hit the top of the ball out in front of the plate. A hit that normally would be a line drive up the center will now become a weak ground ball to the shortstop.

Tim Naehring gets this one right off the barrel of the bat with his hands in the "palm up, palm down" position.

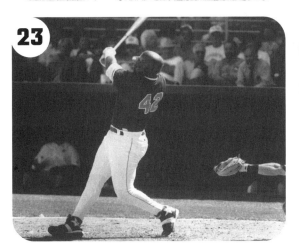

Mo Vaughn shows us his classic home run swing by hitting one over the right field fence. Mo starts with his hands high (Figure 13), then drops them low as part of his coiling action (Figure 15). Vaughn plants his front foot, keeps the front toe closed and begins to rotate his hips by leading with the knob of the bat (Figures 16 through 18). He drops the barrel of the bat down and brings it through the zone on an upward arc to lift the ball into the air. By the time Vaughn reaches the point of contact, he is in full hip rotation (Figure 20). Take note of how little his head has moved from the starting point to the time he makes contact (compare Figures 13 and 20). It starts on the front shoulder and ends up on the back shoulder without moving (shoulder to shoulder). Mo finishes his swing strong with a high follow (Figure 23).

THE FOLLOW-THROUGH

Finally, to complete the swing, you must follow through. Just like a golf shot, a ground stroke in tennis, or a slapshot on goal in hockey, you have to follow through after you strike the ball in order to achieve the maximum velocity and distance. Basically, the follow-through means continuing the swing after the ball has been hit.

Many hitting instructors describe it as "hitting through the ball." Charley Lau and Walt Hriniak recommended that hitters release their top hand after contact and finish with the bat high around their shoulder. Other coaches think that both hands should stay on the bat. All-Star first baseman Fred McGriff finishes high up and wraps his bat all the way behind his head. It works for him. Choose a style that works for you, but make sure you allow the swing to run its course. Don't cut it short at the point of contact.

Hitters also differ in the extent and force of their follow-through. Home-run hitters with long swings generally have a much longer, powerful follow-through, while singles hitters have swings that are smaller. Former Los Angeles Dodger Steve Garvey had a short, quick swing and a compact follow-through, while Hall of Famer Reggie Jackson practically screwed himself into the ground after he swung the bat. He actually "replaced the shoulders," which means that his back shoulder ended up where his front shoulder began.

Your follow-through can also alert you to what you're doing wrong at the plate. If you're in a slump, take a look at your body at the end of the follow-through. Is your head in the middle of your shoulders? You're probably pulling your eyes off the ball too soon. Does your back leg come flying forward? You may be shifting your weight too early. The way you finish is an extension and a telltale clue of the way you hit.

It's important to hit through the baseball, get good arm extension, and finish the swing. If you don't follow through, the ball won't go anywhere. I use a high follow through that was taught to me by Mike Easler. If feel that I get better carry on the ball when I finish high.

— Mo Vaughn

Figure 24: Fred McGriff has had great success with a high follow through after his swing, and a mental approach to hitting that translates into "see the ball, hit it hard." Different strokes for different folks. Figure 25: Paul Molitor's compact swing results in a short, level follow-through. His hip rotation is rapid but also controlled—from start to finish, his hips rotate slightly more than ninety degrees.

Power Flows from Smoothness

I was only 19 when I broke in with the Yankees. I had the incomparable Joe DiMaggio to watch during my first few months with the Yankees in 1951, but Joe decided to call it a career at the end of the season. So in 1952, my first full year with the Yankees, I began to take "double takes" at all of the star hitters. Every time one of them went to the plate my eyes were riveted on him. I studied the stance, the pivot, the swing, every detail. I was learning.

I watched the silky swings of Yogi Berra and Johnny Mize and Ted Williams. I wouldn't know about the great hitting stars of the past like Ty Cobb, Joe Jackson, and Rogers Hornsby, but how in the world can anybody be a better batter—hitter is the word— than Ted Williams?

Here's what I did or tried to do. Since I'm a switch-hitter, I schemed to incorporate the best features of them all in my left- and right-handed swings. However, please don't ask me which is my better side. I'm right-handed naturally, but I feel just as strong from either side. Any kid can master it if he starts swinging alternately early enough. My dad started me out at age six.

A kid can develop the same way as a thrower. I know it will work because I saw one master it right in my hometown of Commerce, Oklahoma. He might have become a big league pitcher from either side, but he gradually drifted away from baseball. I predict that someday we will have pitchers who can throw from either side. Just wait and see.

Now let's go back to hitting. If you love the game, you'll do all right—much better than you think once you get your confidence. That comes with only one thing—playing. Some folks call it experience.

First of all get the right bat, one that feels good, with the weight that's right for your kind of swinging. If you're a "full swinger," experiment with the lighter bat. If you're a "short swinger," test the heavier one.

Don't forget to grasp the bat firmly, but don't try to grip the grain out of it—just enough to feel natural and "be in charge" when you connect. Place the handle across the palms of both hands where they join the fingers. Then "fool around" until you get the "just-right" feeling.

Keep your bat high and shoulders level. Then it's easier to drop your shoulders to meet a low pitch than to raise your shoulders to meet a higher one. Keep your elbows away from your body to give you freedom for swinging. Don't swing for the moon every time. Meeting the ball on a pitch you believe is over the plate is the prime objective in learning how to hit.

A good swing is a level swing, parallel to the ground. Any motion of the bat either up or down during the swing will chop balls for fouls or get you some weak rollers. Always bear in mind, the smoother the swing the better. Power flows from smoothness.

— Mickey Mantle

26

Figure 26: Mickey Mantle was the most powerful switch-hitter of all time. He hit 536 career home runs, including the longest recorded ball to ever be hit at 565 feet.

Slugger Jose Canseco times this pitch perfectly. He's got the barrel of the bat to the ball just as it enters the hitting zones.

27

Hitting is a lot about timing. If you're a split second early or late, you won't hit the ball squarely. That's why even at the major league level you see so many funny swings, or hitters who look foolish at the plate. It's because their timing is off.

— *Paul O'Neill*

TIMING

Now all that's left is timing, and timing is everything. You could have the sweetest swing in baseball, but if your timing is off, it's not going to make a bit of difference to your team. You need to have the ball hit your bat the instant it comes into the hitting zone. If the swing is a fraction of a second early, the ball can hit off the end of the bat. A fraction too late, and you can get jammed. And that's assuming you make contact at all. With the average pitch taking four-tenths of a second, you don't have much room for error.

There are two things you have to worry about when you're trying to time your swing: the pitch speed and your bat speed. The hitter should know his own bat speed through repetitious training, but recognizing the speed of each pitch is much more difficult.

Each pitcher differs in some way in velocity and pitch selection, so you need to pay attention to who's on the mound, how hard he throws, and what he's throwing. You can do this in the dugout, the on-deck circle, and even in the batter's box. Often coaches will ask their hitters to take a pitch, to help them gauge the pitcher's velocity. Even the best hitters in the major leagues will look at the first pitch thrown to get an idea of what the pitcher has.

Every great hitter I have seen has developed this fundamental proper timing to a very high degree. It may be easy to strike fastballs or perhaps curveballs correctly, but to be able to time fastballs, curves, changes of pace, knuckle balls, or any kind of pitch that a foxy pitcher may serve is an accomplishment well worth acquiring, for it will largely determine your rating as a hitter.

— *George Sisler*

28

Juan Gonzalez is badly fooled on this pitch. He has already committed his hands and the lower half of his body. This is undoubtedly some sort of off-speed pitch.

KEEP YOUR HEAD ON THE BALL

You often hear coaches tell their hitters to "watch the ball hit the bat." Although it's not possible to actually see the ball and bat meet, this is sound advice, because it keeps your head down and your eyes focused on the ball all the way from the pitcher's hand into the hitting zone. Stan Musial, Pete Rose, and Wade Boggs are all great examples of players who kept (or keep) their heads down through an entire swing, and you could see it there after the follow-through.

When you start your swing, your chin should be on or right around your front shoulder. As the body rotates through the swing, try to keep your head in the same spot. Your head should finish closer to the back shoulder. Once your hips begin to rotate, the head doesn't move; the hands, arms, hips, and shoulders do. Stop-action photography of the swing shows that the head remains still throughout the rotation of the hips but moves slightly forward and downward during the stride. However, you should practice keeping your head as still as possible—this will help prevent a number of faults, especially a weak rotation of the hips.

Practice holding your head still as you hit off a tee. Keep looking down at the top of the tee for an exaggerated time after you hit the ball. Young hitters often pull their heads up too early so that they can see where the ball is going. This is a good way to break yourself of that bad habit.

The most important single factor, I have come to believe from my observation of great hitters including Joe DiMaggio, Babe Ruth, Ty Cobb, Ted Williams, and others is this: Keep your head still! In nearly all forms of sport that I know, even in fancy diving, the head is the key.

— *Lefty O'Doul*

Even though Frank Thomas misses this pitch, he maintains good discipline of his head position.

THE SWING ARC

When you leave the launching position and start to swing, your bat has three options. It can swing in an upward, downward or level arc. To generalize, a level swing produces line drives, a downward swing creates ground balls, and an upward swing lifts the ball in the air. They each have their advantages and disadvantages, and you can find major leaguers who support each type of arc.

Of course, it is possible to hit the ball different ways with the same arc. For instance, a downward swing won't be a ground ball if you catch the bottom half of the ball. This will send the ball backspinning into the air, often with good carry. Hitting the top of the ball with an upward swing will produce a sinking line drive or even a ground ball. A level swing basically works the same way; it depends where you hit the ball.

A downward swing is very popular among major leaguers. By coming down to the ball from the launching position, they avoid dropping the barrel beneath their hands, which can result in strikes or popped balls.

It's important to understand that having a downward swing does not mean chopping down at the ball. It just means keeping the barrel of the bat above the hands until the top hand takes over the swing. When the top hand comes through the zone, it brings the bat down.

Basically, as I got older I developed a swing that allowed me to hit the pitch I wanted to hit more often. I developed a more level, downward plane swing which decreased my swings and misses and foul balls and put the ball in play more often. . . . Everyone has a slight loop [in their swing]. It's natural. It creates a lot of fly balls, foul balls and swings and misses. When you have a downward plane and swing over the top of the ball, you hit with authority much more often.

— *Mike Schmidt*

Figures 31 and 32 show Tony Gwynn raising his hands to the flight of the ball, and then pulling the knob of the bat forward and down. As he rotates (Figure 33), the barrel of the bat drops slightly, and then he levels it off at the point of contact. Although Gwynn fouls this pitch off, it's a good example of "getting on top" of a ball that's up in the strike zone.

It's important to keep your swing level. Some instructors will say you should even swing down on the ball a little. And you'd be surprised at the way the ball jumps off your bat when you do. The important thing, however, is that you don't uppercut the ball. It wastes your power, and it won't produce home runs.

— *Dick Allen*

The ideal swing is a level swing, but I don't worry about this too much because if the fundamentals are right, the swing will be almost perfectly level. On pitches that are higher than the belt buckle, I have the feeling I'm hitting down on the ball slightly. On pitches that are below the belt buckle, I have the feeling I'm hitting up. I think of it as though I were a woodsman cutting down a tree and chopping the classic "V" in the trunk of the tree.

— *Ted Williams*

Ted Williams felt that a slight uppercut on a pitch at or below the belt was the best approach for a hitter. That way such a pitch could be hit in the air for a home run. Because the pitcher was throwing the ball at a downward angle from the mound, Williams thought an upward angle would be the best way to hit the ball squarely.

Williams's slight uppercut swing would still require the downward dropping of the bat's barrel, an acceleration through a short level plane, and then an upward arc. Many left-handed power hitters, such as the Braves' Ryan Klesko, hit home runs by dropping the barrel and catching the pitch out in front of the plate as the bat starts its ascent. So Williams may be right, but he also may be reporting only half of what he did in lifting a low pitch into the air.

It's hard to argue with Williams's success, but he did have exceptionally long arms, quick hip action, and tremendous bat speed and power. For him, hitting the ball in the air always meant the possibility of a home run—he hit 521 in his career—but for someone who doesn't possess Williams's kind of power, an uppercut swing that lifts the ball would just mean a lot of fly-outs.

If you're going to follow the trunk-of-the-tree "V" cut theory that Williams describes, you need to be careful on that low pitch. The adjustment you make for it should be with your entire body, not just the swing. Lower your legs and

Jim Eisenreich shows exactly how to handle a pitch low in the strike zone. His legs go down with the pitch bringing the bat down into the plane of the ball. Notice how far his head has lowered from Figure 53 to 58.

Ruben Sierra displays exactly how not to go after a low pitch. Sierra just drops the barrel of the bat down, and as you can see in Figure 61, he pops the pitch up in the air.

DIFFERENT SWINGS FOR DIFFERENT HITTERS

In the course of baseball history, fans have witnessed the sweet swing of Ted Williams, the attacking stroke of Roberto Clemente, and the artistic bat-handling of Rod Carew. They were all tremendously successful, yet their swings were radically different. Each was able to find a swing that worked with his particular abilities. You have to do the same. You can't be a home-run hitter if your body and hitting style aren't made for it, so it would be a mistake to try to copy the swing of a home-run hitter. As Hall of Famer Phil Rizzuto liked to point out, the type of hitter you should be isn't always the type of hitter you want to be.

By looking at the way a hitter swings the bat, you should be able to tell what kind of hitter he is. You wouldn't see Hall of Famer Richie Ashburn taking big, long cuts at the ball; he made contact and used his speed to smack singles and doubles. San Francisco Giant Matt Williams, on the other hand, takes a full cut every time; you know he's a power hitter. Harmon Killebrew the former major league slugger was another power hitter who had a big swing. The length of his swing combined with a slight uppercut enabled Killebrew to send a lot of balls out of the yard (573), but he had to trade off 1,699 strikeouts for taking such big hacks at the ball.

When you try to hit the ball for power, sometimes your swing gets a little too long. When that happens, you might be late with your swing, you could get jammed, or you could pull off the ball too soon on a breaking pitch. The best thing to do is to stay back, see the ball first, and then explode through it.

— *Dante Bichette*

Hank Aaron shows why he is one of only three players in major league baseball history to compile over 500 home runs and 3,000 hits. His eyes and head are locked down on the pitch. Aaron has the knob pointed at the ball, and is ready to snap his wrists. Aaron hit a lot of home runs in his career off his front foot, as he is pictured here. His weight has already begun to shift forward, and his hips are leading his swing. The ability to hit for power using this method is a credit to Aaron's strong hands and quick wrists.

Because of this, some home run hitters use a much shorter swing. They create their power with quick wrists and tremendous hand strength. All-time major league home run king Hank Aaron had a very compact swing. Because he used a short stroke and had such powerful forearms, Aaron was able to clear fences even when he was fooled by a pitch. As long as he kept his hands back, Aaron could hit the ball hard and far with just a quick flick of the wrists.

The short power stroke also allows the hitter to hit for average. Aaron finished his career with a lifetime batting average of .305. All-star outfielder Barry Bonds chokes up on his bat and uses a short stroke to maintain a .300 average and hit 25 to 30 home runs every year.

While these rare hitters can use the short swing for power, most short-swing hitters use it for average. They can wait longer on pitches because it doesn't take as long to get the barrel of the bat into the zone, which allows them to get a better idea of pitch type and to see whether it's a ball or a strike. Short swingers, like Wade Boggs, look to put the barrel of the bat on the ball and let the velocity of the pitch supply much of the power. Their swing is used to give the ball direction.

Slap hitters hit for average, too, but they don't worry about power at all. Their goal is just to get to the base, either by slipping the ball past the infielders or by beating the throw to first base. Slap hitters were common in the Dead Ball Era because power hitting was not a factor in a team's offense. Then they were reborn when teams started covering their field with Astroturf. A ground ball moves much faster on carpet than on grass and the weaker, ground-ball hitters gained an advantage. Vince Coleman and Otis Nixon are a few slap hitters who have used their speed to become dangerous offensive threats. Infielders have to play up on hitters with good speed, so the holes in the infield become bigger. It's a great situation for the fast, slap hitter.

Trying to throw a fastball by Henry Aaron is like trying to sneak sunrise past a rooster.

— *Curt Simmons*

I hit 29 major league home runs and after every one of them I worried that I was swinging wrong, that I wasn't staying with my normal pattern of what the strike zone was or how I was supposed to swing. To hit a home run you have to uppercut a little bit and I never wanted to uppercut. My game was built around speed. I was a guy who hit a lot of singles, doubles, and triples, not home runs. I always tried to keep the bat above the ball. I didn't want to hit the ball in the air.

— *Richie Ashburn*

63

If I had played on Astro-turf as often as players compete on it today, I certainly would have changed my stroke. I would have tried to beat the ball down more. When you hit the ball in the air in any ballpark, you've got three guys out there who can catch it. If you get the ball down on the ground, it has a good chance to get through on that quick surface.

— *Brooks Robinson*

DIFFERENT SWINGS FOR DIFFERENT SITUATIONS

Every hitter has his own swing, but there are times when hitters need to change their swings to adapt to a certain situation. (See Chapter 8 for more about situational hitting.) A home-run hitter may need to hit a ground ball to the right side to move the runner. A contact hitter might have to hit a fly ball to the outfield to score the runner at third. While most of the time you can use the swing you're comfortable with, you also need to know how to adjust if your team needs something else.

MOVING THE RUNNER

If you're looking to move a runner who's on second or score a runner who's on third, you want to hit the ball to the right side of the field because this allows the runners on second and third to move up and score respectively. How you do this depends on whether you are a right-handed or a left-handed hitter.

If you're right-handed, you look for an outside pitch and contact it when it's on the back side of the plate. Simple. Unfortunately, most pitchers will suspect that you are planning to do this and they will choose to pitch you inside. Now what do you do? You need to use an "inside-out" swing. In this type of swing, you lead the bat into the hitting zone with your bottom hand. Your top hand plays a much smaller role than it usually does. The barrel of the bat stays back in the zone so it's angled toward the right side of the infield. Your bottom hand pulls the knob of the bat into the pitch and then your top hand pushes it out toward the second baseman. Your front shoulder should stay closed and there is less than full rotation of the hips. Contact the ball toward the back of the plate and try to hit the top half of the ball.

If you're a left-handed hitter trying to hit to the right side, your job is a little easier. You have to pull the ball. Get the head of the bat moving earlier,

64

The key to hitting to the right side as a right-handed hitter is the bottom hand. The bottom hand is the dominant hand in this swing, and has to pull the bat to the ball. The top hand plays a secondary role and merely guides the bat through the zone. The wrists don't roll over until after contact is made. Timing is also important. The hitter has to wait until the ball is back in the hitting zone before he makes contact.

Hillerich & Bradsby Co. makes approximately one million wood bats per year. However, the most bats made in one year was six million.

and keep your arms away from the body, not pulled in tight. Bring the bat out to meet the pitch in front of the plate.

No matter which side you're hitting from, though, it's a good idea to choke up on the bat. Any time you're trying to place hit the ball, you'll want to choke up, because it will make the bat lighter and shorter and give you better control.

SACRIFICE FLY

Sacrifice flies are important to a team's offense and are a way to produce runs without the pressure and difficulty of getting a base hit. Any time there's a runner on third and less than two outs, a deep fly ball to the outfield will allow the runner to tag up and score.

First, you need to get a good pitch. Most hitters find it easier to lift a ball into the air that's located from the belt up. However if you like low strikes for the long ball, wait for a low one, but make sure you contact the pitch in the front portion of the plate. It is difficult to lift a low pitch when the ball is located in the back part of the plate. The key is to look for the pitch that suits the objective. If you just hack at any pitch in an effort to get the job done quickly, you'll most likely end up with a weakly hit ball that fails to get out far enough to enable the runner to score. Keep in mind, though, that if the pitcher gets two strikes on you, the situation changes. You have to protect the plate—that is, swing at anything close to a strike.

When you get the pitch you like, you want to have a slight uppercut at the ball to get it into the air. The uppercut should come from slightly dropping the barrel of the bat with your hands. Try lowering your hands in your stance—it will keep the barrel of the bat below any pitches from the waist up. *Do not drop your back shoulder.* All you'll get is strikeouts, foul balls, and pop flies. Attempt to hit the middle to lower middle section of the ball. Follow through high, keeping your head down at the point of contact.

Sometimes pitch location is just as important as the swing when trying to lift the ball in the air. A pitch at the belt (as shown in this photo), is much easier to hit in the air than the one around the knees.

65

TWO-STRIKE HITTING

If you're faced with the unfortunate situation of the pitcher having two strikes on you, you're going to have to change your approach. If you're normally conservative, get the bat off your shoulder. This is not the time to be particular. If the pitcher gives you a strike, even if it's that pitch on the outside of the plate that you hate, go for it. Be aware, though, that he may try to get you to chase something way out of the strike zone. Even though you have to be less selective with two strikes, it doesn't mean you should swing at everything.

When you get two strikes on you, try to shorten up your swing. Choke up on your bat. A shortened swing will allow you to see the pitch longer, which will improve your chances of making contact.

Basically, you're going to have to bite the bullet and go after the ball where it's pitched. It's a good bet that the pitcher will use his best pitch at this point, so if you know what that is, be aware that he may use it. You should always look for a fastball, but be ready to adjust to something else. You also may make your own adjustments at the plate to subtly "force" a certain type of pitch. You might want to back off the plate if you can't handle inside pitches or move up if you don't like the outside ones. And crouch low if you like them low, and then stand back up just before the release.

Another tactic when faced with a two-strike count is to try to take away the pitcher's best pitch, thus forcing him to alter his pitch selection. Here's how this might work. Against a pitcher with a good breaking pitch and average fastball, move closer to the plate and forward in the batter's box. You are now in an excellent position to hit any pitch that breaks toward the outside corner of the plate. Your objective is to invite the pitcher, who now sees that you're crowding the plate and vulnerable to the inside heater, to throw his second best pitch—the fastball. Choke up, look inside for the fastball, and use a short, quick swing to get the bat barrel out in front. If the pitch is a fastball, you'll be ready. If the pitch is a curveball, you'll be able to hit it before it breaks too far.

Face it. The pitcher has the advantage when there are two strikes on you, but you might be able to grab a little of it back.

Pete Rose drives hit number 4,192 to left-center field, breaking Ty Cobb's career hit mark of 4,191. This is a classic example of an inside-out swing which Rose mastered throughout his career. His hands are leading the barrel of the bat with the bottom hand above the top hand. **Notice Rose's hips are not fully turned, pointing to the area between shortstop and third base.** This keeps him from pulling off the ball too soon, and allows Rose to see the pitch a split-second longer.

66

PRACTICE, PRACTICE

Once you have determined what type of swing is going to work for you, you need to perfect it and make it feel natural. You want your body to react this way without you even thinking about it. The best way to do this is to practice.

Tee and soft toss drills are the best way to do this. Tees are good because if you aren't hitting the ball solidly, it shows at once. If you top the ball, it just dribbles off the tee and if you get under the ball too much, you're going to hit the tee itself. Soft toss is good when you want to quicken your bat speed. The ball should be tossed underhand to you from the side. The object is simply to get the barrel of the bat to the ball. Taking batting practice with the pitcher at half the normal distance (about 20 to 30 feet away) is also a good drill. This forces the hitter to respond quickly to different pitch locations. There won't be time for a big swing at this range, so you're forced to work on contact rather than power.

After you feel good about your basic swing, adjust the pitch or the tee to work on different pitch locations. And have a coach or teammate pay attention to where your ball goes; this might give you some clues to flaws in your swing.

The thing of just swinging a bat cannot be taken too lightly. It helps a great deal. I recall that when I was a boy in grade school playing on Little League teams, I loved to swing a bat, as my mother will testify. I used to knock all the roses off her bushes and the leaves off her plants, imagining they were certain pitches at different levels. I don't believe in beating rose bushes with a bat, but I do believe that regular swinging of the bat helps you get the feel of it and learn to control it.

— *Harmon Killebrew*

Soft toss drills (Figure 67), tee work (Figure 68), and short batting practice (Figure 69) are excellent methods of developing a fundamentally sound swing. Figure 68: Always practice hitting the ball in different locations. Here, the hitter is working on hitting the ball up the middle. Figure 69: Short batting practice works on quickening the hands and getting the head of the bat to the ball. Always remember to put a screen in front of the pitcher. Figure 70: Whenever possible have a coach or teammate analyze your swing. Figure 71: Consistent practice will help develop a fundamentally sound swing, as shown here. Practice makes perfect.

Components of a Good Swing

① **RECOIL.** Go back to go forward. The recoil *can* be as minimal as a light inward turn of the knee or as exaggerated as a front leg kick.

② **STEP.** As the pitcher is releasing the ball, take a short, soft step toward him.

③ **SEPARATE.** As the pitch is released, the hands and the front foot should separate. The hands should move to the back while the lead foot steps out.

④ **VISION.** Pick up the velocity, location, and type of pitch so you can time your swing correctly.

⑤ **ADJUST.** Once you've determined the type of pitch, you need to move your hands and your lower body accordingly.

⑥ **CONTACT.** Bring the barrel of the bat to the ball. On an inside pitch, this would be out in front of the plate; for one down the middle, it would be at the top of the plate; and for an outside pitch, contact would be at the middle to back part of the plate.

⑦ **PALM UP, PALM DOWN.** As you make contact, your top hand should face up toward the sky and your bottom hand down to the ground.

⑧ **ROLL OVER.** Right after contact, your wrists should roll over.

⑨ **FOLLOW THROUGH.** Finish your swing. Young hitters are notorious for cutting their swing short.

⑩ **HEAD DOWN.** Keep your head down on the entire swing. What you can't see, you won't hit.

71

Retired Minnesota Twins fan-favorite Kirby Puckett started his career in style. In his debut game in 1984, Puckett smacked four hits to tie a major league record for most hits by a player in their first game.

I may be 21, but I never felt like a phenom and I hate the word 'potential.' I want to be known as a player, period.

— Alex Rodriguez, after winning the 1996 AL batting title

■ St. Louis Cardinal Lou Brock became the first man to bat in a major league game held outside the United States when he faced the Montreal Expos in Canada on April 14, 1969.

■ Babe Herman of the Cincinnati Reds hit the first home run in a major league night game against the Brooklyn Dodgers on July 10, 1935.

■ 1/8 was the uniform number worn by midget Eddie Gaedel when he batted for the St. Louis Browns in 1951, becoming the smallest hitter in history. Naturally, Gaedel walked on four pitches.

■ 54 is the highest number of hits a team can record and still be shutout. How's that possible? Hint: Major league rules state that whenever a baserunner is struck by a batted ball the runner is out, the ball is dead and runners may not advance and the batter is credited with a hit. So if the first three hitters in each inning get hits to load the bases and the next three batters hit balls that strike their teammates you have six hits with no runs scoring. Nine innings with six hits in each and you reach a total of 54 hits.

■ In 1990 Kansas City Royal George Brett won the American League batting title to become the first player in major league history to be batting champion in three different decades.

■ Joe Sewell, a shortstop for the Cleveland Indians from 1920 to 1928 was the toughest hitter to strike out in the history of baseball. Sewell, a member of the Baseball Hall of Fame, came to bat 7,132 times in his career and only struck out 114 times. So Sewell only struck out once every 62 at-bats! In 1925, he struck out only four times in 608 at-bats.

■ When he homered for the Cleveland Indians during the 1995 World Series Eddie Murray became only the third player in baseball history to hit a home run in three different decades. Murray had previously homered in the 1979 and 1983 World Series for the Baltimore Orioles. Prior to Murray, only Yankees Joe DiMaggio and Yogi Berra had homered in three decades.

■ Four major league baseball teams (all in the National League) have never had a batting champion on their roster. No player from the New York Mets, San Francisco Giants, Houston Astros or Florida Marlins has ever led their league in batting.

To the Parent or Instructor

Here's how to get started in teaching your youngster, one-on-one, how to hit a baseball. It's fun, as all games should be, and you should keep it simple.

This initial session is not really one session, but a series of three or four low-intensity 20- to 30-minute demonstration/play periods during which you gradually lay the groundwork of a correct swing. Rome was not built in a day and neither is a batting swing. Your objective in the early going is not to build a flawless swing. It's to play, to impart the basics of hitting a baseball, to pass along your love of the game to your youngster, and to have some fun.

Figure 1: As difficult as hitting a baseball is, it can be taught on a very basic level. Young hitters should try to work on three different areas when they start out; try to learn the correct form; swing the bat aggressively; have fun while you're practicing.

In each session present the entire swing but select only one technique for emphasis and reinforcement. First time out, simply make sure the grip is correct. Second time around, recheck the grip and make sure your youngster is stepping directly toward the pitcher. In the third session, make sure the hands stay back as long as possible. In the fourth session, pay special attention to proper weight shift (batter must go back before going forward). Keep your corrections simple, repeat them, but don't give the child several things to think about at once. This is not the time to clutter your youngster's mind with excessive details.

By encouraging your child to take healthy (hard) cuts at the ball, you will automatically promote many of the components of a good swing—bat speed, hip and shoulder turn, leg drive, and weight shift. Even the swings that don't connect with the ball should be gut-busters—recall Reggie Jackson's swinging strikes and you've got the picture!

Getting started is just that, a beginning that may—if you approach it properly—lead to your child's enduring interest in the game of baseball and the art of hitting.

What You'll Need

A bat that your youngster can lift and swing without straining (24 oz. to 28 oz). (Here's a way to determine the right size and weight. Have your youngster grasp the bat with one hand at the handle, lift it, and extend the arm parallel to the ground (see Figure 2). If the bat can be held easily in this horizontal position for several seconds, it can be swung easily, too.)

- Baseballs
- Tennis balls
- Platform tennis balls
- Specially made "soft" baseballs (sold in sporting-goods stores)
- Rolled-up athletic socks
- Batting tee

You and your child should read and follow the following instructions. If your child isn't able to read, then explain what to do.

For the Player

The Very First Time (20–30 minutes)

"Grip it and rip it" is your objective, but you cannot hit any pitch with a faulty grip. Here's a simple way to get the proper grip. Place the bat on the ground between your legs with the handle closest to you (at 6 o'clock) and the barrel farthest from you (at 12 o'clock). Lean over, pick up the bat, and lift it directly over your hitting shoulder.

Check the alignment of your knuckles—the second knuckles on the fingers of the top hand should align somewhere between the second knuckles and back knuckles of the bottom hand (see Figure 4).

Here are some tips to make sure you have a proper grip.

1. Don't roll either hand over so far that any sets of knuckles are aligned; this inhibits proper hand and wrist action.
2. Hold the bat firmly but not with a "death grip." The hands will naturally tighten when the swing begins.
3. Grip the bat in the fingers of the top hand—this is the dominant hand in controlling the flight path of the barrel of the bat as it strikes the ball.

I tell parents to make sure their son or daughter takes the bat and puts it right on the shoulder when they begin hitting. What happens when you rest the bat on the shoulder is that as the pitch comes in your first reaction is to push the bat back and up into the perfect hitting position with your hands and wrists cocked just right. There's no thinking about it, you just swing from there. It happens naturally.

— *Steve Garvey*

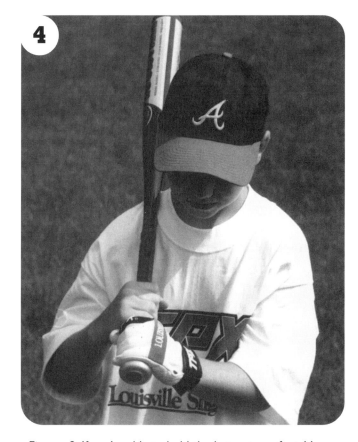

Figures 2: If you're able to hold the bat out comfortably with one arm, it should be light enough for you to swing.
Figures 3 and 4: A good way to find out where your grip is comfortable is to simply pick the bat up naturally.

Figures 5 and 6: Grip the bat more toward your fingers than your palms. You want to have a loose, but firm hold on the handle.
Figures 7 and 8: Start out with the bat on your shoulder. As the pitch is delivered, you'll raise the bat to the launch position instinctively.

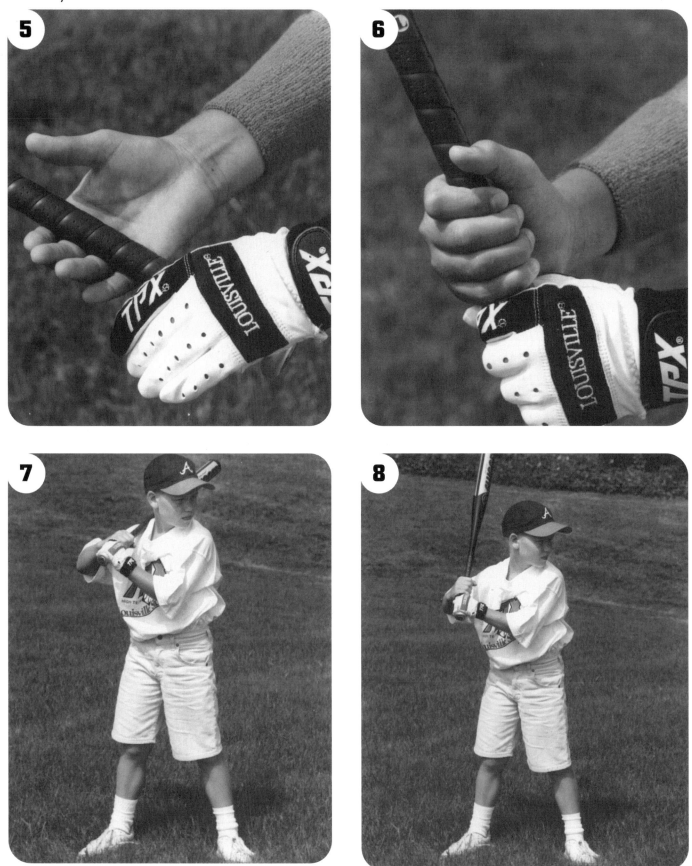

Step 1

Assume the "Athletic Position"

Square your feet and spread them slightly more than shoulder-width apart. Bend at the knees and push down on the inside balls of your feet, with your weight evenly distributed and muscles tense and ready to contract or extend. This has been termed the "athletic position" because in nearly every game—football, basketball, tennis—players get into this balanced position to perform one or more movements. For example, basketball defenders face their opponent in the athletic position. Hitters assume a similar stance.

Figures 9 through 11: Notice the hitter starts out in the athletic position with no bat. There is a little bend in his knees and he's slightly bent forward at the waist. In Figure 10, the hitter puts his hands up as if he was in his stance. His weight has shifted a bit to his back side. Once the hitter has the bat in his hands (Figure 11), he shifts back even more to what he feels is comfortable.

Step 2

Rock, Wiggle, But Don't Roll

From the athletic position, begin wiggling your toes, pressing them downward and then gradually rock your weight from side to side. Do not roll your weight over onto the outer sides of your feet, and do not shift so violently that you lose balance and fall forward or backward. Continue to rock back and forth, lengthening the side-to-side motion but keeping your balance under control.

The purpose of this little drill is to promote the weight shift that is necessary in a proper swing. All the great batting instructors stress the importance of a batter's ability to shift his weight. According to former major league batting instructor Charley Lau, "A hitter must shift his weight back in order to go forward. Balance and rhythm make this possible. Generally, the better the weight shift, the harder you hit the ball." When you begin, learning to hit the ball hard is a priority because so many other components of a proper batting swing will occur naturally when you take a vigorous swing.

Step 3

Step and Swing

Next, imagine a ball coming over the plate, rock your weight back (onto the rear foot), step and swing. Take a hard swing, as hard as you can.

To the Parent or Instructor

It's time to put a live ball into the mix. Put up your batting tee and place a ball on it about waist-high. Have your youngster repeat Steps l and 2, then attempt to hit the stationary ball. Again, get your child to swing hard—this will naturally call upon the legs to drive, the hips to turn, and the hands to propel the barrel of the bat at maximum speed. Encourage your youngster to hit the ball really hard—no need to mention leg drive or any of the other mechanics also at work!

Make a game of it. Award 10 points for every ball cleanly hit and see how many swings it takes to reach 100 points.

Work off the tee until fatigue sets in, then quit. Come back another day!

Components to Add in Future Sessions

In successive "getting started" sessions, introduce hitting a moving ball, hitting balls in various parts of the strike zone, and how to avoid getting hurt when hit by a pitched ball. Review the basics for a few minutes at the start of each session.

Hitting a Moving Ball

Position yourself about 12 to 15 feet from the batter and pitch the ball underhand. Toss the ball waist-high with a very small arc. Encourage a hard swing and don't be shy about giving praise when your youngster connects. Use your imagination to make up a game. Or challenge your youngster to hit the ball over your head. Just duck if he whizzes a line drive at your nose!

Hitting Balls in Various Parts of the Strike Zone

You will need a dozen or so rolled-up socks for this drill. Position yourself on bended knee about 5 to 6 feet in front and off to the side of the batter (see Figure 13). The purpose here is to get your youngster used to hitting the ball in various parts of the strike zone. The strike zone extends between the batter's

Figure 12: Hitting off a tee is one of the best ways to drill the fundamentals of a good swing. Timing, pitch selection, and pitch velocity are taken out of the picture so the hitter can focus solely on his stride, swing, and follow through. This hitter displays good form. His hips are turned, the bat is level, and his head is down on the ball.

13

armpits and knees and is 17 inches wide. Begin tossing the socks into various parts of the strike zone. Move the tosses in and out, up and down. Instruct the batter to take pitches that are balls and to swing at pitches that are strikes. Call out the pitch location, such as,"Low inside strike." When your toss misses the strike zone, call out "Ball, low." This helps the batter to learn the strike zone and promotes eye tracking (see Chapters 4 and 5), which is an important vision skill in batting.

For the Player and Parent

All batters, whether they admit it or not, are afraid of being hit by the ball. Here is a combination rolling/batting drill you can practice. Take a dozen or so tennis balls, or special "soft" baseballs, and position yourself about 25 from the batter and one by one toss the balls gently at your youngster aiming for the upper body. Have the child practice rolling away from the ball, making a quick quarter turn with the upper body, head tucked behind the front shoulder. Then move back another 20 to 25 feet and conduct a normal batting practice. Intermittently, throw the ball at the batter without warning, who should roll away from the pitch. Soon, the rolling action will be an automatic reflex. This drill will develop confidence and reduce fear.

Figure 13: Working on form is very helpful, but eventually a player needs to practice hitting a moving object. A simple, slow toss is sufficient, even if rolled-up socks are used instead of a ball. The hitter trains his hand-eye coordination, and begins to get a sense of timing.

Switch-Hitting—Start Early

A big advantage to any youngster aspiring to become a professional ballplayer is to learn to swing the bat from each side of the plate.

And the sooner a youngster begins converting himself into a switch hitter, the better. I was nine years old and play-ing Knothole Baseball in Cincinnati when I began switch hit-ting. But major leaguers such as Maury Wills and Don Kessinger stand as living proof that the conversion can be made successfully after a player reaches adulthood.

Learning to become a switch-hitter takes practice, prac-tice, and more practice. And it also requires a lot of perse-verance because it's easy to become discouraged. Everyone wants to excel. But youngsters embarrass easily, especially when mom and dad are looking on. So a youngster who's a natural right-handed hitter must learn to swallow his pride

and keep plugging if he strikes out while learning to swing left-handed.

By switch-hitting, a player practically eliminates his chances of being platooned (sharing a position with another player).

There are other advantages. Any batter will tell you that the toughest pitch to hit is the one that moves away from him. The only pitch that moves away from a switch-hitter is the screwball. And how many pitchers throw effective screw-balls? Not many. But every successful pitcher has a curve or a slider. Most of them have both pitches. I didn't have to swing at a Bob Gibson slider or a Jim Bunning curve from the right side of the plate, all because I learned to switch-hit.

— Pete Rose

KNOWING
THE ZONES

4

"*All good balls to hit are strikes, though not all strikes are good balls to hit.*"
— *Dave Winfield*

WHAT IS THE STRIKE ZONE?

Every at-bat is a one-on-one duel between the hitter and the pitcher, with the pitcher getting all the advantages. He already knows what pitch he's throwing and where. It's up to you to figure it out. Knowing the strike zone can make all the difference.

If you develop a good eye, the pitcher is going to have to start giving you good pitches. And good pitches are a whole lot easier to hit. On the flip side, if a pitcher sees you swinging at pitches outside the strike zone, you won't see a strike all day.

Of course, although the strike zone is uniformly and simply defined as the area over home plate and between the batter's armpits and knees, it really changes from game to game because you have different umpires calling it as they see it. And as a result, in every baseball game, you're going to have hitters, pitchers, catchers, coaches and fans complaining about how the umpire is calling the strikes and balls. Calling the pitches is a thankless job. Not only does each umpire bring his own version to the game, but each batter does, too.

Back in 1870, the game actually allowed for batter preferences. Believe it or not, the hitter had a say in deciding where in the strike zone the ball had to be thrown. Until 1887, the hitter would announce to the umpire whether he wanted a high ball, a low ball, or a fair ball. A high ball was a pitch that was to be between the shoulders and the waist, a low ball was between the waist and the knees, and a fair ball meant anywhere below the shoulders and above the knees. The umpire would relay the hitter's request to the pitcher before the first pitch was thrown. After the first pitch, the batter would not be allowed to alter his desired location.

Then, in 1887, the strike zone was set in stone. It was the area over the plate, from the top of the shoulders to the bottom of the knees. This huge strike zone lasted until 1949. In 1950, it shrank to only from the armpits to the top of the knees. For the six years from 1963 to 1968, baseball went back to the big zone; in 1969, the zone shrank again. Finally, in 1996, it dropped to

O bviously, it's important to know the strike zone, but it will change from day to day with different umpires. What a hitter needs to do is pay attention to what the umpire is calling a strike that day. It doesn't matter what you think the strike zone is sometimes. It matters what the ump thinks.

— *Mike Stanley*

The strike zone is defined in the rule book as the space that exists over the plate area from the bottom of the knee caps to just below the arm pits. However, most umpires won't call any pitch a strike that's above the belt.

include the full kneecap, allowing the pitcher more room for error when working a hitter low. The high pitches, though, still aren't given a break; any pitch within five inches of the armpit would no doubt be called a ball.

Despite nearly four decades of uniformity, the strike zone still remains open to interpretation. Some umpires have a low strike zone, and some have a high one. One umpire may call a strike on a pitch that barely skirts the perimeter of the plate, while another may squeeze the pitcher and not give him the corners. Batters need to be aware that the strike zone is going to change with each umpire.

For years, major league players even had to deal with the fact that the strike zone varied between leagues. The American League had a high strike zone and the National League had a lower one. The difference did not stem from a league philosophy but merely from the fact that in the American League the umpire wore a balloon chest protector, forcing him to stand as he called strikes, while the National League umpire wore the inside protector, allowing him to crouch lower. Finally, in 1979, the American League umpires switched over to the inside protector. Now, pitches that looked low from a standing-up position were being called for strikes. It was a major adjustment for hitters and pitchers in the American League.

Regardless of what league you play in, though, it is important to be aware of what calls your particular home plate umpire is making. Simply by being observant when you're on deck, in the dugout, or even in the field, you can get a good idea of what is going to be called a ball and what will be called a strike. This is important, because even if you feel you know what the strike zone is, the umpire might have something slightly different in mind that can make or break an at-bat.

Having learned the legal, personal best, and pitcher's strike zone, the smart batter conforms to the ultimate strike zone: the umpire's.

— *Dave Winfield*

FINDING THE STRIKE ZONE

Obviously, the best place to become familiar with the umpire's particular strike zone is when you're up to bat. If the umpire calls a strike that you felt was high or outside, don't get upset. Instead, store that information in your memory for the rest of the game. When you see that pitch again, get your bat off your shoulder and swing. Chances are good that the umpire is going to call it a strike. Bottom line, it's not going to matter whether the ump's or your judgment is off; the ump is the one making the call.

A big reason why Frank Thomas has so much success at the plate is because of his patience. Thomas rarely swings at a pitch out of the strike zone, and had only 136 walks in 1995 to prove it.

Knowing an umpire's strike zone has other advantages, too. For instance, if you notice the umpire has a small strike zone, make the pitcher work. Be more selective about "borderline pitches," that is, pitches that are on or just off the edges of the plate. Not only will the pitcher be forced to throw down the middle of the plate, but if he's constantly running deep counts, he will tire sooner and become more hittable.

A DRILL TO LEARN THE STRIKE ZONE

Honing your strike-zone judgment should begin even in preseason. While you can also learn from each at-bat in a real game, you want as much knowledge as possible going into the start of the season. There's a good drill for this.

Stand up at the plate while a pitcher is working his pitches. Assume the stance you would if you were batting in a game and treat the incoming pitch as if it were real. Pick up the ball when it leaves the pitcher's hand and try to determine how the ball is spinning, and its velocity and location. (How to distinguish each of these is discussed further in Chapter 5—Knowing the Zones.) Step into the pitch and watch it all the way into the catcher's glove. *Do not swing!* When the catcher receives the ball, have him call out whether it was a strike or a ball and give the location of the pitch (i.e., ball, high and outside). Pay attention to see if you felt the same about the pitch.

Once you've done this for a few days of practice, you're ready to add the next step. You call the pitches. While you are calling these pitches, have someone (a coach or teammate with good strike-zone judgment) stand in the umpire's spot. He should record his opinion and your call on a piece of paper. After about ten pitches, go over the results. See if there's a particular location that you misjudged with regularity.

Be sure to do this with a variety of pitches. Don't just get in the batter's box when the pitcher is throwing fastballs. Learn how you call them when you see breaking balls, sliders, and off-speed pitches.

It came to me when I was in American Legion ball in Nebraska . . . make the pitcher throw. You usually don't think of that until you get to the major leagues. I can remember a particular at-bat in my career against Juan Marichal. I was lead-off hitter in a game in Philadelphia on about a 100-degree day. He must have thrown me 30 pitches before I got a walk. I just kept fouling pitches off. By the second inning he was through. It was the earliest then that he'd ever been taken out of a game.

— *Richie Ashburn*

Stand up at the plate while the pitcher is getting his work in on the mound. Practice calling out whether the pitch is a ball or a strike, and compare your opinions with the catcher's.

4

Everyone has their own specific hitting zone. Some hitters like the ball down, others like pitches inside. Here, Charlie Hayes takes a hack at a pitch up around his letters.

If you want to be a consistent hitter, you've got to know the strike zone. Swinging at strikes not only increases your chances to hit the ball well and reach first base, but it also makes the pitcher work harder.

— Lenny Dykstra

WHAT IS THE HITTING ZONE?

There's a bottom line for hitters. In order to be successful at the plate, you have to be able to make contact with the ball. You may be a perfect judge of the strike zone, with a beautiful swing to boot, but if you can't hit the ball, the pitcher is going to throw it right over the plate and get you out.

That's why you need to be aware of another zone—your hitting zone. You won't find the hitting zone in any baseball rulebook. It's a personal preference zone that varies from batter to batter. There are certain pitches that you will be able to handle best, and you need to recognize what they are in order to maximize your potential.

Some batters are high-ball hitters; others are low-ball. Some like the pitch inside; others like the pitch away from them. In some extreme cases, batters have a hitting zone that isn't even in the strike zone. The hitting zone is merely the spot where you can drive the ball. The key is to recognize where your zone is, so that when you see a pitch heading there, you can jump on it.

It sounds simple, but mastering it is a little more complicated. You have to work hard to create a large enough hitting zone so that pitchers can't just pitch around you (pitch both strikes and balls at which you won't swing because they are not in your hitting zone), and you even have to reevaluate your zone depending on the type of pitch. Most batters like their fastballs to be low, the breaking balls to be in the middle, and the off-speed pitches to be high. Discovering all the nuances of your personal hitting zone can take a long time, but once you know it, you can sit back and choose your pitch with confidence. Drills that can help you distinguish your hitting zone are presented later in this chapter.

My hitting zone is a little tighter than my strike zone. There are great bad-ball hitters in this game, like Kirby Puckett, guys who swing at everything and still hit .300. I can't have success that way. I try to hit only strikes.

— Wade Boggs

Ken Griffey, Jr., watches as his towering drive sails toward the right-field bleachers.

5

THE HITTING ZONE FOR POWER

It's funny how, whenever you hear a youngster dreaming up that heroic baseball fantasy—bases loaded, two outs in the bottom of the ninth, tie score—he never imagined singling to right field for the game-winning hit. Nor is it ever clear how those bases got loaded in the first place. It's always a game-winning homer that caps the imaginary at-bat and steals the glory.

Home runs are undoubtedly one of the most exciting events that can occur in a baseball game. A dramatic home run in a tight game is a moment that players and fans will savor for years. But home runs do not come as frequently as you might think. The average for major leaguers is only once in about 40 at-bats. And these are the guys who are paid to play the game!

Trying to be a "power hitter" greatly reduces your effectiveness as a hitter. You become one-dimensional, and your hitting zone is small—basically right down the center. When you go to the plate thinking, "This one's over the fence," you'll be looking for a ball to pull. And that kind of thinking will more often than not result in your pulling your shoulders and head off the ball too soon. If the pitch is right where you want it, you may succeed. But if it's anywhere else in the strike zone, you'll swing and miss.

This is the basic reason why home-run hitters strike out so often. And strikeouts are the worst. If you can at least make contact, even just an infield dribbler, the fielder might boot it or throw it away. Getting on base that way may not help your statistics, but it certainly helps the team. Striking out does not.

It is true that there are players who hit home runs far more frequently than once every 40 at-bats and yet still maintain a great average. Players like Ted Williams, Stan Musial, Ken Griffey, Jr., and Frank Thomas are in a very small class of major leaguers who hit for both power and average. But most of that elite group will tell you that they rarely went up to the plate trying to hit a home run. They just wanted to make good contact—and the ball went out of the park.

In 1912, J.F. Hillerich and Son hired Frank W. Bradsby as its sales manager. Bradsby went on to become one of the most dominant figures in the sporting goods business and in 1916, J.F. Hillerich and Son was changed to Hillerich & Bradsby Company.

6

Rod Carew compiled 3,053 career hits, and was a master at hitting the ball where it was pitched. Carew liked to adjust his swing to what and where the pitcher was throwing.

I hit only .261 in 1974, so during the following winter, I made up my mind that I would hit to right field the next season. Well, I hit .318 in 1975 and drove in 102 runs by going with the pitch and hitting singles to right field.

How does a right-handed hitter learn to hit to right field? You just prepare yourself mentally and then learn the technique. For example, I learned to sit on the breaking ball. In other words, just wait for the breaking ball. That's the key: wait, wait, wait.

— Thurman Munson

THE HITTING ZONE FOR AVERAGE

If you shift your focus from home run to base hit, you miraculously enlarge your hitting zone. Now that you don't have to wait for a pitch in that central power spot, you can be productive with a variety of pitches. Now your goal is just to hit the ball to an open space, but it can be right, left, or center field, depending on what pitch the pitcher gives you.

The ability to hit well to all parts of the field will also make it harder for the opponents to defend against you. A predictable hitter can be stopped by a simple shift in the defense. An unpredictable hitter gets hits.

For instance, if you're a left-handed hitter who likes to pull the ball to right field, the defense will shift to their left, tightening up the holes in that area. On top of that, the pitcher will probably try to pitch you inside, making it even more likely that you'll pull the ball. On the other hand, if you demonstrate you can hit to all parts of the field, the defense can't shade their positioning to one side of the field and the pitcher has to give you a variety of pitches.

Easier said than done, though, right? You want to become a spray hitter, but your zone is just as limited as a power hitter's—right in the middle. The answer is training. Figure 7 shows you where you want to make contact with the ball, depending on the pitch. Work on this. A ball down the middle should be met in the front half of home plate. An inside pitch should be swung at a little sooner and be met out in front of the plate. An outside pitch should be a fraction of a second later and contacted a little farther back. It's important to practice hitting the baseball in all locations, not just the ones you have success with.

One of the most difficult pitches for hitters to handle is the pitch on the outside part of the plate. The single most important detail to remember, though, is merely to wait. By waiting a split second longer, you will keep your body closed, which will prevent you from pulling off the ball. Too often, hitters will commit too soon and open up, forcing them to swing "all arms" (a swing with premature weight shift and minimal hip rotation) at an outside pitch—most likely producing a weak infield hit.

The best advice I can give young hitters is to constantly swing the bat, work hard, and practice on your weaknesses. If you have trouble with the curve ball, practive against curves. You'll never learn to hit a curve merely by swinging at fastballs. That's a common failure, even in the majors.

— Stan Musial

Timing is a key factor in hitting the outside pitch to the opposite field. However, when you're looking to hit the inside pitch that way, you have to alter your swing. Jim Eisenreich illustrates this by keeping the barrel of the bat behind his hands.

I try to lean out over the plate and have my eyes looking for the pitch away. I want to have my whole body heading toward the shortstop [Thus keeping the front shoulder closed and hips cocked], and if they come inside, that's the one I just rotate on as quickly as possible and pull to right field.

— Mo Vaughn

If you wait on the pitch you also allow yourself to take a full swing. Many hitters have the misconception that if the pitch is away from them, they can't take a full cut. It's not true. The distance from where you start your swing to the point of contact is shorter and you won't have as big a follow-through, but you can and should still swing the bat with authority.

Knowing your hitting zone helps with some of the finer points of baseball strategy, too. Sometimes you're going to get a specific assignment. You might be charged with the task of providing a sacrifice fly to score the runner at third. You're going to have to look for a pitch that falls into the area in your hitting zone that allows you to send a ball long and high to the outfield. Hitters often become too anxious when given a task like that and they swing at the first strike they see. Chances are the pitcher knows what you want to do and that first strike is probably not the pitch you want to hit.

In Figures 8 and 9, notice the difference in where Eisenreich is making contact with the ball. In Figure 8, he's pulling the pitch and meets the ball way out in front of the plate. Eisenreich hits the ball up the middle in Figure 9. The point of contact is much further back in the hitting zone.

Although the pitch in this picture may appear to be out of the strike zone, it may be a part of Stan Musial's hitting zone. **Musial does an excellent job getting the bat on the same plane with the ball.** Stan's weight has shifted forward to enable him to raise his hands more easily.

10

THE HITTER'S CORNER

MOVING YOUR HITTING ZONE

If you've tried to expand, but you still have a fairly small and obvious hitting zone, your only option is to move your hitting zone. *Move* is not the same as *change*. You've discovered that your abilities as a batter limit your flexibility for change, but the chalk line is the only limit you have in the batter's box.

If the pitcher knows you like the ball out over the plate, and is therefore pitching at your hands, back away from the plate a bit. Now when he throws that same pitch, you can extend your arms and get a good whack at the ball. And keep in mind that you moved, but the strike zone stayed the same; now a pitch heading for your wrists will be way inside. Take the pitches and take the walk.

SOMETIMES YOU JUST HATE THE PITCH

At some point, you're going to realize there's a certain pitch you'll always have trouble handling. You might have trouble with the high fastball, for instance. If you notice that you almost always get poor results going after those high strikes, you probably just want to avoid swinging at them. Remember that you're given three strikes to work with. If you have enough patience, it's likely that the pitcher will eventually come in with a pitch that's in your hitting zone. Obviously with the count at two strikes, you have to swing the bat and make contact, but otherwise let it go. Being patient and intelligent at the plate will make you a better hitter.

In the years 1994 and 1995 Frank Thomas hit a total of 78 home runs. Of those 78, 61 of them were hit when he was even or ahead in the count.

Nearly every hitter has a certain type of pitch in a particular spot in his strike zone which he finds hard to hit. For some it's high and inside while other have trouble hitting anything that's low and away. On this kind of ball, and if the count is less than two strikes, take that pitch.

— *Ted Williams*

John Mabry takes this pitch. The hitter should always remember to follow the ball all the way into the catcher's glove even when he decides not to swing.

MAKING WALKS WORK FOR YOU

A base on balls is nothing but a positive at-bat for an offense. The team gets a runner on base, the other hitters get to witness at least four pitches, and the pitcher is just a little bit more tired and disappointed. The old slogan, "A walk is as good as a hit," is very accurate. In fact, sometimes a walk can be better.

Walks are often an unnoticed stat, yet they are quite important. A runner can't score unless he gets on base first. One study revealed that three of every four batters who led off an inning with a walk came around to score. That statistic alone gives credibility to the walk. It's no wonder pitching coaches say, "Walks will kill you, every time."

Players who earn those bases on balls are experts on the strike zone. Ted Williams had more knowledge of the strike zone than any player of his time. Even though his career batting average (.344) was lower than that of the all time leader Ty Cobb (.366), Williams had a better on-base percentage (.483 versus .433). The "Splendid Splinter's" 2,109 walks made all the difference. For a team, it matters not how you get to first base, just so long as you get there. Williams was one of the greatest hitters who ever played the game, but his ability to draw walks made him even more valuable.

There are many ways to work the count into a walk. One way is not to swing until you've seen a strike. Pitchers often like to throw perfect pitches early in the count for fear of hitters sitting on a fastball, that is, when a hitter is just waiting for a fastball in the strike zone. If the pitcher is missing, the count gets to be 2-0 and the pressure is on. That alone might rattle him enough to throw the 3-0 pitch.

Another technique frequently used at higher levels of play is simply not to swing until you get a pitch you like. Obviously if the count is 0-2, you can't be picky, but before that, lay off. If you continually wait for your pitch, not only will you get it frequently, but you'll also find yourself going into deeper counts, always good for a base on balls. With two strikes, you can still battle the pitcher for your pitch if you learn to foul off balls. Eventually, he'll either give in or give you your walk.

TWO HITTING ZONE DRILLS

The first drill is just a variation on the drill used to learn the strike zone. Have someone stand behind the plate during batting practice and record the pitches you're given and the results of your hits. A pattern may emerge to show you which pitches you have trouble with, and you may find that you're not hitting certain balls well because you're judging them to be strikes when they are not.

Pepper is the other great drill. It's played by two or more players, and one player bats medium-speed pitches to the other players, who are standing 20 to 25 feet away. The swing should be crisp but controlled, with the idea of directing the ball to a player in mind. It not only helps you expand your hitting zone

> When the pitcher is in a tough spot he will do his best to get you to go for bad balls. But always remember, a walk is as good as a hit.
>
> *— Joe DiMaggio*

by teaching you how to hit to all parts of the field, but it proves an interesting point. In pepper people don't strike out, and in fact they almost always make good contact, because no one is trying to hit for power.

Hall of Fame third baseman Mike Schmidt captures this idea in his book, *The Mike Schmidt Study*:

> Have you ever noticed how the pepper hitter always gets a piece of the ball? We need to ask ourselves why. The answer is obvious. *Because he doesn't try to hit the ball out in front of the plate.* He waits for the ball to come to him and makes square, center field contact over the plate. He pushes out the inside pitch and centers the rest. He is hitting the way Harry Walker recommends hitting. Waiting as he does, *he can't get fooled.* If the object of pepper was to *pull* the ball, he would be fooled as easily as the hitter at home plate. We can learn from this.

Pepper is a great drill to improve your skills as a contact hitter. By attempting to direct where you're hitting the ball, you get a feel for how to handle pitches in different areas of the strike zone.

Study the Slugger

At 19, just graduated from high school, Waite Hoyt began his 21-year major league pitching career which included seven World Series and 243 victories. He wrote these tips for high school pitchers more than 50 years ago. Today's aspiring sluggers can benefit from learning how a Hall of Fame pitcher advised other pitchers on how to gain an edge.

Professional teams have clubhouse meetings to learn about opposing batters, but a non-professional pitcher must do all his own thinking and analyzing. Here are some pitching tips in a nutshell.

1. **Study the feet of the batter.** Notice how far from the plate he stands, and how he steps. If he is slow to shift or follow the ball, then he's a sucker for a curve.

2. **Watch a batter's eyes.** You may discover where he is trying to hit by the way he is looking. If he's right-handed and seems bent on hitting to right, pitch inside.

3. **Watch his stride.** If the batter takes a long stride, he can't hit a change-of-pace or other slow pitch.

4. **Watch the way he leans his weight.** If he leans out over the plate as he swings, pitch him inside.

5. **If your opponent takes a very long swing,** so much so that he jerks his head away from the ball, try slow ones. A change of pace is poison for the long, irresponsible swinger.

6. **If he holds both arms very high,** try low outside pitches.

If you see a batter coming to the plate who is a poke hitter—someone who is just trying to get the wood on the ball and punch it to spots in short left, center or right or through the infield—give up thoughts of striking him out. Try to fool him with a curve or drop. Make him hit the ball into the ground where the infielders can grab it.

If you ever pitch against anyone who can swing a bat like Ty Cobb, or Honus Wagner, my advice would be, "Pitch and pray."

Diamond Dust

Baltimore Orioles leadoff hitter Brady Anderson smacked 50 home runs during the 1996 season, 12 of them leading off his team's first at-bat. The latter figure in a major league record.

*I've had pretty good success facing
Stan (Musial)—by throwing him my
best pitch and backing up third base.*

— Former Dodger pitcher Carl Erskine

- During the 1995 season Oakland Athletic Mark McGwire hit 39 home runs in only 317 at-bats, or nearly one home run every eight at-bats, the greatest home run ratio ever. McGwire, who hit an all-time record 49 home runs as a rookie in 1987, followed his prolific 1995 season with a major league-leading 52 home runs during the 1996 season.

- Ted Williams went into the final day of the 1941 season with a .39955 batting average, good enough to finish the year at a rounded-off .400. But Williams refused to sit out a season-ending doubleheader to protect his average. Instead, he played in both games and went a combined 6-for-8 to finish the season at .406. Williams is the last man to hit .400 in the major leagues.

- Ty Cobb won an all-time record 12 American League batting titles, including nine straight from 1907 to 1915. Nobody has ever had more in a row.

- When Alex Rodriguez of the Seattle Mariners won the American League batting championship in 1996 he became the first shortstop in either league to claim a batting crown since Pittsburgh Pirate Dick Groat turned the trick in 1960.

- Going into the final day of the 1929 season New York Giant slugger Mel Ott needed one home run to catch Chuck Klein of the Philadelphia Phillies for the league home run championship. To make sure that Ott did not catch their teammate, Phillies pitchers intentionally walked Ott a record five times.

- During his career Babe Ruth hit 714 home runs, the second highest total of all-time. On 72 occasions the Babe hit two or more homers in the same game.

- On April 30, 1996 in a game against Cincinnati, Pittsburgh Pirate Jeff King hit two home runs in the fourth inning, a solo shot and a grand slam. In doing so, King became only the third player in major league history to hit two homers in the same inning twice. King had done it in 1995 in a game against the Giants. The other two players to hit two home runs in an inning twice are Willie McCovey and Andre Dawson.

- In 1989 Kirby Puckett of the Minnesota Twins collected more than 200 hits for the fourth consecutive season. In doing so, he became only the fifth player of the century to accomplish the feat, joining Wade Boggs, Al Simmons, Paul "Big Poison" Waner and Bill Terry.

TRAINING
THE EYES

5

"See the ball, hit the ball."

— *Pete Rose*

HAVING VISION

Vision is very important in hitting. Our guys get tested every fall by an optometrist on their vision and eye skills such as depth perception. Very few guys have well-trained vision coming out of high school. They have a lot of difficulty identifying pitches early on because they simply haven't seen a wide variety of pitches at the high school level. Some guys are able to learn how to do it while others just can't seem to get it and struggle because of it. One thing we do try to teach with everybody is to make sure they're seeing the pitch with both eyes.

— *Ron Polk*
head baseball coach,
Mississippi State
University

Have you ever seen the television clip where Chicago Bulls superstar Michael Jordan takes a shot from the free-throw line with his eyes closed? Jordan, perhaps the greatest basketball player in the history of the game, made the shot, then casually retreated back to the opposite end of the floor.

In 1993, Jordan turned in his basketball shoes for a pair of baseball cleats and suited up for the Birmingham Red Barons, the Double A affiliate of the Chicago White Sox. When asked what he would have said to attempting an at-bat with his eyes closed, Jordan replied: "I would say you're crazy. The difference is that the basket is not moving like a baseball. Once you can visualize the rim in your head, a free throw with your eyes closed is not that hard. Hitting a moving baseball with your eyes closed is a different story. It can't be done, and shouldn't even be tried."

Vision is an absolute necessity in hitting, but there's far more to "baseball vision" than just seeing the ball. If you're going to be a successful hitter, your eyes need to pick up every little detail about that baseball. You have a fraction of a second to learn the speed, location, and type of pitch, and your eyes are the only tool you're given. They are as important to the batter as strong wrists and good bat speed.

"Vision is certainly critical to one's success as a hitter," says Paul Berman, a Hackensack, New Jersey, optometrist who has worked with amateur baseball players at all levels. "Hitting a baseball is the quintessential act of hand-to-eye coordination. The eye tells you where the ball is and when to swing. It's possible to shoot baskets blindfolded and it may be even possible to complete a pass in football blindfolded. But there is no way you can hit a ball without seeing it from release to contact, because vision is the timing device. A hitter can have the best swing in the world, but it's vision that tells you when the pitch is coming and where it is."

A hitter can pick up several clues from a pitcher when his delivery is frozen in time as shown in this picture. However, he has very little time when standing in the batter's box.

On average, when a pitcher delivers a pitch to the plate, it takes four-tenths of a second to get from the pitcher's hand to catcher's glove. Half of that time—in other words, two-tenths of a second—the hitter spends on physically swinging the bat. It takes another tenth of a second for the brain to tell the body to swing. That leaves the hitter with one-tenth of a second to identify the pitch—fastball, curveball, change-up, slider—and its location—high, low, inside, or outside. At higher levels, when pitches such as split-fingered fast-balls and knuckleballs are thrown into the fray, it becomes even more difficult.

So how is a batter supposed to put it all together in four-tenths of a second? Well, no one ever claimed it was easy, not even for a world-class athlete like Michael Jordan. But it's not impossible. Like most other aspects of hitting, zeroing in on a pitch can be broken down into smaller steps: analyzing the pitcher, knowing his release points, focusing at the right time, and identifying the type of pitch.

Against a knuckleballer, all you can do is hope the ball is in the vicinity of where you're swinging. If it's up in the zone, you swing. If it's down, you just let it go.

— *Mickey Tettleton*

KNOW THE PITCHER

Suppose you're a major leaguer who has to face Randy Johnson in Seattle one day and Tom "Flash" Gordon in Boston the next. The fact that you have to adjust to a different repertoire of pitches, their velocities, and facing both a right-hander and left-hander, makes your at-bats challenging enough. But there are other factors that need to be taken into account.

Six-foot, ten-inch Johnson will throw a fastball that's traveling on a down-ward plane. It's going to look like it's heading straight down, and unless you adjust for that, you're going to get a strike called on you.

2

Major league pitcher Todd Stottlemyre has a three-fourths overhand delivery and uses a four-seamed fastball that has minimal movement. His slider has a short, sharp beak, and he throws it more often than his fastball when he needs to make a batter put a ball in play. This is information a hitter should know about the pitcher he is facing.

The hitter has to immediately pick up the pitcher's release point. Pay attention if the pitcher has different release points for different pitches. It may clue you in on what pitch is coming.

3

J. Frederich Hillerich, father of John Andrew "Bud" Hillerich, who made Pete Browning's first bat in 1884, opposed this new enterprise. J.F. Hillerich's business thrived on turning roller skids, bed posts, ten-pins, wooden bowling balls, and a swinging churn. But son John persevered, and eventually grew bat-making into a major part of the Hillerich family business.

The next day, when you play five-foot, nine-inch Gordon, you have to make an equivalent mental shift, because his pitches are going to appear higher. The ball will seem to be coming straight out of his hand.

And height is just one factor. While the pitcher is warming up in the bullpen or out on the field before the game, watch him. Study the pitches he gives your teammates who go up to bat in front of you. Get as many clues as possible before you step into the batter's box. Does the breaking ball have a big break or a slight, sharp one? Does the fastball have movement or is it flat? And, most importantly, where is the release point?

RELEASE POINTS

One of the most important things to look at when you're analyzing a pitcher is the release point or points. You have to know exactly where the ball is going to come from in order to maximize every tenth of a second you have after the pitch is delivered.

Other pitchers who don't have good command of all their pitches may vary their release points. This can be difficult on the hitter because he's never sure at what point the pitch will be released. Smart hitters can, however, use this as an advantage. If a pitcher throws his fastball straight over the top, and his curveball from a three-quarters delivery, the batter will know the pitch type just by recognizing the release point.

DRILL FOR FOCUSING ON THE RELEASE POINT

Ron Polk, who coached current major league stars Will Clark and Rafael Palmeiro during their collegiate days at Mississippi State, spends a lot of time with his players in the pre-season drilling them on pitch identification and picking up release points.

4

"It's very important to pick up the ball and the release point right away and to track it into the hitting zone," he says. "One thing we do when we practice inside is use colored baseballs to pick up release points during batting practice. We paint the balls black, blue, and white and have the hitter call out the color when the pitcher releases the ball."

In another drill, Polk has his pitchers go into their windup, but they do not have a baseball. Instead of throwing a ball, they flash either one, two, or three fingers, or a fist. The hitter immediately calls out what he sees.

FOCUSING

Whether it's in the middle of a ballgame or during batting practice, coaches can often be heard shouting, "Keep your eye on the ball!" It seems like obvious advice, but when should you start? Do you focus in on the ball the entire time the pitcher is shuffling around on the mound? Definitely not. If you try to keep track of the ball through the pitcher's entire motion, your eyes can become tired. They might blink or lose focus.

The alternative that many hitting instructors, eye specialists, and hitters have come up with is something called a "soft center" followed by a "hard focus." A soft center is a general awareness of what is going on in the field. The center would be something like the pitcher's hat or a sign in center field that you can focus lightly on while the pitcher walks around on the mound, grabs the resin bag, or starts his windup. You should be attentive in the direction of the pitcher and observe what he is doing, but there is nothing you should zero in on yet.

Having a soft center will help you avoid being fooled by a herky-jerky type of motion. Pitchers will often have some sort of awkward motion that distorts the hitter's timing or they may try to hide the ball as long as possible. None of this should bother you as your attention is on your soft center and your focus is on finding the pitcher's release point.

I've got sights when I go up to the plate. In Fenway, I put my sights on that left-center field wall. I'm looking to aim myself to hit the ball at that spot.

—— *Mo Vaughn*

The fastball appears to leave the pitcher's hand at a slight, downward angle. The rotation on the ball is a backward spin. The hitter should recognize that the palm of the pitcher's hand is facing him, which indicates a type of fastball or change-up.

Rotation

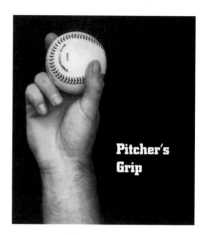

Pitcher's Grip

Nothing stops my concentration. A bomb could go off between the mound and home plate and I'll still hit a line drive somewhere. You can't ever take your eye off the ball. I'm lucky—I've always had this. I think I can hit anyone, and if he gets me out, I give him credit. But if I get a hit off him, I expect that he'll give me credit, too!

— Al Oliver

When the pitcher is almost ready to release the ball, it's time to switch to your hard focus. A hard focus is when the hitter finds the pitcher's point of release and concentrates on seeing the ball coming out of his hand. The hard focus should receive 100 percent of your attention and concentration. If you give anything less than that, then the pitch's four-tenths of a second will seem like a flash of light.

THE PITCH

If you've ever played whiffle ball, you know how difficult it is to hit a ball with a lot of break or movement. You see the ball in one location, prepare your swing to hit the ball in that spot, and then, all of a sudden, it swerves or dips and eludes your bat. When two Cy Young Award winners, Greg Maddux and Orel Hershiser, dueled it out in the 1995 World Series, it did appear as if they were using a whiffle ball. Every pitch they threw seemed to curve, drop, tail, or slice. The only way to avoid swinging blindly at pitches like these is to identify the pitch as soon as it comes out of the pitcher's hand. This isn't an easy task. You might be thrown anything from knuckleballs, screwballs, split-fingered fastballs, and forkballs to palm balls, "slurves," and "cutters," but the four most commonly used pitches are the fastball, the curveball, the slider, and the change-up.

THE FASTBALL

A fastball is undoubtedly the most common pitch in baseball at all levels. It is the fastest pitch thrown and the easiest one to control. If the pitcher you're up against has a good fastball, you're going to have to look for it. If you look for anything else, such as a curveball or change-up, you're going to be in big trouble when the pitcher comes in with the hard stuff. Your strategy should be to look for the fastball and adjust to anything else.

6 **Curveball**

Rotation

Pitcher's Grip

The curveball appears to leave the pitcher's hand with a slight upward and outward arc. The rotation on the ball is a forward spin. Here, the palm of the hand is pointed toward first base (third base for a left-handed pitcher), and the side of the hand is facing the batter. This always indicates some sort of breaking pitch.

Know where to look for the ball. If you can't see it, you'll never hit it. Finding the pitcher's point of release, seeing the ball come out of his hand, and knowing how each pitch looks coming out of the hand is a skill every hitter must have. Without this skill, the best mechanics in baseball become useless.

— *Mike Schmidt*

There are two basic ways a pitcher holds his fastball: across the seams or with the seams. Most pitchers seem to prefer to grip across the seams because they get a little more velocity that way. Notice what the pitcher does. Just changing to that grip might be all the clue you need.

Regardless of the grip, though, a fastball comes out of a pitcher's hand at a downward angle, the degree of which depends on the pitcher's height. Because the pitch rolls off the tips of the pitcher's fingers, the fastball will have a backward spin (see Figure 5).

THE CURVEBALL

Hitting would be a lot easier if pitchers just threw fastballs, but the curveball has been complicating the game since shortly after the Civil War. As baseball lore has it, a man named William Arthur "Candy" Cummings, a Baseball Hall of Fame inductee, is credited with the curveball's introduction.

Pitchers use the curveball to throw off the hitter's swing and timing and very possibly to fool him. While the fastball is predominantly straight, the curveball goes down and to one side or the other, depending on the pitcher. The curveball has a slower velocity than the fastball and this can fool a hitter who is counting on a fastball into shifting his weight much too soon. Even if a hitter recognizes the curveball and keeps his hands and weight back, he still has to calculate how much that ball is going to break in order to get the meat of the bat on the ball.

A curveball is almost the opposite in appearance from a fastball. The spin on the ball is a forward rotation (see Figure 8) instead of backward and it's traveling upward rather than down. While the fastball explodes out of the pitcher's hand, there is a slight delay when the curveball is released. That delay is noticeable if you can pick up on the slight arc the ball travels just as it is released (see Figure 7).

A good hitter, too, will always look for the fastball, [because] he can adjust his timing for the slower curve and change of pace. But if he's looking for the curve, the fastball will be thrown by him.

— *Lefty O'Doul*

An overhand breaking pitch, like Tom Gordon uses in this photo, will have slight arc out the pitcher's hand. A hitter should look for the immediate downward angle of a fastball, but if he sees that brief delay, he knows it's off-speed.

The two main breaking pitches are the curve and the slider. The purpose of both pitches is to create the illusion in the batter's mind that a fastball is coming. If the pitch has a noticeable break on its journey to the plate, the batter's timing will be disrupted and he won't be able to recover in time to hit the ball with authority. The curveball's velocity is significantly slower than the fastball's, perhaps as much as 10 miles per hour as measured by our radar guns. A good curve breaks downward between 10 and 20 feet from the hitting zone, confounding the hitter who had been expecting a harder pitch in a higher plane.

— *Tom Seaver*

If there was one pitch that gave me the most difficulty, it was the slider. It's a very deceiving pitch. The key to hitting it is to recognize the spin before you commit yourself to your swing.

— *Stan Musial*

SLIDER

The key to hitting a curveball is recognizing it as soon as possible. Because it's a pitch with lesser velocity than the fastball, you can delay your swing and use the extra time to find the ball's location. Your batting problems appear to be solved . . . until you're given a slider.

The slider lies between the fastball and the curveball. The pitch has high speed and a break, although the break is slighter and sharper than a curveball's and breaks a bit later.

The slider is very tough to pick up. The release point is almost always the same as a fastball, and it doesn't have that upward arc after the release that a curveball has. In fact, the pitch looks just like a fastball until the last 10 feet, when it appears to take a sharp, lateral break. There's not a lot of time to adjust your swing.

Picking up the spin is probably the only way to detect a slider. A slider produces many more revolutions than a curveball, which give it a tighter spin. With the spins turning rapidly, a small illusionary dot is formed in the middle of the ball. If you have a good enough eye to notice this small dot, then you know the pitch is a slider.

Another reason why sliders are so difficult to deal with is because they aren't used in the younger levels of baseball. Throwing a slider can be very damaging to a young arm, so a hitter may not see one until college or the big leagues. It takes time and experience in order to master a skill, so it might be some time before a batter feels comfortable with a slider.

CHANGE-UP

A straight change-up is a pitch with the same release point and rotation as a fastball but a markedly different velocity. It's thrown with the same arm speed as a fastball but it moves with less velocity because of a mechanically disadvantaged grip that is not effective for speed.

A good change-up, one that looks just like the fastball, can be very effective because players will jump on it as soon as they see the backward rotation,

Figure 8: The spin of a slider will form a small, illusionary dot in the center of the ball. The palm of the hand is turned slightly inward. This is hard to recognize, so concentrate on the spin of the pitch. Figure 9: The rotation of a change-up is the same as the fastball, but it doesn't explode out of the pitcher's hand. Mike Mussina has one of the best change-ups in baseball.

Slider

Rotation

Pitcher's Grip

and they'll be way ahead of the pitch. Left-hander Tom Glavine, who won 62 games for the Atlanta Braves between 1991 and 1993, is famous for his outstanding change-up. Glavine has a good fastball and breaking ball, but it's his change-up that he goes to when he needs to get himself out of a jam.

The way you can distinguish a change-up from a fastball is to observe the explosiveness of the ball coming out of the pitcher's hand. When a fastball is thrown, it's like the ball is being shot out of a cannon. The change-up kind of floats out. Like the curveball, the slower speed of the change-up gives you

The slider does not break as much as the curveball. It also starts out like a fastball and appears to be one until it is less than 10 feet from the hitting zone. When well thrown, it breaks across the plate and slightly down. The slider has been called a "nickel curve" because the break is less than for the curveball. But it is a very deceptive pitch because the breaking action takes place so near the hitting zone.

— Tom Seaver

Most pitchers hide their grip in the glove as Mike Mussina does above (Figure 9). However, a pitcher can get careless and give away his pitch by exposing the ball (Figure 10).

Tony Gwynn watches this pitch all the way into the catcher's glove. By doing this, he improves his sense of timing, becomes more familiar with the pitch type, and heightens his knowledge of the umpire's strike zone.

The value of taking a long, good look at every pitch cannot be emphasized too much. Don't make up your mind whether to swing or not until you know definitely where the ball is coming and whether it's high or low and to what corner. So many men strike out a lot because they think they've got a pitch tabbed, and find it's not where they thought.

— Rogers Hornsby

Rusty Staub was the best at recognizing a pitcher tipping his pitches. One time, he noticed Nolan Ryan was tipping off his pitches. When he'd look at you, it was a fastball. When he'd look down in his glove as he started winding up, it was a curveball.

One year, Ed Whitson was giving away his change-up. When he was coming forward to throw the ball, if he spread his glove open it was going to be a change. For a split second, just before he threw, you could see his glove and that was enough.

Then Rusty spotted one year that Mark Langston was giving his pitches away. When his glove was straight up and down in his windup, perpendicular to the ground, it was a fastball. When he had it cocked, running from 10 o'clock to 4 o'clock, it was a curveball.

— Keith Hernandez

time to adjust. The key is not to commit yourself too early. If you do, your weight will move forward prematurely leaving you with nothing but your upper body in your swing. Change-up pitchers are notorious for getting a lot of weak ground-out balls.

LOOK THE BALL INTO THE GLOVE

There are a number of times at bat when you won't be swinging at the pitch. The coach may have put the take sign on, the pitch might not be to your liking, or it might be a ball. Whatever the reason, when this occurs, it is important to look the ball all the way into the catcher's glove.

Watching the ball all the way into the catcher's mitt makes the average hitter a wiser one. There are a number of things your brain will compute as you follow the ball. You will have a much better sense of the speed of the fastball. You will have a better sense of the break on a pitcher's curveball. And you'll get a handle on the timing of the change-up.

Even if you sense immediately that this will be a bad pitch, don't take your eyes off the ball until it's safely in the glove. You get a free, up close and personal opportunity to analyze your opponent. At the very least, this gives you one more opportunity to learn the umpire's strike zone (see Figure 11).

WHEN THE PITCHER TIPS OFF A PITCH

In the course of a game, you may notice that the pitcher is tipping off his pitches. He may do something that alerts the hitter to what he's throwing before he even throws the ball. Look for this. Try to discover if the pitcher makes a particular movement, gesture, or change in delivery that sends a message to onlookers as to what he's going to throw.

There are a number of common errors that pitchers make that can tell the hitter what's to come. An obvious one is the change in release point. If your opponent has an overhand fastball and a three-quarter-arm breaking ball, you

12

Juan Gonzalez still has his eye on the ball as he watches it travel over the left-field fence.

You can also see what type of windup the pitcher has and where his release point is. Perhaps you'll be able to determine that he has one release point for a fastball and another for a curve, and that could help you tremendously.

— Rod Carew

know what he's throwing before the pitch is even out of his hand. The speed and style of a wind up are often other clues.

Even before the pitch, there are signals a pitcher can send. He may hold his hand a different way in his glove. He may grip the ball across the seams for a fastball and with the seams for a curveball. When the pitcher comes to a stop in the stretch, he may alter the way he lines up his feet.

Other players may give the pitch away, too. The catcher might go through the pitching signs in the same order. You can tell what's coming by the number of times the pitcher shakes the pitch off. The infielders might adjust once they see the sign from the catcher. For example, say a right-handed batter is at the plate and after the catcher gives the sign, the shortstop quickly shifts closer to third. It's likely the shortstop thinks the hitter will pull it, so it's probably something off-speed. And if he shifts over toward second, the hitter can look for a fastball.

Trying to pick up what the pitcher is throwing can be like a game, but for some it's a game they don't want to play. Many hitters would prefer just to rely on their reactions at the plate. It comes down to what makes a hitter feel most comfortable.

Northern white ash is particularly desirable for the making of baseball bats because it is strong, stiff and has high resistance to shock.

TRAINING YOUR EYES

The good news is that now you know how to use your eyes to identify a pitch. The bad news is that identification is just a small part of the eye exercises you need to do to develop excellent baseball vision. You have to be concerned with your dominant eye, your dynamic visual acuity, your eye tracking ability, your depth perception, your peripheral vision, your visual reaction time, and your visualization. While understanding, much less improving, these vision components may seem like a daunting task, they are really quite basic.

YOUR DOMINANT EYE

Everyone is born with a dominant eye, which is the stronger of the two eyes. If you want to learn which of your eyes is the dominant one, just take note when you're looking through a camera. The eye you keep open is your dominant eye.

In this photograph of Mickey Mantle, you can see Mantle's eyes are not looking directly at the baseball, but where the ball was a split-second earlier. **He is actually using peripheral vision to hit the ball.** His back shoulder has dropped down to give his swing an upward arc. Mantle's weight is still on his back side, leaving him with plenty of power.

13

THE HITTER'S CORNER

Most people are what optometrists call same-side dominant, meaning if you're right-handed, your right eye is probably your dominant eye. Unfortunately, this is exactly what you don't want in baseball. A same-side dominant hitter would have the weaker eye closer to the pitch. The lucky few who are opposite-side dominant will have their stronger eye closer, allowing them to recognize the pitch sooner. Ted Williams, in addition to having 20-10 vision, had a dominant right eye. As a left-handed hitter, it gave him even better vision at the plate.

Dr. Berman, the optometrist, agrees. "A hitter can pick up the ball one-hundredth of a second sooner with his dominant eye. If his dominant eye is his front eye, then he is going to be in a better position than someone who is same-side dominant. A lot of times with young hitters who are same-side dominant, we recommend that they use an open stance. The open stance forces a hitter to turn his head toward the pitcher and brings his dominant eye into the field of view."

DYNAMIC VISUAL ACUITY

When a doctor gives you an eye exam he is measuring your static visual acuity (SVA). It's a measure of how well you can see a stationary chart while

Vision Training

According to an article by Jim Catalano in *Coaching Management*, the U.S. Air Force Academy Falcons baseball team added vision training to their off-season work-out program following the 1993 season. Since 18 of 21 players on the '94 squad were returning players, it was easy to observe the progress of the team from one season to the next.

Each player went through a six-week program that required a one-hour session twice a week. The exercises were focused on improving eye-hand coordination, peripheral vision, eye tracking, near-far focusing, vision and balance, and eye movement. The players were tested before their training and then after the program was completed. The post-tests on the six visual skills showed a 20 to 70 percent improvement, depending on the skill. The results on the field were even more stunning. The Falcons team batting average jumped from .319 to .360; team slugging percentage went from .487 to .623; and their home run total more than doubled, going from 32 to 76. The Air Force Falcons led the nation's NCAA Division 1 schools in team batting average and slugging percentage during the 1994 season.

you are sitting still. Unfortunately, in sports there are not a whole lot of things that sit still. Either you're moving, your opponent is, or the ball is. Sometimes everything is moving at once. How well you can see an object in this situation is called your dynamic visual acuity (DVA). Very few people start with good DVA. It's something that needs to be trained.

Drill for DVA

Get a softball or small beanbag and tape letters and numbers to it. Stand about six feet back and throw it against a pitchback. As the object comes back to you, call out as many of the symbols as you can see before you catch it. Each session you should change the letters and numbers. When you can call out about four of them, your DVA is sharp.

EYE TRACKING

Eye tracking is a skill that entails conditioning the eye to remain focused on an object in its movement toward you. A receiver catching a football, a hockey goalie stopping a puck, and a batter hitting a baseball all require eye tracking.

14

Mike Greenwell tracks the ball right into his bat. Keeping the head and eyes locked on the ball until the point of contact is essential in being a good hitter.

Figures 15 through 18: Here's another possible way of stealing the pitch type before the ball is thrown. Many pitchers take their grip on the ball before they put it in their glove when throwing from the stretch. Get a good look at how he's holding the seams if he does this. Figures 15 and 16 show the pitcher holding the ball across the seams. He's about to throw a fastball. In Figures 17 and 18, he's gripping it with the seams. Be ready for a curveball.

A common problem for hitters is that they have trouble tracking the ball because they move their heads excessively when they're in the box. The rhythm and movement in a hitter's stance should only include a slight movement forward and downward of the head (accomplished as you plant your front foot and before you rotate the hips). Moving the head more than two or three inches will throw off the hitter's balancing system, making it more difficult to track the pitch.

Drill for Eye Tracking
Get a basketball, tennis ball, or soccer ball and throw it up into the air. Follow its course as it goes up and all the way down. Every time it hits the ground, call out "Ball." Gradually throw the ball higher in the air.

19

If a pitcher shows you the ball during his windup, look for his grip or how he's holding the ball.

DEPTH PERCEPTION

Hitting is said to be one of the finest acts of eye-hand coordination, and to have it, you need good depth perception. Your depth perception judges distance and the spatial relationship between objects. It's basically the reason that you have two eyes. Try flipping a coin and catching it, while holding a hand over one of your eyes. Chances are you'll miss, because you no longer have depth perception. In other words, when you're up to bat, make sure you're looking at the pitch with both eyes.

Drill for Depth Perception
Sit down and have a friend or a teammate hold a straw horizontally about an arm's length away. Hold a toothpick in your hand and concentrate on the straw. Only paying slight attention to the toothpick, slide it into the straw.

PERIPHERAL VISION

When Magic Johnson played basketball for the Los Angeles Lakers, it sometimes looked as if he had eyes on the sides of his head. He had great peripheral vision and often made pinpoint passes while it appeared he was looking in another direction. Peripheral vision is this ability to see what's going on outside your central field of vision.

Several eye specialists have said that baseball players hit using peripheral vision. Because the ball is traveling toward the hitter at such a high velocity, it's impossible to actually see the bat hit the ball, even though that's what coaches tell their hitters to do. The batter actually sees it connect in his peripheral vision—so that's what you really need to train.

Drill for Peripheral Vision
Tie a ball to a string and hang it from the ceiling. Sit in a chair and have the ball hang down so that it's at eye level. Swing the ball so it circles around your head. Every time the ball comes into your vision, yell "Ball." Do this in one-minute intervals, the first minute clockwise, the second minute counterclockwise.

F ind something that works for you. Hit objects, any kind. I hit an awful lot of rocks with broom handles in my time. I've been blessed with good eyesight and hand-eye coordination. You can only improve your hand-eye coordination by constantly swinging a bat.

— Wade Boggs

PLAYING OTHER SPORTS

Repetition of prescribed drills is great for improving your vision, but you can improve in other ways, too. You can play sports that promote repeated tracking of a ball, such as racquetball, tennis, Ping-Pong, or squash. Play them and you'll improve your baseball vision.

The .230 hitter in baseball, the tennis player who has failed to make it to the quarterfinals, the golfer who has trouble making the cut—all may be professionals, but none is succeeding. They have mastered the game well enough to outdistance the amateur but not well enough to excel on the professional level. There may be several reasons—from lack of mechanical ability to family problems—but visual skill certainly needs to be taken into account, and it is a factor that can be enhanced through training.

— Dr. Arthur Seiderman
sports vision specialist

VISUAL REACTION TIME

An athlete's visual reaction time measures how fast his eyes can focus and pick up on something. A hitter needs to pick up the location and type of pitch in less than two-tenths of a second, and send a message to his brain to swing if he likes the pitch. A hitter who can't do it this quickly is going to have a tough time at the plate.

Drill for Visual Reaction Time

Write a series of numbers (about seven or eight digits) on a piece of paper and tape it to the wall. Have a friend hold another piece of paper in front of the numbers so they're covered. Have him flash the numbers and see how long it takes you to read them all. Change the numbers with each session and increase the speed he flashes the numbers as you progress.

VISUALIZATION

Visualization is the ability to see an image in the mind's eye. Most of the time, visualizations are of things you've already seen, but visualization in sports is a combination of memory and positive thought. Thinking of something positive tends to help the hitter relax and builds confidence, which can enhance performance. On a more advanced level, hitters may be advised to visualize a particular at-bat or to swing in an attempt to repeat that same activity.

Drill for Visualization

Simply close your eyes and visualize yourself in a peaceful spot under a tree watching the sunset for 30 seconds. Then visualize the clothes your teacher or girlfriend was wearing a day ago, for 30 seconds. Fianlly, visualize the last good at-bat you had in a baseball game and try to remember what you did correctly and how it felt. Just spending time in the batter's box, whether it be in the gym, in the cage, or outside, is always a good way to train the eye as long as you're focused on a vision purpose. You can work on finding a soft center and switching to a hard focus, you can work on picking up a release point, or you can look for the spin of the pitch. No matter what, vision is just as important as any other skill when hitting a baseball and time for training it should be set aside.

In the Old Days

Earlier players in the major leagues didn't have the benefit of participating in formal vision training programs. Most had to devise tactics of their own if they wanted to improve their eyesight. Ted Williams used to hit bottle caps with a stickball bat in a dimly lit room. Harmon Killebrew would hit the roses off his mother's bushes and the leaves off her plants to practice seeing objects at different levels.

"Shoeless" Joe Jackson, a lifetime .356 hitter who played for the Chicago White sox in the early 1900s, would hold his hand over one eye in a dark room and stare at a candle flame with the other. Once his vision became so blurred that he could hardly see, he would switch and exercise his other eye. Jackson claimed the procedure not only exercised his eyes but also helped him pick up a pitched ball better.

Kirby Puckett combines weight shift and rotational hitting. Here he takes a weight shift swing in batting practice. Puckett starts out in a square stance. He gets his trigger action by cocking his knee inward (Figures 20 and 21) just before he strides. Puckett's weight begins to shift forward (Figure 24) before hip rotation as he watches the pitch come in. Look closely at Figure 30 and you'll see that Kirby is using peripheral vision when he makes contact with the ball. His hands are in the "palm up, palm down" position, and his front leg is now rigid. Puckett's hips come through with his swing and do not fully rotate until his follow through (Figure 36).

Diamond Dust

During the 1996 season Colorado Rockies teammates Andres Galarraga, Ellis Burks, and Vinny Castilla all hit at least 40 home runs. The 1996 Rockies became only the second team in baseball history to feature three players with 40 or more homers during the same season. The first was the 1973 Atlanta Braves who featured Davey Johnson (43 homers), Darrell Evans (41 homers), and Hank Aaron (40 homers).

My approach is: see something I like and attack it.

— *Dave Parker*

- St. Louis Cardinal Rogers Hornsby is the only player to hit .400 and slug 40 home runs in the same season. In 1922, the "Rajah" batted .401 and hit 42 home runs.

- In 1996, San Diego Padre outfielder Tony Gwynn won his 7th National League batting crown, and third in a row. Gwynn's 1996 title was won even though he did not collect the necessary 502 plate appearances. The crown was awarded to Gwynn based on a never-before-used rule which states that any player without the required plate appearances who would *still* have the highest average if they had the required plate appearances will be declared the batting champion.

- In 1996, New York Mets catcher Todd Hundley broke the all-time record for home runs in a season by a catcher by rapping out 41 round-trippers. He also caught more than 150 games, joining his father, Randy Hundley, as one of the few receivers in baseball history to catch more than 150 games in a season.

- The great Willie Mays really shined in baseball's All-Star Game. Mays played in 24 All-Star contests (tied for the most) and he holds the record for runs scored (20), hits (23), stolen bases (6) and is tied for most triples (3) and total bases (40).

- The great Japanese slugger Sadaharu Oh is the world's all-time leading home run hitter with 868 to his credit. Hank Aaron is second with 755, a full 113 dingers behind Oh.

- In 1993 Toronto Blue Jay Joe Carter became the first man to end the World Series with a home run since the Pittsburgh Pirates Bill Mazeroski beat the Yankees with a Game 7 homer in 1960. In his first year with Toronto in 1991, Carter also accomplished a first when he knocked in 100 or more runs for the third season in a row with three different teams. He had previously reached the 100 RBI level with Cleveland and San Diego.

- In 1991 Toronto's Manny Lee set a dubious major league record by recording the most strikeouts in a season (107) by a player who failed to hit a home run.

- Though it has played host to great Yankee sluggers such as Babe Ruth, Lou Gehrig, Joe DiMaggio, Mickey Mantle, and Reggie Jackson, Yankee Stadium in New York remains unconquered. No man has *ever* hit a baseball out of Yankee Stadium, though Mantle came close on many occasions when his towering drives struck the facing of the third deck in right field.

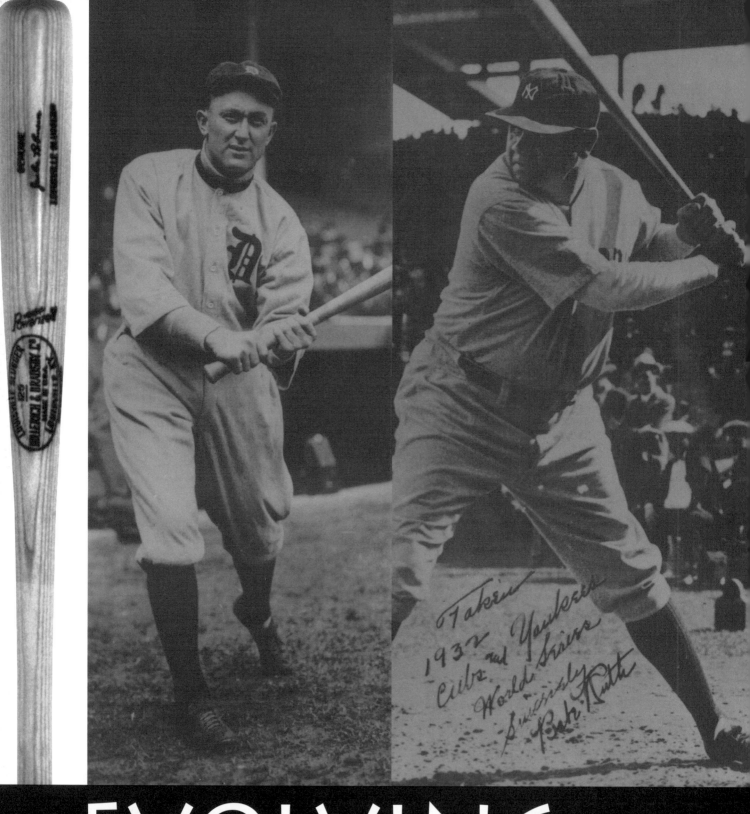

The signature on the photo reads:
Taken
1932
Cubs and Yankees
World Series
Sincerely
Babe Ruth

EVOLVING
THEORIES

6

"What's happened to those grand old, one-run, last-inning finishes?"

— *Ty Cobb*

Over the years, hundreds of different styles, methods, and theories of how to hit a baseball have developed, but unfortunately, some instructors remain limited in their knowledge. One may preach strictly "top hand, top hand"—a reference to rolling the top hand as the barrel of the bat makes contact with the ball—and nothing else. One may preach weight back; another weight forward; still another, hitting the ball back up the middle. The problem with these theories is that the people who put them forth speak in absolutes, as if their way is the only way to hit.

— Rod Carew

All I can tell 'em is I pick a good one and sock it. I get back to the dugout and they ask me what it was I hit and I tell 'em I don't know except it looked good.

— Babe Ruth

Rogers Hornsby is considered by many as the greatest right-handed hitter of all time. He still holds the single-season record for highest batting average, posting a .424 clip in 1924. Hornsby's approach to hitting changed dramatically with the emergence of Ruth. He totaled just nine home runs in 1920, then socked 42 in 1922.

On September 11, 1985, Pete Rose drove his career 4,192nd hit to left-center field off San Diego Padres pitcher Eric Show to eclipse Ty Cobb's long-standing total hits record. With 4,256 to his name, Rose still stands as baseball's all-time hit leader. A young player starting out might figure that if he could just copy Rose's batting style, he might have similar success. But that's not even remotely true. What works for one hitter doesn't always work for the next.

Looking at the great hitters of baseball—Rose, Cobb, Ted Williams, Babe Ruth, Hank Aaron, Willie Mays, George Brett, and many more—you'll notice as many different hitting styles as there are players. They each discovered something that worked for them, but not one can say that they found the definitive best way to hit a baseball. It truly depends on the individual. However, if you study the principles behind good hitting and understand the various styles, you'll be one step closer to finding what works for you.

THE EVOLUTION OF HITTING THEORIES

Over the years, two major hitting theories have dominated hitting philosophy: The Modern Weight Shift System and The Rotational Hitting System. Because each one serves a different purpose, it's difficult to say which one is more effective. Both styles are still present in the game today, but preferences have changed over the years because the game of baseball has changed, too.

During the era of Ty Cobb and Tris Speaker, from 1900 to 1920, offensive strategy was based on intelligence and craftiness with the bat. Hitters were aggressive at the plate, and they looked to beat defenses with bat control and running speed.

In the early years of baseball (The Dead Ball Era), balls didn't travel with nearly the same distance that they do today. The "dead ball" almost assured that contact hitting (hitting singles or doubles) would be more successful than power hitting (swinging for a home run), and the weight shift system was ideal for this kind of hitting. Almost everyone used it.

Different Hitting

Take a close look at Cobb. His feet are close together with little or no bend in his knees. He is bent over at the waist, which leaves his upper body leaning out over the plate. There is a three- to four-inch gap between his hands, which are held unnaturally low. Nobody in baseball today looks like him, yet he still holds the highest career batting average in the history of the game (.367) and has the second highest number of hits (4,191).

How did he do it? Well, Cobb played (1906–28) during an era when baseball was very different from the game played today. His slap-and-punch style wasn't radical at all. In fact, a lot of players looked just like him at the plate. Their game centered around a number of factors that are no longer present in the game. Outfielders played deeper because there were no fences. The gaps were many, and a player who could make contact with the ball would have success.

2

What Ty didn't know as his mind whirred and clicked and processed information was that his style of hitting was endangered. The old-fashioned thinking-man's batter was being shoved out of the spotlight and into the orchestra pit by a muscular stage-hand named George Herman Ruth.

— Richard Bak
author of "Ty Cobb—His Tumultuous Life and Times"

I think the styles changed dramatically in the 1960s and 1970s to using the whole field. There was a combination of a lot of different guys that did that such as Rose and Carew. What you had in the 1940s and 1950s were ballparks that were built to pull the ball, 320 down the lines. Once the players went out and played in the bigger stadiums, it brought about a different style of play. Speed became more important with the emergence of Astroturf. Playing on such a quick surface, it became much easier for hitters to get the ball through the infield on the ground. Infielders had to play deeper, allowing fast runners to utilize their speed to get on base. The strike zone moved down and away, which forced hitters to hit the ball the other way. For a while, you would only see Aaron and Mays hit that ball out of the ballpark, but now, with bigger and stronger players, you see guys do it all the time.

*— Peter Gammons
ESPN baseball analyst*

When George Herman Ruth hit the scene, he brought with him a whole new approach that featured a walloping swing and the glamour of home runs. This was the start of the rotational hitter.

People loved the power game, and baseball owners took notice. The Dead Ball Era was over and in 1920 the new tight white ball that was introduced was jumping off the bats. Suddenly, everyone was copying The Babe, and control hitters were out of fashion.

Once Cobb retired, he considered the new generation of hitters as soft in dedication, guts, and brains. He even criticized Boston great Ted Williams, who many considered to be in the same class as Cobb as a hitter, for taking too many close pitches and for not punching singles to left. Conceding that Cobb was the greatest ballplayer of all time, Williams admitted the two were completely different hitters. "When he talked hitting," said Williams, "he talked Greek to me."

Despite Cobb's indifference with the new brand of offensive baseball, players, owners, and fans all thrived on the long ball. Owners became aware of the crowd's hunger for high-scoring affairs, and entertained them by putting up short fences in the outfield. Hitters realized the opportunity to sign bigger contracts through home run production, and they modified their approach to hitting as a result. Speed and hitting the ball on the ground were replaced by power and lifting it into the air.

When Astroturf and larger stadiums entered the game in the 1960s and 1970s, the gap hitter, and therefore the weight shift hitter was reborn. Hitting the ball down on the swift surface allowed place-hitters and running speed back into offensive baseball. Hall of Fame players like Lou Brock and Maury Wills were just as important to a team's lineup as Willie McCovey or Frank Howard. Because the outfields were bigger and the fences stood at a greater distance, teams had to produce runs instead of waiting for that one big swing of the bat.

Today, there's room for both the power hitter and the control hitter in the lineup, and room for the Modern Weight Shift System and the Rotational System in the instruction books. Many major league hitters use just one system, and others combine depending on the situation; pitcher, pitch count, runners on base, etc. Here's a look at both systems of hitting and the advantages and disadvantages of each one.

THE MODERN WEIGHT SHIFT SYSTEM

The weight shift system is primarily used to improve contact and to hit for a high average. It's not a power system. The weight shift hitter transfers his weight from his back leg to his front leg and basically throws his body and swing into the ball.

Most weight shift hitters like to stand deep in the box, so they can wait on the ball longer and hit the ball to all fields. The greater the distance between you and the pitcher, the more time you have to see the ball and swing the bat. Because hitters tend to wait on the ball, most pitches are hit up the middle or to the opposite field. They pull the ball only on inside strikes.

If you are going to be a weight shift hitter, your stance should include a slight bend at the waist with your feet square. Your weight is primarily on the back leg. As the pitch comes in, you want to shift your weight back even more, before bringing it forward. Charley Lau, a great endorser of the weight shift theory, often said, "You've got to go back in order to go forward." Many weight shift batters cock their front leg and knee in a "coiling" motion. This puts all of their weight on that back leg, and the movement creates the rhythm to begin the swing.

The stride is the main power element to this form of hitting. It's the movement that shifts your weight forward. Despite this, though, the stride is a soft, small step. It should go directly toward the pitcher, with your toe closed, pointing at the plate. Stepping with the toe closed will prevent you from opening your hips too early.

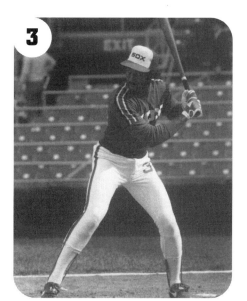  

Figures 3 through 14: Harold Baines was a student of Charley Lau's with the Chicago White Sox. Baines liked to use the weight shift swing especially with two strikes to improve his chances of making contact. Just after he gets to the launch position (Figure 5), Baines begins to shift his weight forward. His front leg becomes rigid as his body continues forward, but he keeps his hands back (Figure 6). Baines stops his forward momentum when he starts his hands, and rotates his hips slightly into the pitch (Figure 7). As the barrel enters the hitting zone, his back foot raises off the ground. This helps keep the front shoulder in and allows the bat to remain in the hitting zone for an extended period of time. After contact is made, the top hand releases the bat in the follow through, and the head stays down.

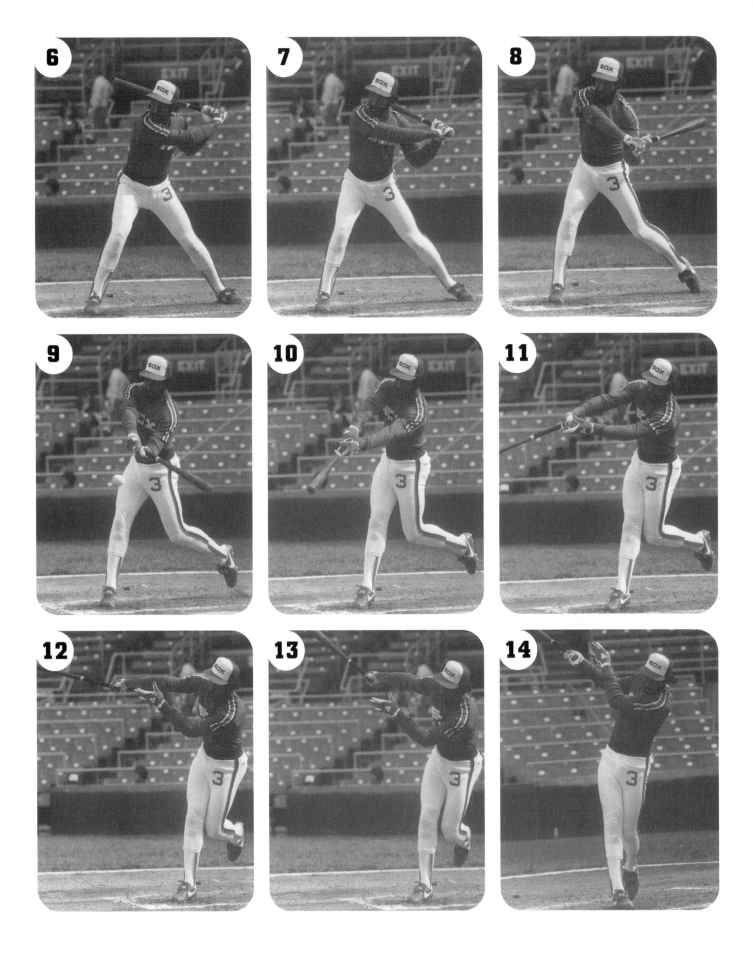

15

George Brett was Charley Lau's most successful student. Here he is shown hitting a home run in 1985 against Toronto. He releases his top hand *after swinging the bat through the contact area.* The top-hand release indicates that he achieved full extension and weight shift during the swing. Brett's striding foot is closed and his head is down, eyes following the flight of the ball—both "absolutes" of proper hitting taught by Lau.

I think the most important hand in hitting is the bottom hand. I don't believe in the top hand theory. If the top hand works too much it will roll the bat out of the way of the ball. We emphasize the bottom hand so the top hand doesn't have to do too much of the work.

— Walt Hriniak

Your front leg should remain stiff. It holds the weight and does not bend or give. This allows you to rotate your hips somewhat and get some of your lower body into the swing. Although the hips do rotate, this movement is limited compared to the hip rotation in the rotational style of hitting.

During the swing, the bottom hand is the one in charge. It pulls the bat through the zone. The speed of the barrel or bat head is not a critical concern; in fact, the idea is to have the bat in the hitting zone (the area in which you are striking the ball) as long as possible. Your hands move as quickly as possible, however, the top hand does not accelerate the barrel. The barrel passes through the hitting zone even with or slightly behind the hands (see Figure 9). If your hands are rolled over and out in front of you, the barrel only covers a portion of the plate. When the bat is square in the hitting zone, it covers the entire plate.

Major league batting instructors Charley Lau and Walt Hriniak, also taught hitters to release their top hand after they made contact with the ball. Their idea was that this would promote full arm extension and avoid pulling their shoulders and head off the pitch. A level swing with a top-hand release (which means the hitter releases his top hand from the bat after contact is made) also creates an elongated arc, which leaves the barrel of the bat in the hitting zone for a longer period of time. Hriniak also feels that it keeps the hitter from rolling his top hand over and hitting a lot of ground balls.

WHAT YOU GET

The weight shift system improves the frequency of contact with the ball, so it's not surprising that its most obvious influences can be seen in increased batting averages. Because the barrel of the bat is in the hitting zone on the swing plane a bit longer, you can make solid contact without timing the pitch perfectly. This puts you on base more and you'll be striking out less, both results hugely beneficial to your team.

Willie Mays was a weight shift hitter on some pitches, and a rotational hitter on others. Here he uses a weight shift swing to smack a triple to right-center field to win the 1959 All-Star game. **Mays has shifted his weight forward onto his front leg, and is in position to get a good jump towards first base.** He's released his top hand and has a high follow-through with the bottom hand.

16

Speed naturally was a big thing for me, at bat as well as on the bases. But, you know, when I'd hit to left field, as I often did, I'd lose just an instant, going into the pitch. By contrast, right-handed hitters like Alex Johnson and Roberto Clemente, going to right often would actually go off just as quickly because they were moving toward first base with their swing.

— *Lou Brock*

When your head moves too far forward, you're in big trouble. Fastballs look faster so you think you have to be quicker, and you don't trust yourself to sit back and wait on a breaking ball. Too much head movement or drifting into the pitch is a major problem at any level of hitting.

— *Tony Gwynn*

You also have good coverage of the plate with this system, and that enables you to hit to all fields. Fielders are going to have trouble adjusting to you, which just creates more openings.

If you're right-handed using the weight shift system, you'll also get a good jump out of the batter's box because your motion is already in that direction. In the rotational system, your body has swung all the way around, and you end up with your back facing first base. In the weight shift system, your body is moving forward, with much less rotation. All you have to do is keep moving forward. How many times do you see a runner get thrown out at first base by a half-step during a season? A good jump out of the batter's box can make up at least a full step for the runner and that close out at first base now becomes a base hit.

WHAT YOU GIVE UP

Reduced power is the most obvious shortcoming of the weight shift system, but there are other difficulties with it as well. If you move your head too far, vision can be impaired slightly. The pitches will appear to have a greater velocity because your eyes cannot track the ball as easily while moving.

And if you have trouble distinguishing between pitches, the weight shift system can be disastrous. If you're fooled, you might find yourself flailing at a

17

Releasing the top hand can work against the hitter if he lets go too soon. The release should be after the shoulders have rotated, as shown here.

pitch with one arm. With a controlled yet positive stride forward, you've started your commitment to the pitch. If you're fooled, you have lost your body's momentum and have only your arms left in the swing. If you are the type to release the top hand, you're left with just your bottom hand to drive the ball. Not likely.

Some may point to Chicago White Sox first baseman Frank Thomas as a weight shift hitter who also hits for power. But at six feet and four inches and 240 pounds, he's an unusual case. Thomas is so big and strong that he can be fooled on a pitch and still hit the ball out of the ballpark with just his arms.

The top hand release can also affect bat speed. Letting go basically creates a sweeping motion through the hitting zone. It keeps you from snapping your wrists through the zone and generating a lot more bat speed.

The high finish may also cause you to top a lot of balls, producing lots of easy ground-ball outs.

Weight shift hitters also have more difficulty on inside and high strikes. If you're going to use this method, you need quickness in your hips and hands to adjust and drive the inside strike. You can shorten the arc, not quite fully extending your arms, and get the barrel of the bat on the ball out in front before it gets to the plate.

ROTATIONAL HITTING SYSTEM

The rotational hitting system, introduced by Babe Ruth and perfected by Ted Williams, revolutionized the game of baseball. Prior to this, only players with tremendous arm strength were able to hit home runs. The rotational system draws its power from a strong lower body, powerful wrists, and good bat speed, so the long ball is a possibility for a lot more players.

That doesn't mean the rotational system can't be used for base hits. Singles and doubles hitters can use the system effectively as long as they understand their capabilities. The rotational system will allow a player to hit longer and farther than he can with the weight shift system. How a player uses this is up to him.

I think it [the weight shift method] really hurts a lot of guys who could hit for power. It helps some become better hitters for average, but one of the reasons is that the pitchers aren't afraid to pitch to them because the best they'll do is hit a single.

Lead-arm [weight shift] hitters are not as effective in the upper part of the strike zone. To hit the high pitch effectively, the top hand needs to take an active role.

— *Al Kaline*

A batter's hands should never leave the bat until the entire follow-through process has been completed. Occasionally, it will happen, but this should only be accidental and only after leaving the impact area of the swing. Players who exaggerate the hand-release technique can easily fall into sloppy habits and lose that sensitive bat control that is so vital to getting base hits. The release of the top hand is a misconception of the late Charley Lau's teaching. Lau often had players practice releasing the top hand to emphasize full extension, which produces the hardest hit balls. I advocate full extension too, but try to get the players to achieve it with both hands on the bat.

— *Tony Oliva*

Babe Ruth had the baseball world in disbelief when he brought his thunderous cut and snapping of the hips onto the hitting scene back in 1919. Ruth revolutionized the game by turning on the ball and lifting it in the air for power. In this photo, Ruth practically spins himself into the ground with his "corkscrewlike" turning motion. **Ruth actually replaces his hips (the rear hip ends up where the front hip began), and rotates them so far that they are facing foul territory.** He has pulled out his head and front foot. Although Ted Williams controlled and perfected this method of hitting, Ruth was the innovator and never got cheated when he took a swing.

18

THE HITTER'S CORNER

Barry Bonds has one of the quickest swings in baseball. Bonds begins with his feet close together and his hands low. He hitches the bat forward a little as a trigger action as he strides (Figure 21). Bonds has a very short stride, and he begins to rotate his hips right after he's in the launch position (Figure 23). In Figure 25, Bonds is nearly in full hip rotation, and he's just started pointing the knob at the ball. His swing has a slight upward arc. He pulls this pitch, making contact well out in front of the plate. Even after contact, much of Bond's weight has not moved past the ball/bat point of impact (Figure 29).

If you're going to use the rotational system of hitting, your stance should be evenly balanced, with your front foot slightly opened. Hold your hands around chest level and keep them in toward your body.

Timing is of the utmost importance in this system, so you want to keep your movements limited, short, and precise. As the pitch is released, there should

be some sort of slight recoil in the front knee that "cocks" the hips. Some players simply turn their knee slightly in, while others, such as Baltimore Orioles star Brady Anderson or New York Yankee Ruben Sierra, actually pick their front foot up off the ground and bring their knee up to their waistline. Whatever you use is fine as long as you leave yourself enough time to plant your front foot and get a good swing.

The planting of your foot is actually a short stride, shorter than in the weight shift system, after which you need to plant and lock your front leg with the foot slightly open. As the pitch approaches, your back foot and hips pivot, turning your body into the ball. The pivot snaps your body and the bat through the zone, bringing your hips all the way through without stopping. The bat and upper body slightly follow the hips. This is where you generate most of your power.

The angle of the swing is a point of controversy. Mike Schmidt preaches a downward arc. Ted Williams thought a slight uppercut was effective. "If you swing up," says Williams, "you have to have the hips leading and then out of the way, generating speed and power, and you will find your top hand is in the strongest possible position: wrist snapping but not yet rolled over and directly behind the ball at impact."

Because of the tremendous bat speed and explosive hip movement, the time the bat is actually in the hitting zone is very short. This makes timing crucial for the rotational hitter. If you don't time it right, the bat will be across the plate before or after the ball gets there. Strike one. If you're going to be a rotational hitter, you absolutely must be aware of the pitcher's velocity, pitch patterns and movements. Pay close attention to these things when the pitcher is warming up, throwing to your teammates, and even during your at bat. In this system you have to know what to expect because you are committing your hips early. It's hard to stay back after that.

WHAT YOU GET

Power is obviously the most beneficial aspect of the rotational system of hitting. Power can mean hitting home runs, but it can also mean hitting the ball hard with authority. A hard hit ball, that is, a ball with some pop, is much more likely to make it through the infield or into the outfield gaps than a weakly hit ball. And the ability to hit the ball with some pop will help you out

A powerful, rotational swing, such as Jose Canseco's, will leave a right-handed hitter's back facing the first baseline.

before you even get a pitch. The infield plays deeper on strong hitters, which makes it a tougher play on them to throw you out at first if you hit a ground ball. The outfield also plays deeper, giving you more gaps in which to drop the ball.

Also, if you're a power hitter, pitchers will try to pitch around you, that is, they will stay away from giving you pitches that play to your strength. This gives you a number of advantages. First, you'll run deep counts, which means you get to see a lot of pitches and it tires the pitcher out. Second, you may draw a lot of walks. Williams led the American League in walks in eight different seasons and drew 2,019 in his career. Third, if the pitcher gets behind in the count early, he's got to come in with better pitches to hit.

Finally, your head moves less, for the most part, in this type of hitting system. Without your head lunging forward with the rest of your body, as it does in the initial part of the weight shift system, you can get a better "read" on the ball.

WHAT YOU GIVE UP

More than anything, it's the batting average that suffers with a player who uses the rotational style of hitting. Because the hips start earlier and the bat flies through the zone so quickly, there's less chance of its contacting with the ball. That's why strikeouts are common with big hitters. In fact, until Ruth came along (1,330 strikeouts), strikeouts were few and far between and were considered humiliating events.

Even if you don't hit the ball well, contact is better than a strikeout. At least with contact, there's a chance the ball will sneak through a gap or the fielders will make an error.

Rotational hitters also tend to pull a lot of pitches, which creates a number of problems. First, it causes a lot of balls to be hit off the end of the bat. If the pitch isn't where the hitter thinks it will be, he'll have trouble making square contact. Second, the fielders know how to play the pull hitter, so they close up the gaps on that side. And third, pitchers know how to pitch to him. Outside strikes are, for the most part, harder to pull.

The right-handed rotational hitter also loses a step on the way to first base. He has swung his body almost completely around, so his back is facing where he wants to go (Figure 33). The good news is that left-handed rotational hitters have it easier.

COMBINING SYSTEMS

Both the Modern Weight Shift System and the Rotational System of Hitting have been used successfully by hitters of varying levels and abilities. And it's obvious that there are advantages and disadvantages to each style. Given that, is it possible to take the best of both systems and eliminate the negatives? Hall of Fame third baseman Mike Schmidt certainly seems to think so.

A pure power hitter early in his career, Schmidt experimented with Lau's and Williams's hitting techniques to make himself into a more rounded player. He finally settled in between, switching systems depending on the pitch. His statistics of two similar years (158 games with 562 at-bats in 1975 and 160 games with 552 at-bats in 1986), one early in his career and one later after he employed both systems, tell the tale of his success:

Hillerich & Bradsby Co. manufactures more than one million wood Louisville Slugger® bats each year for professional and amateur players. Nearly 1.5 million Louisville Slugger® aluminum bats are sold annually.

Mike Schmidt combined both systems of hitting which made him a better all-around hitter. Here he hits a game-winning home run off reliever Lee Smith. In Figure 35, you can see that Schmidt has taken his stride and keeps a bent front leg. By keeping the front leg slightly bent, it allows him to rotate or weight shift depending on the pitch. Schmidt rotates on this pitch (Figure 38), and locks his wrists at the point of contact (Figure 40). Schmidt has a short, compact swing for a power hitter and exercises a low follow through. The ball leaves the bat at the optimum power angle of forty-five degrees (45°).

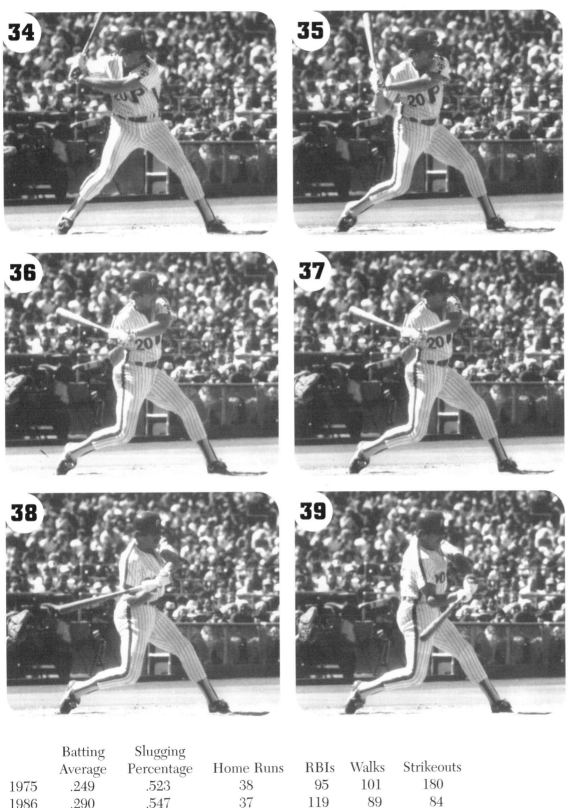

	Batting Average	Slugging Percentage	Home Runs	RBIs	Walks	Strikeouts
1975	.249	.523	38	95	101	180
1986	.290	.547	37	119	89	84

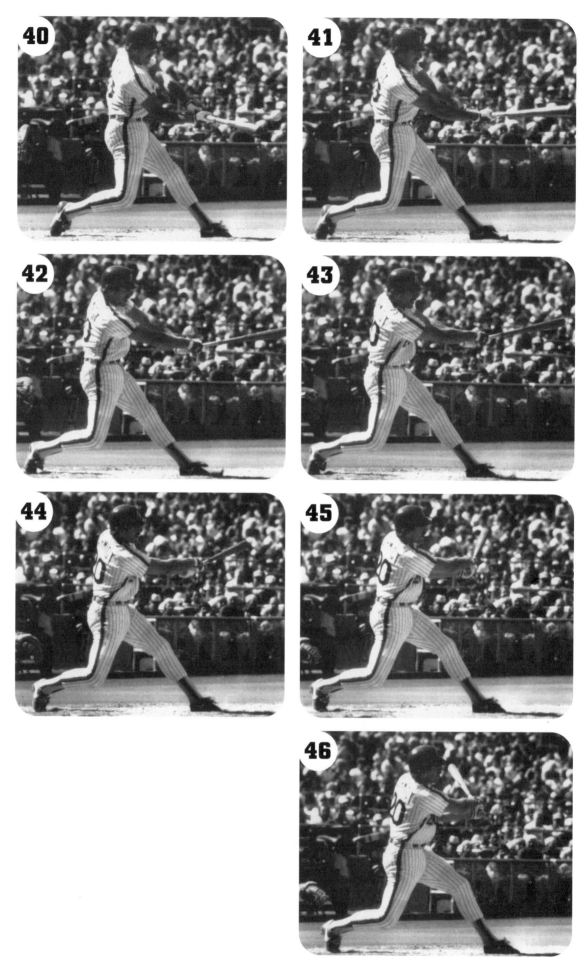

Looking at these numbers, you can see that Schmidt sacrificed no power while improving his average and reducing his strikeouts dramatically. His idea was to go with the percentages, so for each pitch he chose the style that was most likely to produce a hit. And percentages told him that the fastball was the most common pitch, so he went to the plate prepared for a fastball.

To use a combined method of hitting, your swing should be level, with the top hand pushing and the bottom hand pulling. Because it's easier to push than it is to pull, your top arm should be the stronger force as it is in the rotational system. This will provide the bat speed you need in order to wait on the ball longer.

Schmidt also recommends angling the front leg about 10 to 15 degrees after the stride, yet still keeping it rigid. This angle allows you to be a rotational hitter on the inside pitch and be a weight shift hitter on the pitch out away from you. You can switch between systems depending on the location of the pitch.

Rod Carew was another player who used a combined system of hitting for tremendous success. During his 19 years in the major leagues, Carew won seven American League batting titles, batted over .300 fifteen years in a row, totaled 3,053 career hits, and compiled a lifetime batting average of .328.

If there was one thing Carew was famous for in his playing days, it was the fact that he could change his stance right in the middle of an at-bat. Instead of making the pitcher adjust to the way he hit, Carew would adjust his hitting to the style of pitching he was facing. He might open or close his front foot, stand taller or crouch more, or move his hands (choke up on the bat). He'd do everything but change his grip.

Now, as the Angels' hitting instructor, Carew is teaching a variety of players how to hit. Although he didn't hit for a lot of power in his career, he is able to tutor players such as Jim Edmonds and Tim Salmon, both of whom have long ball capabilities. Despite this, Carew is mainly a supporter of weight shift hitting and stresses contact as the foundation of a good hitter. Carew teaches his players to hit to all fields, driving the ball wherever it's pitched.

Carew departs from the weight shift system when it comes to the hands, though. While weight shift hitters put the emphasis on the bottom hand and rotational hitters endorse the top hand, Carew believes in flat-hand hitting. This means neither hand is dominant during the hit. He feels that flat-hand hitting will give increased flexibility to a number of different pitches, more leverage to drive the baseball, greater ease getting the bat and ball on the same plane, better arm extension, a more natural rolling of the wrists, and the ability to wait longer on the plate. Sounds like a can't miss proposition.

It's obvious that there are a wide variety of theories when it comes to hitting, and it's naive to say that one is better than another. Some of the greatest hitters in the game differ wildly in their approaches. The best advice for a young hitter is to keep an open mind and experiment with different ideas in batting practice. Even if you disagree with most of what your coach is saying, stay attentive. There might be one piece of information that you can use. A combined approach can be a good one. Whether you get your hitting system all at once or in bits and pieces over the years, it's most important to find a style that feels comfortable for *you*.

My approach is to hit the ball to all fields. I struggled early in my career because I tried to pull everything out of the ballpark. Now, I stay back behind the ball and look to hit it the other way. If they come inside, I just rotate my hips as quickly as possible. It's a natural reflex, and it gets the barrel of the bat into the right position for the inside pitch—out in front of the plate. By hitting to all fields, they don't know how to pitch you or defend you.

— *Mo Vaughn*

I rotate and weight shift all the time. The guys who are real successful on this level are the ones who can cover the whole plate. Depending on the situation and location of the pitch, sometimes I use more weight shift and others I rotate more.

— *Will Clark*

During the 1993 season Seattle Mariner Ken Griffey, Jr., hit a home run in each of eight consecutive games, joining Dale Long and Don Mattingly as the only players to accomplish the feat. On September 14, 1990, Ken Griffey, Jr., and his father, Ken Griffey, hit back-to-back home runs in a game for the Seattle Mariners, becoming the only father-son combination to ever do so in the major leagues.

Confidence is everything. Consider what the highest possible goal you can attain is and then convince yourself you can attain it.

— Joe Morgan

■ Many baseball fans know that Joe DiMaggio hit safely in 56 straight games during the 1941 season to set the all-time record. Not everyone knows, though, that after being held hitless for a game, DiMaggio went on another 17-game streak. DiMaggio also holds the Pacific Coast League's record for hitting streaks. In 1935, playing for the San Francisco Seals, the Yankee Clipper hit safely in 61 straight games!

■ During a game in 1989, Darren Daulton went 5-for-5 with no runs batted in. The following day, Tony Gwynn went 0-for-4 with three RBIs (two infield groundouts and a sacrifice fly). The two performances illustrate how funny a game baseball can be.

■ A player wins the Triple Crown when he leads his league in home runs, RBI and batting average in the same season. The last player to perform the feat was Carl Yastrzemski of the Boston Red Sox in 1968. Two players, Ted Williams (1942, 1947) and Rogers Hornsby (1922, 1925) have won the Triple Crown twice.

■ Paul Molitor of the Milwaukee Brewers hit safely in 39 consecutive games during the 1987 season, the longest such streak in the American League since Joe DiMaggio set the all-time record (56) during the 1941 season. Molitor surpassed the 3,000-hit mark during the 1996 season, a sure ticket into baseball's Hall of Fame.

■ In one game during the 1902 season, Nig Clarke of the Texas League's Corsicana team went 8-for-8 with eight homers.

■ On June 23, 1971 Rick Wise of the Philadelphia Phillies made history by hitting two home runs and pitching a no-hitter against the Cincinnati Reds on the same day. That is producing in style.

■ Robin Yount is the only player to have two four-hit games in World Series competition. The two-time American League MVP got four hits in Games 1 and 5 of the 1982 World Series while playing for the Milwaukee Brewers against the St. Louis Cardinals. It was the only World Series appearance in Yount's career. He made the most of his opportunity.

THE MAKING OF A
LOUISVILLE SLUGGER

Louisville Slugger® wood baseball bats are made from Northern white ash which has the needed strength, resiliency, and density. Hillerich & Bradsby Co., makers of the Louisville Slugger since 1884, harvests its white ash from Pennsylvania and New York, where the terrain, soil, and climate are most favorable to producing these characteristics. The trees are first cut into 40-inch sections or bolts.

Each bolt is marked for splitting into billets, which are then sawed into rounds, that is, smooth-surfaced, cylinder-shaped sections. The rounds are stacked and cured, and air is circulated freely around each round in modified dry kilns for six to eight weeks.

(Above) The average major league player uses seven or eight dozen bats each season. They are turned on a "tracer lathe" that uses a metal template, that is, a pattern of a particular model.

(Below) After curing, the rounds are inspected for defects. Although only the highest quality timber, free from defects and blemishes, goes into Louisville Slugger bats, the bats are, nonetheless, graded to determine which are best-suited for the various models.

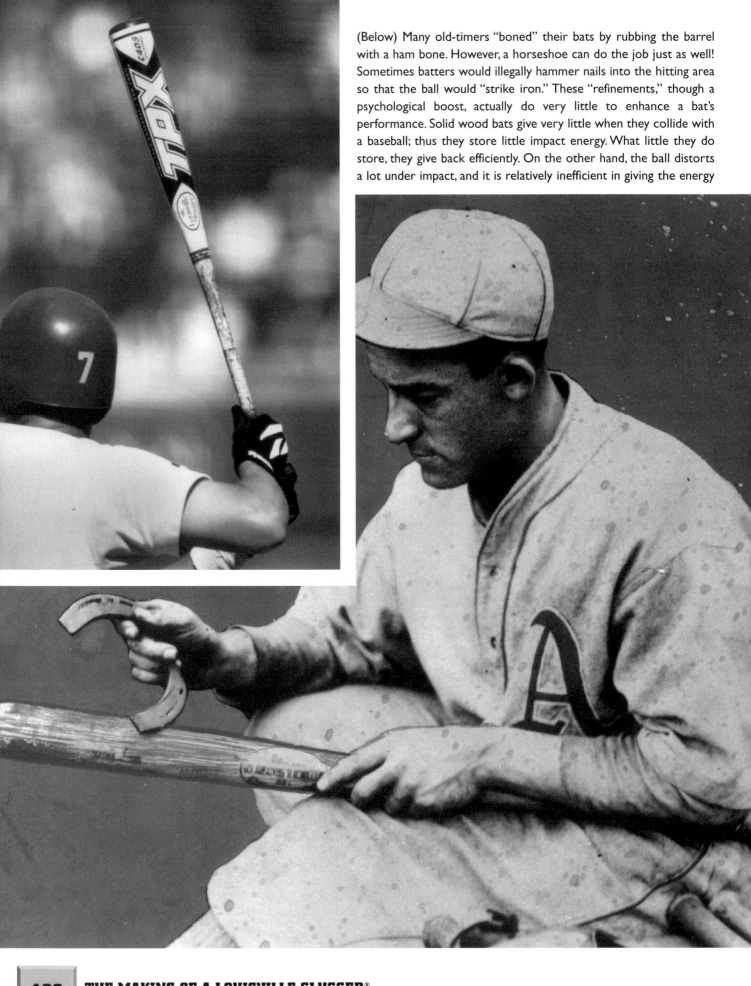

(Below) Many old-timers "boned" their bats by rubbing the barrel with a ham bone. However, a horseshoe can do the job just as well! Sometimes batters would illegally hammer nails into the hitting area so that the ball would "strike iron." These "refinements," though a psychological boost, actually do very little to enhance a bat's performance. Solid wood bats give very little when they collide with a baseball; thus they store little impact energy. What little they do store, they give back efficiently. On the other hand, the ball distorts a lot under impact, and it is relatively inefficient in giving the energy back, that is, as it compresses and then recoils into its rounded shape it loses a lot of energy. Players have discovered—and laboratory tests have confirmed—that the larger barrel diameter, the more efficient the energy exchange is with the ball and the faster the ball comes off the bat. The rules of professional baseball allow one-piece wood bats up to 2¾-inch maximum diameter and 42 inches long.

(Left) Unlike wood, aluminum bats are hollow. Aluminum alloys are much stronger than wood and much stiffer. Adult aluminum bats used in college baseball can be made as much as five ounces less than the length; for example, a 32-inch bat can weigh as little as 27 ounces. The significantly lighter aluminum bat allows college players to generate faster bat speed. By contrast, the lightest major league wood bats weighed 30 ounces, which were used by Cincinnati Red Joe Morgan and Boston Red Sox Billy Goodman. Among today's players Tony Gwynn uses a bat weighing 30½ ounces. Aluminum bats perform uniquely when striking a baseball. They don't break. They employ more of the bat's full weight in propelling the ball, even on off-sweet spot hits. At the same time, the barrel gives under impact, then springs back—like a trampoline—to help propel the ball at higher speeds and for longer distances. Because the giving of the

wall reduces distortion of the ball, less energy is lost at impact. In selecting an aluminum bat, a player will get maximum performance from a bat with the biggest barrel (max. 2¾ inches) and lightest weight, provided the player can swing comfortably and still maintain some feel (for the head or barrel of the bat).

(Below) First Bat Factory. In 1884, John Andrew "Bud" Hillerich fashioned a new wood bat for Pete "The Old Gladiator" Browning, star player with Louisville's Eclipse baseball team of the old American Association. Browning cracked consecutive hits in his first three at bats with what was then called a "Falls City Slugger" (by 1894, changed to Louisville Slugger) and put the Hillerich woodworking shop in the bat business. Hillerich and his fellow wood workers turned the bats of Browning's teammates according to player preferences of weight, length, and style, which they committed to memory. They branded each bat with the Louisville Slugger trademark and player names, which replaced the practice among the players of carving their initials into the knob or barrel of their bats. Before the turn of the century, nearly every legendary baseball player—including Wee Wille ("Hit 'em where they ain't") Keeler, Hugh Duffy, John McGraw, and Honus Wagner—used the Louisville Slugger. Today, it is the oldest and largest such business in the world.

DEFINING YOUR ROLE

7

"*Mike Schmidt could crush you with power, Rickey Henderson will beat you with speed, and Tony Gwynn will run you ragged all over the field.*"

— Wade Boggs

If you're a football fan, you've probably seen a highlight clip of San Francisco's Steve Young dropping back and hitting wide receiver Jerry Rice in the end zone for a touchdown pass. Young and Rice are two of the best at their positions and deserve the attention, but what about the nine other guys who made that play possible? Their roles aren't any less valuable.

The same is true for baseball. The power hitter gets the glory on the 11 o'clock news as a clip of his grand slam home run is shown, but what about the other three guys on base who made that grand slam possible? Who is the most valuable to the team? Is it the guy who hits .270 with 35 home runs and 100 RBIs? Or is it the guy who hits .333 with only 10 home runs but scores 100 runs? It's 100 runs scored either way.

Just as there are different styles of hitting, there are also different types of hitters, each with his own role to play to ensure the team's success. Contact hitters, power hitters, spray (to all fields) hitters, slap (and run) hitters, gap hitters, and hybrid hitters (part power, part contact) all play integral parts in sustaining a productive offense.

TAKE AN HONEST LOOK

Sometimes the role you *want* to play and the role you *are able* to play don't match. Not everyone is born with the natural ability to hit home runs like Mickey Mantle or Jose Canseco or to hit consistent line drives like Wade Boggs or Tony Gwynn. Your job is to figure out what your body is capable of doing and what would make you most dangerous to the opposing teams.

It's important to be completely honest with yourself. You will in no way enhance yourself as a hitter if you're trying to do something you're incapable of doing. You'll waste time trying, time that could be spent perfecting your strengths. Kenny Lofton might dream about being a home-run hitter, but he knows he's going to have more success and be more valuable to the Cleveland Indians if he gets on base and uses his tremendous speed. Albert Belle, Manny Ramirez, and Jim Thome get the job of hitting the ball off and over the wall to drive him in.

First baseman Cecil Fielder might be able to increase his batting average to get on base more often, like one of his speedier teammates, but he would be

You are the only one who knows your own possibilities and limitations. But you must be honest with yourself. So I advise: Analyze yourself. Decide what you can do best. Then go all out to obtain the maximum results for yourself and your ball club. And bear in mind at all times: In all baseball history no player has been able to hit 60 home runs and chalk up a .400 average at the same time. So it's one or the other.

— Ralph Kiner

If Cecil Fielder didn't hit he couldn't play at all. Toronto gave up on him as a hitter. He went over to Japan and became more patient at the plate because over there they throw more breaking pitches, and it helped him a great deal.

— Harry Minor
New York Mets Scout

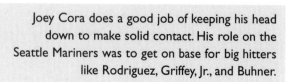

Joey Cora does a good job of keeping his head down to make solid contact. His role on the Seattle Mariners was to get on base for big hitters like Rodriguez, Griffey, Jr., and Buhner.

Matt Williams watches one leave Veterans Stadium. Williams' primary job is to hit the long ball and clear the bases.

sacrificing what he does best and what the team needs from him, his power. His value comes from his home run, which became obvious early on in his career.

ANALYZING YOUR SKILLS

You know your capabilities better than anyone, but sometimes it's still hard to pinpoint where your strengths might lie. Pay attention when you're at batting practice or during a game. What do you do well with a bat and what do you have trouble doing? Do your long fly balls frequently go out of the park or just occasionally? Do they only reach the warning track the majority of the time? If that's the case, then your long ball is more of a liability than an asset. Concentrate on contact instead.

Look at your size, strength, running speed, bat speed, bat control, and hand-eye coordination. These are all characteristics that will help you define your role.

How do you find out what kind of hitter you are? First you try to hit for average, hit with consistency. You keep your eye on the ball, you make good contact and you swing aggressively. Then the balls you hit will either drop in for singles and doubles, or they'll end up over the fence. If they go over the fence, you know you're strong enough to be a power hitter. If this is what you want, you can develop your power stroke.

— *Johnny Bench*

Once you accept your limitations, then you can work to overcome them and to improve your strengths. For instance, shortly after I began playing pro ball, I became a good pull hitter. But it didn't take me long to realize that I had to learn how to use the entire field, and I wasn't really capable of doing that at that time. But I worked on it, and later it became one of my strengths.

— *Tony Oliva*

Mike Piazza possesses great physical strength. At six feet, three inches, 200 pounds, Piazza is capable of hitting the ball out of any part of the ball park.

CONFRONTING THE OBVIOUS— PHYSICAL SIZE

I was fortunate enough to have a high school coach who taught me about the pitfalls of the little man. He would take me aside and say, "Look, you have no power." I didn't like hearing that. He said, "You can't steal first base. You have to learn how to bunt, learn how to hit, learn all the little things to help the team." He worked with me. He taught me the push bunt and the bunt down the third base line. I kept practicing. I got so many hits bunting and they led to so many runs, either me scoring them or driving runs in with squeeze bunts.

— *Phil Rizzuto*

Picture Ozzie Smith, Eric Young, PeeWee Reese, and Brett Butler standing next to Jose Canseco, Lou Gehrig, Duke Snider, and Mo Vaughn. All these players have experienced tremendous success in baseball. All of them could teach you a thing or two about swinging the bat, but the first group is a whole heck of a lot smaller than the second.

Physical size is a major factor in determining the potential and the limitations of a hitter. In most cases, a bigger player is going to hit the ball with more authority and power than a smaller player. There are exceptions, but on the average, it's the big guys who hit for distance. Think of home-run hitters Frank Thomas, Mickey Mantle, Albert Belle, Babe Ruth, Mark McGwire, Harmon Killebrew. All big.

Smaller players tend to put the bat on the ball with more consistency and hit line drives. A shorter, quicker stroke allows them to wait on the ball longer and use the entire field. The shorter swing allows them more time to see the pitch, helping them contact the ball more and strike out less. Also, the smaller the batter, the smaller the strike zone. There are smaller holes in their hitting zones and pitchers don't have as much success throwing their pitches into these areas of weakness. Bigger players have larger strike zones to cover and pitchers have bigger areas of weakness to aim for.

Assess your body type. Although you might think you can turn yourself into a different body type through weight training and conditioning, for the most part, you really can't. While you might get stronger, which will improve your game, weight training is not going to change your height or your frame. It's not going to change the length of your arms, which give a power hitter longer extension and therefore more power. And it's not going to change the size of your hands. That's not to say that weight training and conditioning aren't beneficial. Quite the contrary. Building strength and muscle mass—provided it does not limit a full range of motion—is beneficial to every type of player.

All-star second baseman Chuck Knoblauch would not be as successful in the Major Leagues as he is if he tried to be a power hitter. Though his five feet, nine inch, 175-pound frame puts a charge into many balls, his value comes from hitting line drives and getting on base.

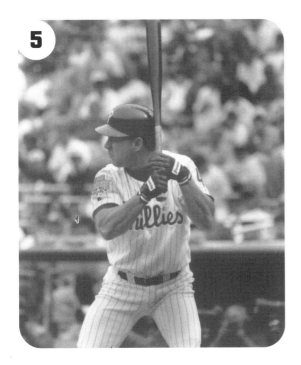

5

In 1993, Lenny Dykstra drew 129 walks and rapped out 194 hits. When Dykstra led off an inning, his on-base-percentage was a whopping .433.

THE CONTACT HITTER

A hitter who knows how to get on base consistently (at least 40 percent of his at-bats) is arguably even more valuable than the home run hitter who clears the bases. Take a look at the Philadelphia Phillies with and without Lenny Dykstra. When Dykstra was acquired by the Phils in 1989, he gave them good speed, lots of hits, and lots of walks. He was the leadoff hitter with a knack for getting on base, and when he did the fans knew something was going to happen. He was an offensive catalyst for the team, and when he was in the lineup, the Phillies compiled a record of 244-210. When he wasn't, they were a dismal 122-168.

Obviously, Dykstra was integral to the Phillies' success in those years. His job was not to hit home runs but to make contact, put the ball in play, get on base, and score runs.

Putting the ball in play may sound boring, but making contact makes all the difference. A strikeout or a lazy fly ball to the outfield doesn't really challenge

A guy who gets on base can be just as important, if not more important, than a power hitter. Teams have always looked for guys that hit for power, but guys who get on base cause havoc for the defense. They do a lot of things that may not show up in the statistics, but are of great value to a team's offense.

— Maury Wills

6

Having a runner on first base forces the defense to make adjustments.

Roger Maris cracks his record-breaking 61st home run of the 1961 season. A startling statistic shows that Maris was not intentionally walked once during that entire year. Why not? The hitter behind him was Mickey Mantle.

I've used the same swing since Little League. Shaving points off your average to hit 30 home runs doesn't make sense to me. If you hit 30 home runs in 500 at-bats, what do you do the other 94 percent of the time? You have another 470 at-bats in which you have to do something else.

— *Wade Boggs*

I've never heard of any ballplayer adding power. I've never seen a young boy come up to the major leagues who could not hit with power and watched the coaches work with him and then seen the day come when he could hit with power. You cannot add power. You cannot add it to a runner or a pitcher or put it in the arm of an outfielder. A man is born with power. And that is it. You can teach a man who has power to use it— and that is an art. Power is inborn, and its control and explosive use are instinctive.

— *Branch Rickey*

the defense and does nothing for your team's offense. But if you hit a solid ground ball, many things can happen. The ball might find a gap. It might take a bad hop. You might be able to beat a throw. To field your ball, a lot of things have to go right for the defense. The fielder must pick it up cleanly, get rid of it quickly, and make an accurate throw to first base. The first baseman has to catch it and keep his foot on the bag. If any of these things go wrong, and they often do at the amateur level, you're on first base. Contact hitters make the other team play, and this puts a lot of pressure on their defense.

Some contact hitters have power potential but have given it up to concentrate solely on developing their swing for high average. Lenny Dykstra, Wade Boggs, and Rickey Henderson are three players who gave up their pop. In 1993, Dykstra hit 19 homers during the regular season and 6 more in the post-season. Boggs hit 24 home runs for Boston in 1987, which is three times as many as he's hit in any other year. And in 1986, with the Yankees, Henderson hit 28 taters, and then hit 28 again in 1990 for Oakland. All three players have shown they have the power to hit home runs, but they understand they're the best player they can be when they are just focusing on being contact hitters.

THE POWER HITTER

Since Babe Ruth turned the home run into a potent weapon, baseball has never been the same. Ever since, teams have wanted power hitters in their lineups. Hall of Famers Frank Robinson, Ralph Kiner, and Reggie Jackson are just a few of the players who made a career out of hitting the long ball. Every time they stepped up to the plate, the fans knew there was a good chance the ball was going out of the park. These players brought excitement to the game because of this anticipation and the fact that they could change the score with just one swing of the bat.

Hitting the ball for power is a natural ability. It is a combination of hand-eye coordination and great strength that cannot be taught. It's possible to make yourself into a good contact hitter, but you can't show up at practice one day and decide to be a power hitter.

Statistics will show you baseball's trade-off for power. Reggie Jackson had 563 home runs, but he's also the all-time record holder for strikeouts with

Figure 8: Harmon Killebrew really gets his legs into this swing as he launches a grand slam home run. Although he gets all of this one, there was a price to pay for such a big swing as he struck out 1,699 times in his career. Figure 9: Joe Morgan could hurt you a number of different ways. Here he's shown hitting a lead-off homer in the 1977 All-Star game.

2,597. Killebrew launched 573 homers but struck out 1,699 times. And Mickey Mantle had 536 homers with 1,710 strikeouts. A comparison can be made with the power pitchers. Nolan Ryan holds the career record for strikeouts with 5,714, but he also tops the list in bases on balls, allowing 2,795 of them. Right behind him on both lists is Steve Carlton with 4,136 strikeouts and 1,833 walks. It's obvious that whenever an athlete puts all of his power and strength into something, he's gong to give up some degree of consistency.

Just because statistics are telling a tale of lower averages for power hitters, it doesn't mean their plight is hopeless. Power hitters need to work on the same things contact hitters work on: getting the bat to the ball, going with the pitch, adjusting to breaking balls, and many other intricacies that make hitting an art.

You should always strive to be more consistent, power hitter or not. If you're looking to increase your home run total, a good place to start is bat contact. The more balls you hit solidly, the greater chance you have of putting one in the seats. If you swing and miss, there's no chance at all.

EXCEPTIONS TO THE RULE

If it were laid down that big hitters should hit for power and small hitters should just try to make contact, then Joe Morgan wouldn't have two National League Most Valuable Player Award trophies. Morgan is an exception to the rule. Despite being five foot and seven inches and 150 pounds, the former Cincinnati Reds second baseman belted 268 home runs in his career. Morgan was the full package, as he hit for average, hit for power, had good speed, and had great discipline at the plate. In 1976, Morgan won his second straight MVP award, leading the Reds back to the World Series after they won the World Championship in 1975. During that 1976 season, when the Reds needed Morgan to get on base, he did, with a .320 batting average and 114 walks to his credit. When they needed him to steal a base, he did, swiping 60 of them during the regular season. When a game was on the line, and the Reds needed a big hit, "Little Joe" was there with 27 homers and 111 RBIs (Figure 9).

I never really go up to the plate looking to hit the ball for power. I just see the ball and try to hit it hard. Whether my high follow through gives me more carry on the ball or not, I don't know. I just do what comes natural and sometimes it just goes.

— Fred McGriff

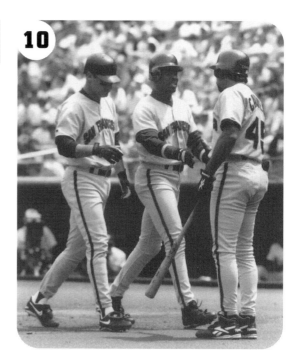

With Lenny [Dykstra] on first base so much, my role is to get him to second or to hit that hole between the first and second baseman and get him to third. I look for the pitch on the inner half of the plate early in the count and use a little more top hand in my swing to try to pull the ball to the right side. I won't swing at anything on the outside part of the plate unless I have two strikes. If Lenny doesn't get on, then I just become the next leadoff hitter.

— *Mickey Morandini*

Morgan is a perfect example of a hitter who maximized his potential, using all his assets. He used his speed to hit for average and steal bases, he used his quick hands and strong wrists for power, and he used his small strike zone to draw walks.

Willie Mays and Kirby Puckett are two other players who put up impressive numbers in all categories. Mays had a career batting average of .302, belted out 660 homers, knocked in 1,903 runs, and stole 338 bases. Puckett was only five feet, eight inches, but he, too, could hit the ball with authority. The Twins All-Star had a career batting average of .315, but he could also hit the long ball, as he proved in 1986 when he banged out 31 dingers.

These players defy the odds. They show you that physical size doesn't have to be a barrier if you make the most of what you have. Even a big player can learn a lot from observing their careers.

HYBRID HITTERS

As a player moves up the ranks into more advanced levels of baseball—high school, American Legion, college, and professional baseball—his duties as a hitter in the line up become more defined. Little League and Babe Ruth players should simply concentrate on hitting the ball hard every time up. But once they advance in their careers, each batter in the lineup inherits certain responsibilities at the plate and those who are most valuable are the hybrids who can perform more than one role, as needed by their team. A leadoff hitter should try to see a lot of pitches and get on base any way he can. The number two hitter should have good bat control and be able to move runners if necessary. The number three hitter should be your best hitter and have the ability to combine power, average, and speed in his offense. The cleanup and number five hitters need to hit for power and drive in runs, while the six and seven hitters should also possess RBI capabilities and hit for a decent average. The eight and nine hitters are usually the weakest and need to try and get on base any way they can so the top of the order can bring them home. A major

Earl Combs . . . The "Waiter"

During his playing days with the Yankees, Hall of Famer Earl Combs was best known in New York as the "Waiter," waiting to be driven around the bases by the explosive bats of Murderers Row. As a leadoff batter, he could wangle a base on balls, bunt in any direction, or line a base hit to the outfield. With names like Ruth and Gehrig behind him in the lineup, Combs' number one priority was to simply get on base any way he could and "wait" for the Big Boppers to bring him home.

league player who hits in the number two spot, such as Boston Red Sox shortstop John Valentin, may be capable of hitting the long ball (27 homers in 1995), but that's not always what the Red Sox need from him. He very well could be a five hitter on another team, but the Red Sox can use him better in a different role.

Placement in the lineup is not the only factor that determines what a team might need a hitter to do. When a hitter can hit for both power and average, he also needs to take a look at the game situation. Game 6 of the 1993 World Series is a perfect example.

The Toronto Blue Jays trailed the Phillies 6-5 going into the bottom of the ninth inning. Rickey Henderson led off the inning with a walk. After Devon White popped out, Paul Molitor came to the plate. Molitor had had 22 home runs during the regular season and two homers in the series, including one already in that game. He had the capability to go for the long ball and possibly end the game with just one swing. Instead, Molitor looked to do what he does most consistently: drive the ball around the field and hit it where it's pitched. As a number three hitter, it was his job to drive the ball hard and get on base

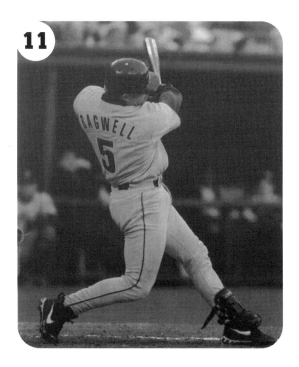

During his 1994 MVP season, Jeff Bagwell hit .368 with 39 home runs and 116 RBIs in just 400 at bats.

for the number four and five hitters. He lined a pitch up the middle for a base hit, bringing Joe Carter up to bat. The rest is history, as Carter hit a 2-2 fastball over the left-field fence to give the Blue Jays their second straight World Championship.

Offenses can't just rely on the long ball to supply all the runs. There are times when a team has to build a run by drawing a walk, stealing a base, moving the runner with a ground ball to second, and then scoring him on a sacrifice fly. A good offense should have balance throughout the lineup to counter any pitcher who takes the mound.

The 1995 Cleveland Indians might have won the World Series against Atlanta if they had thought this way. Instead, their lineup was stacked with power hitters. After Kenny Lofton and Omar Vizquel led off the game, the Indians bombarded their opponents with power: Baerga, with a record of 15 home runs, Belle (50), Murray (21), Paul Sorrento (25), Manny Ramirez (31), Jim Thome (25), and Sandy Alomar (10). Against a hard thrower like John Smoltz, the Indians had great success, but when they were matched up against control pitchers like Tom Glavine or Greg Maddux, they had trouble adjusting. They needed a couple more guys who could stay back and hit the ball where it was pitched.

Teams at every level need all the different types of hitters to compete. It is the responsibility of the individual to be the best kind of hitter he can be for that team at that time. Most hitters need to concentrate on hitting for either average or power, some have been able to do both. Here's a list of 25 classic hybrid hitters who have had great seasons over the past 25 years. Each one of these players has had the ability to get on base with a single, drive in a run with an extra-base hit, or clear the basepaths with the long ball.

The longest Louisville Slugger® was used by Philadelphia Athletic Al Simmons, a 38-inch bat.

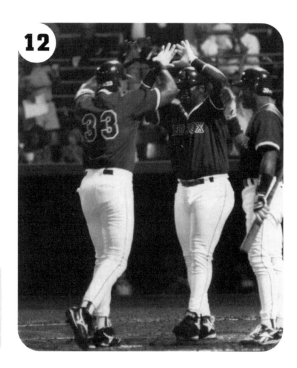

From one MVP to another—Jose Canseco (1988) and Mo Vaughn (1995) have both won American League Most Valuable Player awards. Both are capable of turning a game around with one swing, but they can also be counted on to hit for average.

25 Hybrid Hitters Over the Past 25 Years

Mo Vaughn—Red Sox
1996 .326 BA, 44 HR, 143 RBI, 118 RS

Paul O'Neill—Yanks
1995 .300 BA, 22 HR, 96 RBI, 82 RS

John Olerud—Blue Jays
1993 .363 BA, 24 HR, 114 RBI, 54 2B, 107 BB

Paul Molitor—Blue Jays
1993 .332 BA, 22 HR, 111 RBI, 211 hits

Mark Grace—Cubs
1993 .325 BA, 14 HR, 98 RBI, 38 2B

Barry Bonds—Giants
1993 .336 BA, 46 HR, 123 RBI, 126 BB

Cal Ripken—Orioles
1991 .323 BA, 34 HR, 114 RBI, 46 2B

Ryne Sandberg—Cubs
1990 .306 BA, 40 HR, 100 RBI, 25 SB

Will Clark—Giants
1989 .333 BA, 23 HR, 111 RBI, 104 RS

Alan Trammell—Tigers
1987 .343 BA, 28 HR, 105 RBI, 21 SB

Don Mattingly—Yanks
1986 .352 BA, 31 HR, 113 RBI, 53 2B, 238 hits

Al Oliver—Expos
1982 .331 BA, 22 HR, 109 RBI, 43 2B, 204 hits

Bill Madlock—Pirates
1982 .319 BA, 19 HR, 95 RBI, 18 SB, 92 RS

Eddie Murray—Orioles
1982 .316 BA, 30 HR, 110 RBI, 70 BB

Robin Yount—Brewers
1982 .331 BA, 29 HR, 114 RBI, 46 2B

George Brett—Royals
1980 .390 BA, 24 HR, 118 RBI, 22 SO

Steve Garvey—Dodgers
1979 .315 BA, 28 HR, 110 RBI, 92 RS

Keith Hernandez—Cardinals
1979 .344 BA, 11 HR, 98 RBI, 48 2B

Jim Rice—Red Sox
1979 .325 BA, 39 HR, 130 RBI, 39 2B

Dave Parker—Pirates
1978 .334 BA, 30 HR, 117 RBI, 20 SB

Dave Winfield—Padres
1978 .308 BA, 24 HR, 91 RBI, 21 SB

Carlton Fisk—Red Sox
1977 .315 BA, 26 HR, 102 RBI, 75 BB

Joe Morgan—Reds
1976 .320 BA, 27 HR, 111 RBI, 60 SB, 114 BB

Tony Oliva—Twins
1970 .325 BA, 23 HR, 107 RBI, 204 hits

Hybrid hitters are players who can do it all at the plate. They're special because they can hurt you in more than one way. A hybrid hitter may be a power hitter, but also a threat to steal a base. High totals in doubles, walks, runs scored, etc., are all different ways that a hybrid hitter can help his team's offense.

In 1991, Baltimore Orioles shortstop Cal Ripken became the first shortstop in American League history to hit .300 with 30 or more home runs and 100 or more RBIs. Ripken led the league in total bases (368) and was second in hits (210) and doubles (46).

*Sometimes I hit him like I used to hit Sandy Koufax,
and that's like drinking coffee with a fork.*

— Willie Stargell on Steve Carlton

- Kirk Gibson of the Los Angeles Dodgers was the National League's MVP for 1988. But due to a serious leg injury, Gibson was able to make only one plate appearance during the 1988 World Series between the Dodgers and the Oakland Athletics. Gibson made the most of his one trip to the plate when he ended Game 1 with a dramatic two-out, two-run homer off A's ace reliever Dennis Eckersley. Gibson's heroics inspired the Dodgers to a 4 games to 1 World Series triumph.

- Bo Jackson played major league baseball from 1986 to 1994. During that time he hit 141 home runs, including 32 in 1989. Jackson is the only man to hit more than 100 major league home runs and rush for more than 100 yards in a National Football League game. Jackson's baseball career was shortened by a hip injury sustained playing football.

- Most baseball fans know that Roger Maris holds the all-time record for most home runs in a season with 61, and that Babe Ruth had previously held the record with 60. But the 60-home run barrier has been reached and passed several times in the minor leagues. The all-time minor league home run record is 72, accomplished by Joe Bauman for Roswell in the Longhorn League in 1954.

- Joe Hauser holds two minor league single season home run records—the American Association (69) and the International League (63). Ten times in his minor league career Hauser hit more than 20 home runs for a season. Hauser hit 79 major league home runs, mostly for the Philadelphia Athletics. The A's released Hauser after the 1928 season, just before they won two World Series in a row.

- In his 21-year career, Hall of Famer Frank Robinson hit 586 home runs, the fourth highest total in history. As a Cincinnati Red, Robinson was the National League Rookie of the Year in 1956, and National League MVP in 1961. He went on to play for the Baltimore Orioles and won the American League MVP in 1966 making him the only player to ever win that award in both leagues.

- When the 1996 season ended Tony Gwynn and Wade Boggs were the only two active players in the top 50 career batting average leaders. Eddie Murray and Paul Molitor are the only active players in the top 50 in career hits and runs scored.

- Joe DiMaggio had a reputation for being a tough hitter to strike out. His brother Dom, however, led the National League six times in strikeouts during his career.

SITUATIONAL HITTING

8

"*I think I'm a better hitter when there are runners on base, because you can somewhat dictate what the pitcher is going to throw.*"
— *Mo Vaughn*

Situational hitting is an advanced form of hitting. When you reach the higher levels of baseball, you need more than just good hitting skills. You need awareness. Every time you go up to bat you need to know the score, what inning it is, how many outs there are, who, if anyone, is on base, what their capabilities are, who's on deck, and if there's any sign on. You're part of a team, and your strategy at the plate should reflect that.

Teamwork is often an underestimated concept in the game of baseball. With the way individual performances and personal statistics are scrutinized, people tend to overlook how important the players are to each other. But at any level of baseball, it's the little things that often win games. In fact, with the exception of a home run, every hit or walk needs another hit, walk, groundball or flyball to score a run, so a good situational hitter can be irreplaceable to a team.

Even teams that play a power game occasionally have to scrap for runs. In 1962, the New York Yankees had names like Mickey Mantle, Roger Maris, and Frank Howard through the meat of their order, but in Game 7 of the 1962 World Series against the San Francisco Giants, the three went a combined 1 for 11 and were not an offensive factor in the deciding game. With Yankee pitcher Ralph Terry and the Giants' Jack Sanford locked in a scoreless tie in the fifth inning, New York looked to the bottom of the order to score a run.

First baseman Bill Skowron singled to left to lead it off. Clete Boyer moved him to third with a base hit to left-center field. And then Terry, batting ninth, walked to load the bases. Tony Kubek came up to the plate, looking to put the ball in play anywhere to get a run on the scoreboard. He grounded into a 6-4-3 double play. Though it sounds like a rally killer, Skowron scored on the hit, giving New York a 1-0 lead. It was all the Yankees needed as Terry pitched a complete game shutout, giving the Yanks another World Series title.

THE LEADOFF HITTER

If you're the first hitter of an inning, it doesn't matter how you get on base, it just matters that you get there. You can draw a walk, get hit by a pitch, smack a base hit, or get on with an error. Any way you do it, it will help your team.

Brett Butler's ability to make consistent contact and get on base makes him one of the best lead-off hitters in the game.

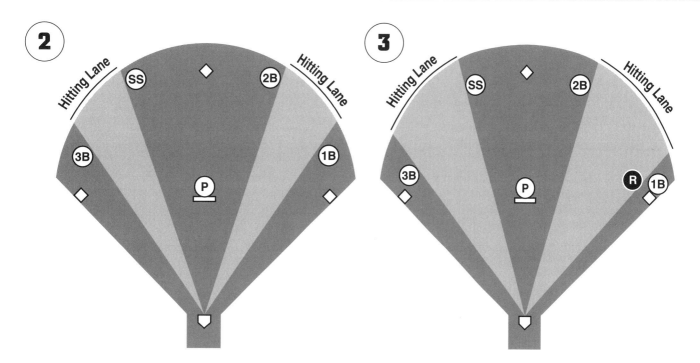

Remember, the lineup card only possesses the leadoff hitter for the first inning. Once the game is in progress, any hitter can become a leadoff hitter. Just because you hit cleanup doesn't mean you're released from the responsibility of trying to get on base if you lead off an inning. Good hitters show versatility in assuming different roles throughout the course of a game, and the leadoff role is a crucial one.

The face of the game changes drastically when the leadoff hitter finds a way on base. Getting on base opens lots of doors for an offense and forces the defense to adjust.

The pitcher now has to pitch from the stretch position (as opposed to the windup), an obviously inferior option or pitchers would do it all the time. They may lose velocity and accuracy without their windup, and they may lose some of their concentration if they have to worry about holding the runner. Facing someone who is less than 100 percent focused on the plate is an advantage to you and the rest of your team.

The infielders have to adjust their thinking as well. The first baseman is forced to hold the runner on the bag until the pitch is thrown. The second baseman needs to move toward second to defend the steal or turn the double play. With these two players closer to the bag, there's quite a large gap in the right side of the field. The shortstop also slides toward second for the same reasons as the second baseman, and the third baseman moves up, even with the bag for a double-play ball, or on the grass to defend the bunt. This leaves a big gap in the left side of the infield. As you can see, the leadoff hitter has opened up quite a few possibilities for a good place hitter in the second spot.

A baserunner who is a potential base stealer has a tremendous adverse effect on the pitcher. It divides his attention. The baserunner also has a great effect on the defense. It takes them out of character and makes them do things they haven't practiced. The third baseman is pulled in, the middle infielders may be jockeying a runner on second base to keep him close. All these things contribute to creating larger holes in the infield for the hitter to hit through.

—— *Maury Wills*

I had good success at fouling pitches off and spoiling pitcher's pitches. I might foul off four or five pitches in one at-bat, mostly to the third base side. One time I hit a lady sitting behind the third base dugout—I got her right between the eyes with a line drive. She was wearing glasses. The ball broke them and her nose, too. They carried her out on a stretcher, cut and bleeding.

The next day I heard from her husband. He asked if I'd come visit her in the hospital. I said, "Sure," and went over to see her and talk to her. As I was leaving, I told her how sorry I was that I hit her with the foul ball.

"You hit me twice," she said. "You probably don't know it, but when they were carrying me out on the stretcher you hit me again."

She pulled up her hospital gown and there imprinted on her thigh was Ford Frick's signature and the stitches from the ball where I got her again.

— Richie Ashburn

O ne of the most common—but bedeviling—situations in the game. The object seems simple: Hit the ball on the ground to the right side, moving the runner into scoring position. It becomes more important when moving a runner from second to third, where he can score on a wild pitch, error, ground out, sacrifice fly, or base hit.

— Rod Carew

A well-executed bunt can play an important role in scoring runs for your team. Bunting is an art that should be perfected by every good hitter.

The gaps in the infield, combined with a less focused pitcher, create wonderful offensive opportunities. In fact, statistical evidence proves without a doubt that hitters experience greater success when pitchers and fielders have to worry about a runner on base. For example, in 1993, major league hitters batted .259 with nobody on, but they hit .273 with runners on. Fourteen points higher!

As the leadoff hitter, you also have another responsibility. Make the pitcher work. You have to be selective, run a deep count, maybe foul off a couple of good pitches. If you're a tough out, it lets your teammates see what the pitcher has, and it tires him out.

AFTER SOMEONE IS ON BASE

When a teammate has gotten on base ahead of you, your role is considerably different from that of the leadoff hitter. It's your job to advance that runner. Unfortunately, there's no award at the end of the season for "Most Runners Advanced," nor will you get headlines in the newspapers for a "spectacular" bunt, but moving the runner is a feat that is very much appreciated by coaches and teammates.

A runner on first needs two hits to get him home, while a runner on second usually only needs one. Any coach will tell you that the player who moves the runner into scoring position is just as important as the hitter who drives him home.

Advancing the runner doesn't always have to mean a sacrifice, however. Many times the coach will just let you swing away. But if he doesn't, you have to leave your ego in the on-deck circle and do what's best for the team.

SACRIFICE BUNTING

Bunting is a skill that is often neglected, but it's one that should be practiced right from the start in baseball. A team is limited if only a few of its hitters know how to bunt.

Bunting Tips

There's a difference between bunting for a base hit and bunting to advance a runner into scoring position. The latter is called a sacrifice and it means just what the word implies.

When I'm sacrificing, I square around at the plate, facing the pitcher. My bat is held letter-high. I do this for two reasons: (1) I know that any pitch above the letters is a ball, and (2) it's much easier to drop your bat down to make contact with a pitch than it is to move the bat up.

A hitter should lay off high pitches when he's sacrificing. If he doesn't, the chances are he'll bunt a pop-up. If he's drag bunting for a base hit, he can go for a high pitch because he's chopping down at the ball as his body is falling away from the plate. He's trying to hit the ball hard enough to get it past the pitcher.

— Pete Rose

Sacrifice bunting is usually used either early in the ball game, to get a few runs on the board, or late, when you're playing for one run. It's the most common use of the bunt. The hitter sacrifices his at-bat for the opportunity to move the runner to the next base (usually second). When executed correctly, it's a safe method of putting a runner in scoring position, while swinging away has only about a 30 percent chance of succeeding.

The job of getting down a successful bunt starts with your attitude. Once the sign is given, you must be totally devoted to carrying out that assignment. Thoughts like "Maybe if I foul one off, he'll let me swing away" have no place here. Do what's best for the team.

There are two methods to execute the sacrifice bunt; the square around (Figure 5) and the pivot (Figure 6). Either way is acceptable. Remember, keep the bat out away from your body, give a little with the pitch, and most importantly, *make sure it's a strike.*

You should square around to bunt when the pitcher comes to a set in his motion. Once he does, you pivot on your back foot, bringing your shoulders square to the mound. Your top hand slides up to about label height; hold the bat in your thumb and index finger, and make sure you keep your hand behind the barrel. Bend your knees and crouch over, bringing your eyes into the strike zone. Extend your arms away from the body and hold the bat at eye level. The barrel of the bat should be angled slightly higher than the handle and out over the plate.

If the pitcher gives you a strike, try to "catch" the ball with the barrel of the bat. Hold the bat firmly in your hands but "give" a little with the pitch. Don't poke at the ball. You want to allow the bat to absorb the energy of the pitch. You'll end up hitting it too hard.

Look for a pitch that's in the middle to lower half of the strike zone. Try to bunt the middle to upper half of the ball to avoid popping it in the air. Bunting the ball in the air not only fails to get the job done, but it could result in a double play.

The placement of the bunt should be down the third or first baseline, keeping the ball away from the pitcher. The pitcher is the closest player on the field and may have a chance to throw out the runner. With a runner on first, try to make the first baseman field the ball. Because he has to hold the runner on, he won't be in close and will be late getting to the ball. With a runner on second, make the third baseman retrieve it. The object is to get the runner to third, so you want to pull the third baseman off his post.

Don't start running until the ball is actually on the ground. If you try to run too soon, it can affect your contact with the ball, its direction, and how hard you hit it. Remember, your job is to advance the runner. Do that part right, and don't worry about racing down to first base.

BUNTING FOR A BASE HIT

If you learn how to be a good bunter, there are times when you can use the bunt without sacrificing an at-bat. On top of that, you'll improve your average for your other hitting as well. Fielders will always have to be on the alert for the bunt base hit and be forced to move up on you, making bigger holes in the infield. If they don't move up, bunt. If they move up, hit away.

Like the sacrifice bunt, the base-hit bunt should only be used at certain times in the game. Leading off an inning is a good time. A hit can ignite a rally, and you might catch the infielders off guard. Another good time is when you or the team are struggling at the plate. Not only will it give your team an emotional lift, but it might disrupt the pitcher's rhythm, especially if he now has to pitch from the stretch.

There are a few times when it's better not to try for the bunt base hit:

- If you're up by a lot of runs, it's considered unsportsmanlike to lay down a bunt.

- If there's a runner on third with less than two outs, you want to swing away to bring him home.

- If you have two outs, you're looking for a bigger hit that will put you in scoring position (2nd or 3rd base).

- If you're not a good bunter or if you don't run very fast, this is not the hit for you.

7

Delino DeShields has his momentum going towards first base before he even bunts the ball.

The key to making good contact as a bunter is the exact opposite of what we teach for making good contact as a hitter. In hitting, the action we initiate thrusts the head of the bat toward the ball. In bunting, we want to let the ball come toward the bat. A big mistake bad bunters make is trying to jab the bat toward the ball. Once you've moved your bat into the bunting zone, the only time that bat, or any part of your body, should move is when the ball actually makes contact with the bat.

— Rod Carew

Bunting for a base hit should be disguised as long as possible, so the pitcher can't alter his pitch and the fielders won't have a lot of time to react. As the pitcher releases the ball, you make your move.

Position your feet in a way that feels comfortable to you. Some right-handed players like to drop their back foot, which keeps them facing toward first base. Others will step forward, to get a jump toward first, although this makes it harder to deal with an inside pitch. Lefties tend to run away from the pitch toward the base. This gives them a great jump, but it does cut down on their control.

Players also have varying opinions on where the hands should go. Some like to slide both hands up near the barrel to increase bat control, while others move only the top hand up. Rod Carew, one of the greatest bunters of all time, didn't move his hands at all. He felt as if the bat was an extension of his hands, and he didn't want to choke up. If you're having difficulty with the bunt, however, choking up is your best bet. Once you're having success, then you can experiment.

There are two basic ways to bunt when you're going for a base hit: the push bunt which is an opposite-side bunt (righty to right and lefty to left), and the drag bunt, a same-side bunt (lefty to right and righty to left).

For a push bunt, angle the head of your bat back, with your arms almost fully extended. Even though it's called a push bunt, you don't want to give it much force, maybe just slightly more than a sacrifice bunt. Look for a pitch that is up and away in the strike zone. This allows you to get your arms out away from your body, which helps you to see the ball hit the bat. Also, stay away from curveballs. Just as in regular hitting, it's a lot easier to hit a straight ball than one that breaks.

The hardest thing for me on a baseball field has always been to hit. I could always run, and bunting just emphasized that. I make it a point of trying to bunt at least once a game.

— Brett Butler

The drag and push bunt differ from the sacrifice because you want to try to bunt the ball with your body already in motion towards first base. Righthanded batters should drop their rear foot back so they're positioned in a direct line towards first base. Lefthanded hitters should time the pitch so when they make contact, they're crossing over with their back foot as DeShields is doing in Figure 7.

The one down the third baseline was the one I liked best. You make believe you're hitting, even pivot a little. Then when the ball gets there, you don't turn, you just move your right hand up just below the trademark. When the ball hits the bat, it has backspin. If you can keep the third baseman from cheating in, you have yourself a base hit.

— *Phil Rizzuto*

A right-handed hitter wants to use the push bunt if the first baseman is playing deep or is slow on his feet. Also, if he's holding the runner on, aim between him and the pitcher, because it could cause just enough confusion to get you on base. If the pitcher is left-handed, you can get pretty close to him. His follow-through takes him the other way, and it's unlikely that he'll be able to react.

A left-handed hitter always has a good push bunt toward the third baseman. If it's well placed, it almost impossible to defend because of the long throw and the good jump a lefty gets out of the box. He also has the same option of going near the pitcher if the pitcher is right-handed.

The drag bunt is probably the more common bunt among hitters going for a base hit. It takes more skill, but if you can master it, it's more effective. You should look to place the ball just inside the foul line, and if you miss, you'd better make sure you miss foul. A bunt too far off the line is an easy out.

On the drag bunt, you need to angle the head of the bat out toward the pitcher. If you're a left-handed hitter, look for a pitch from the middle of the plate in and no higher than the waist. If you're a right-handed batter, look for a pitch out over the plate, not inside, and never higher than your waist. Again, position your feet and hands in the way that is most comfortable.

It doesn't matter if you're hot at the plate or if you're slumping—if you're a good bunter, lay one down. If you're hot, the infield is back, defending against your hits. If you're slumping, it's a good way to change your focus, take some pressure off, and gain some confidence.

THE SQUEEZE BUNT

Typically, a squeeze bunt is called late in a close game with a runner on third and less than two outs. The beauty of it is that it's almost a guaranteed run if it's executed right. But if either the batter or the runner makes even the tiniest error, a good scoring opportunity can be an easy out.

During a squeeze play the runner should break from third just as the pitcher releases the ball. The batter must also remain in his normal stance until the moment of delivery. The pitcher must have no knowledge of the squeeze play until it's too late, because if either the runner or the hitter move too early, the pitcher can pitch out and nail the runner.

Once the ball is released, the batter *must* bunt it. In this case, a failed attempt isn't going to help at all. No matter where the pitch is, the batter has to get a piece of it or the runner's a dead duck.

For the squeeze bunt to succeed, the batter merely needs to get the ball on the ground and make sure it's fair. As long as the runner is breaking, there's not enough time for the defense to throw him out, no matter where the ball is bunted. The best place for the bunt is up the middle. You can't risk a foul ball in this situation, because you'll have lost your chance for the squeeze. Just make sure you hit down on the ball. A pop-up on this play would be disastrous.

THE SLASH

The slash, an offshoot of the bunt, is another excellent way to get a hit and move the runner along. The slash is when the hitter shows bunt but then pulls back and swings away . When defenses set up to cover the bunt, their coverage is limited for other types of hits. The slash not only gets them out of position, but it also catches them off guard.

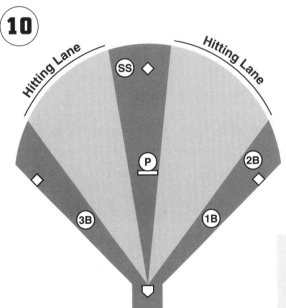

With the infield rotating for bunt coverage, a slash can be extremely effective. The first and third baseman are charging in while the shortstop covers second and the second baseman moves to first. This leaves the entire middle of the field open.

11

Work on bat control. There is always a place on any team, anywhere, for a guy who can handle the bat. For the greatest degree of bat control, however, the middle finger joints of both hands should be roughly aligned. This position affords one the greatest wrist freedom. One other thing to remember: the fingers do more holding than the palms, just as in the case of a golfer and his club.

—— *Harry Walker*

When you go to execute the slash, pivot and face the pitcher when he is set and about to go into his leg kick. *But do not pick up your back foot to square around.* Your feet should remain planted. Your top hand should slide up to the barrel of the bat, while the bottom hand should move up just a little on the handle. Extend the arms to show bunt and as the pitcher is about to release the ball, pull back into your stance. Slide your top hand back down, but leave your bottom hand where it is, so you're a little choked up to give you better bat control.

The best place to hit a slash is on the ground. With bunt coverage, the third and first baseman are charging, the second baseman is covering first, and the shortstop is on second. Virtually the entire infield is wide open (Figure 10).

The slash sounds like a can't miss play, and when executed well, it is. But it's a difficult hit to master, so infielders are relatively safe when they cover for the bunt.

PLACE HITTING TO THE RIGHT SIDE

If there's a runner on second, with no outs, your job is to hit a ground ball to the right side of infield. In this situation, you don't even have to worry about finding the gaps, although it is obviously a nice bonus if you do. But even if the fielder picks your hit up cleanly, a runner with a good jump should have no problem reaching third base safely, especially as it's not a force play. The main thing you need to worry about as the hitter is keeping the ball on the ground.

In the batter's box, you have to make a full commitment to hitting to the right side of the field. Be patient and look for a pitch you can hit to the right side. If you're right-handed, look for a pitch away. If you're left-handed, look for one you can pull.

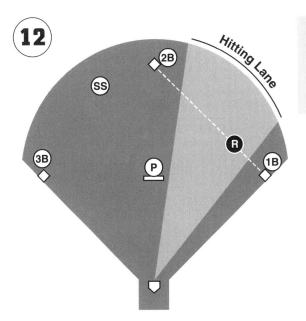

12

With the runner breaking, either the shortstop or second baseman has to leave his position to cover the bag. This diagram illustrates where the infielders are positioned when the second baseman covers the steal. Notice the large hole on the right side of the infield. Good bat control can translate into base hits.

One of the prettiest and most valuable plays in baseball is the hit-and-run, in which a runner on first breaks for second and the batter does whatever is necessary to contact the ball. If executed properly, it will get the runner over to third or, at least, will avoid a double play. It's one situation in which it's imperative to try to hit the ball on the ground.

— *Joe Torre*

If you're a good place hitter, you might even want to try this if the runner is on first. But in this case, you must hit the ball into the gap or you're likely to be hitting into a double play.

THE HIT-AND-RUN

When a manager has Willie Mays or Mike Piazza or Ken Griffey, Jr., coming up in his lineup, he can often sit back and watch their natural abilities take over, but most of the time he has to be figuring out the best way to put runs up on the scoreboard. He might want to try to manufacture some runs, and the hit-and-run is a great instigator.

The hit-and-run can create a lot of opportunities for an offense simply by putting the runner in motion and the ball in play (Figure 12). Before the ball is even released, the baserunner is running, the fielders are moving, the pitcher and catcher are distracted and the hitter is definitely swinging. It's a recipe for chaos and some good offense. When a team is struggling to score runs, the hit-and-run can act as a good jump start.

If you've gotten the signal for the hit-and-run, you have an obligation to swing the bat, no matter how bad the pitch is. Whether it is in the dirt, in on your fists, or even a pitch out, you have to attempt to make contact, because protecting the runner is your primary responsibility. If you don't swing, he's in big trouble. If you swing and miss, you've at least gotten in the catcher's way a little bit, giving the runner a chance. If you swing and connect, though, who knows what might happen.

Try not to let the hit-and-run sign change your hitting approach. You should just concentrate on making solid contact, as usual, and hitting a ground ball. With all the movement on the field, there's a very good chance of the ball getting through a gap. If it is fielded, though, at least the runner will have advanced into scoring position.

The hit-and-run only makes sense when a pitcher needs to throw a strike or close to it, for his own purposes. Thus the count in the at-bat is everything with the hit-and-run. The counts on which the batter has the best chance of getting a decent pitch are 1-0, 2-0, and 2-1. The basic idea is to force the shortstop or the second baseman to cover second base, opening a large, inviting hole, usually to the opposite field, for the batter to shoot a hit through on the ground.

— *Keith Hernandez*

If you have the ability to place hit, however, by all means go for the gaps. There will be a huge hole in the infield with either the shortstop or second baseman covering, and if you can take advantage of this, do it. You'll have to notice ahead of time, however, who covers on a steal. Some teams will have the second baseman covering the bag for righthanded hitters, the shortstop for lefties. Other teams will do the reverse.

Sometimes a team will adjust their playing because of your hitting tendencies. If you're a dead-pull hitter, chances are the opposite field will be wide open for you. If you can manage to hit that way, you'll get a hit for sure.

The hit-and-run can also be used to help a slumping player. Slumps can make a hitter more tentative. With the hit-and-run sign on, though, the hitter must swing. It takes away the chore of decision-making. Mike Schmidt, a three-time National League MVP, used to request that coaches put a hit-and-run on for him when he was having problems. It got him swinging the bat and kept him from worrying too much about what pitch was coming.

Just remember to hit the ball on the ground. A perfectly executed hit-and-run has the strong possibility of turning the situation from a man on first with no outs to a man on first and third with no outs. But one that puts the ball in the air could easily turn it into nobody on, two outs.

One of the greatest clutch hitters of all time, Reggie Jackson launches his third home run of the day in Game 6 of the 1977 World Series at Yankee Stadium. **Notice Jackson's foot remains closed just before contact**, and his head is locked down on the pitch. Jackson possessed great power and bat speed, but more importantly, he hits this pitch right on the "sweet spot" of the bat.

13

THE HITTER'S CORNER

THE RUN-AND-HIT

The run-and-hit is more for the batter than the baserunner. For the baserunner, it's a straight steal. The hitter then has the option of swinging the bat, to take advantage of the newly created gaps in the field, or not. Because the runner is on his own in this situation, the batter is relieved of the responsibility to protect him and only has to swing at strikes.

SCORING THE RUNNER ON THIRD

With a runner on third and less than two outs, it's your job to score the runner. This is what wins ball games. The hitters before you worked hard to get that runner to third. It's up to you to finish the job and bring him home.

Rafael Palmeiro puts a good, level swing on this pitch to drive in a run. With the infield back, simply putting the ball in play is all the hitter needs to do.

You've got to score the runner from third any way you can. One of my most memorable at-bats of my career came in one of the last games of the 1951 season that practically won us the pennant. Joe DiMaggio was on third base and Mickey Mantle, who was in his first season, was in the on-deck circle. DiMag later told me that Al Rosen, who was playing third base, said to him before the pitch, "I think he's going to bunt." And DiMaggio said to him, "I know he's going to bunt."

I laid a bunt down the first baseline and DiMaggio scored to win the game. The pitcher, Hall of Famer Bob Lemon, was so frustrated that he picked up the ball and threw it up on the screen along with his glove. They all knew I was going to bunt, but if you get a good one down, it doesn't matter.

— *Phil Rizzuto*

First, look at the infield. There are three basic positions they can be in: normal depth, "corners up" (that means the third and first basemen move up even with the bag), or on the grass. Your choice of hits changes with each formation.

If the infielders are back at normal depth, it means they probably are going to concede this run and play for an out. This makes your job a little easier. All you need to do is hit a deep fly ball to the outfield or put the ball in play on the ground. In most cases, if you just hit the ball hard, it will take care of itself. What you want to avoid are shallow fly balls, a pop-up in the infield, a ball back to the pitcher, or, of course, a strikeout isn't a hit.

If the defense is playing corners up, they are hedging their bets. They'll go for the play at the plate if the ball is hit to first or third, otherwise, they'll go for the out. You have to hit up the middle on this one. A long fly ball to the outfield will still do the job, but aiming for the middle is safer.

If it's a close game, and your opponents aren't willing to give up a run, you'll find them pulled up close on the grass. Their number one concern is to prevent the runner from scoring. Rod Carew terms this scenario "the easiest way to hit .500." A lot of people think they have to hit the ball in the air in this situation, and this *will* work as a sacrifice fly. But you can also hit the ball hard on the ground and slip it past the infielders for a hit. With the defense playing in close, their range is so severely limited that only a ball hit directly at them is catchable.

Jay Buhner, who drove in 121 runs during the 1995 season, keeps his front shoulder in and drives the ball to the opposite field.

STAYING AWAY FROM THE DOUBLE PLAY

Bases loaded, one out. The score is tied late in the game and your team is on the verge of a big inning. A hit from you means at least two runs and you've been seeing the ball well all day. Your opponent brings in a relief pitcher, and you know he likes to get ahead with a fastball on the first pitch. You're relaxed, confident, and aware of the situation in the batter's box. It doesn't get any better than this.

The pitcher delivers, and, sure enough, it's a fastball. It's low in the strike zone so you go down with the pitch to drive it. Although you hit the ball right on the nose, it's a hard ground ball to shortstop. He flips it to the second baseman, who pivots and fires to first base to complete the double play. The inning is over and the game is still tied.

You feel cheated. You think you did everything right and the worst possible outcome happened. But, in actuality, the pitcher cast out his bait and you swallowed it hook, line, and sinker. Though you swung at a strike, it was a low one, which induced you to hit a ground ball. Two outs. No runs scored.

Former Minnesota Twin Gene Larkin was in a similar situation in Game 7 of the 1991 World Series. With one out, Larkin knew he had to stay out of the double play. Even though he considers himself a low-ball hitter, he was looking for something up in the strike zone to lift into the air. He got a high strike on the first pitch and lofted it over the left-fielder's head to win the series. Here's how Larkin remembers it:

Louisville Slugger® nicknames include Timber, Lumber, Stick, Black Death, and Black Betsy.

I'd been watching [Alexandro] Peña throw all series and he was going after everybody with high fastballs in the strike zone, so I pretty much knew he was going to throw me something hard, high and tight, or high and away. I'd always been a low-ball hitter, but in that situation I could have grounded a low pitch into a double play and the game would have continued. If that first pitch was low, I probably would have taken the first pitch. But fortunately it was up and it was an ideal pitch to hit.

19

CLUTCH HITTING

When you're up at bat with runners on but two outs, the pressure builds. Your team can't afford anything less than a base hit in this situation. It's a whole new ball game when it comes to hitting in the clutch.

Clutch situations make the showdown between the hitter and pitcher much more intense. Either the pitcher is going to get out of a jam or the batter is going to put some runs on the board. Some players struggle in clutch situations, others revel in them.

Players have different philosophies when it comes to clutch hitting. Some like to jump on the first good pitch they see. Others like to take the pitcher deep into the count, to see a lot of pitches.

The most important thing you can do in the clutch is to stay calm, positive, and have confidence in your ability. There's no room for doubt. Go up to the plate determined to do your best and you'll have some success. Remember, baseball is a game of averages. If you live up to your potential, sometimes you'll get that clutch hit. And sometimes you won't. Even the very best clutch hitters don't always succeed.

TWO OUTS AND NOBODY ON

When there are two outs and nobody has gotten on base, you're facing a field that looks remarkably similar to the one the leadoff hitter faced. Your job description, however, is radically different.

Unless you're a Rickey Henderson who can basically steal bases at will, you need to look for a hit that will get you farther than first base. If you just get to first, you'll most likely need two other hitters to come through to score you. The odds of that happening without an out are slim.

The number one way to succeed in hitting with men in scoring position is to keep from going to two strikes in the count. I say that and, in the same breath, I say you have to be patient. I know that's contradictory but here's what I mean. Don't wave at the first thing you see but hit the first good pitch you get before you get two strikes.

The other thing is, you must stay geared up the middle on the ground. You can't think about pulling the ball with men in scoring position because, most of the time, a pitcher will try to trick the hitter there or throw him off stride by throwing a breaking ball. The guys who go for the home runs and try to go for too much too early in the count become easy outs. That was my problem the first five or six years of my career.

— *Mike Schmidt*

So the extra base hit is the goal in this situation, and to do that you need to find a pitch that you can drive into the gaps in the outfield. If the pitcher serves up a "fat pitch" early in the count, hoping to get ahead, you'd better jump on it. Chances are good, too, that this will happen. With two down, the pitcher is looking for that third out. The last thing he wants to do is walk you.

Assuming you do deliver a pitch into the outfield, this is the time to try to stretch it into a double. You might even catch the outfielders off guard, if the hit isn't a clear double.

No matter what the circumstances are, situational hitting takes intelligence, patience, concentration, and most importantly, an unselfish attitude. If, instead, you put yourself in front of your team, the only situation you may find yourself in is spectating from the bench.

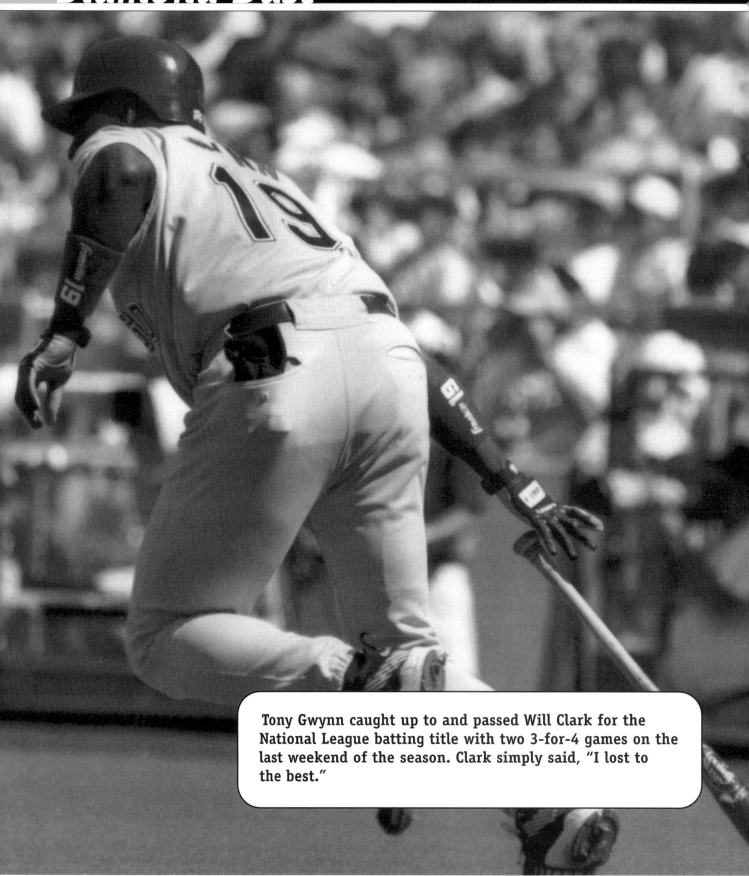

Tony Gwynn caught up to and passed Will Clark for the National League batting title with two 3-for-4 games on the last weekend of the season. Clark simply said, "I lost to the best."

There are two theories on hitting the knuckle ball.
Unfortunately, neither of them works.

— Charley Lau

- The name Spencer Davis is to minor league baseball what Pete Rose is to major league baseball. For his career Davis is the all-time minor league hits leader with 3,617 safeties. He also leads in doubles with 743 and runs with 2,287 and he is fourth in RBIs with 1,769.

- Carl Yastrzemski won the American League batting title in 1968 with a .301 average, the lowest average to ever win a batting crown.

- Jimmy Foxx, Babe Ruth and Hack Wilson are the only three players to record 200 hits and 50 home runs in the same season. Their record is an uncommon blend of power and batting average.

- On April 17, 1976 the Philadelphia Phillies, led by a record-tying four consecutive home runs by Mike Schmidt, rallied from a 12-1 deficit to defeat the Chicago Cubs. The rally ties a record for overcoming the largest deficit to win a game. See, you're never out of it until the last out is made.

- September 25, 1990 is a date the Baltimore Orioles pitching staff would like to forget. They yielded eight straight hits (six singles and two home runs) to the Yankees before recording an out. The onslaught tied records for most consecutive hits to start a game and most runs scored to start a game before an out is recorded.

- Willie Mays was baseball's original 30/30 man. In 1956, the "Say Hey Kid" became the first player ever to hit 30 home runs and steal 30 bases. He went on to lead the National League in home runs four times and also stolen bases four times.

- Ted Williams made a triumphant return to baseball after spending three seasons in the service during World War II. On the first pitch thrown to him in three years, Williams hit a 418-foot home run, and later led the Red Sox to their first pennant in 28 years.

- New York Yankee Bernie Williams hit home runs from both sides of the plate in the same game in both the 1995 and 1996 American League playoffs.

THE MENTAL
GAME

9

"*Once you get to this level and do so many drills and take as many swings as we do, hitting becomes all mental.*"

— *Will Clark*

There was the infamous home run against the Cubs in the fourth game of the '84 playoffs. It was a situation where Tony Gwynn was on. I know Lee Smith isn't going to throw me a change-up or a curve. It's power against power and it's up to me to hit. The first pitch was a fastball, up and away, which told me he was just going to keep right on with that fastball, trying to get me to pop it up. I was 0 for 8 against him that season, but I'd been hitting the ball, not striking out. I said OK, I'm going to look away, get my hands up, and sure enough there it was. I hit through it and the rest is history.

— *Steve Garvey*

In Game 5 of the 1984 World Series, the Detroit Tigers were leading the San Diego Padres three games to one and needed just one more victory to clinch the world championship. With Detroit batting and leading 5-4 in the bottom of the eighth, Kirk Gibson came to the plate with runners on second and third. A hit would drive in two runs and basically sew up the series for the Tigers.

The Padres had the legendary Goose Gossage on the mound, an imposing figure who had been clocked in the high 90s during his career. The manager, Dick Williams, signaled to Gossage to intentionally walk Gibson, thereby loading up the bases, and creating a force play at any base. Gossage wanted nothing to do with this and the team met at the mound.

Gibson, meanwhile, waited patiently, listening to manager Sparky Anderson shouting in disbelief, "They don't want to walk you!" Gibson looked at the situation. If they weren't going to walk him, Gossage was going to try to strike him out. His strikeout pitch was the fastball, and because his ego may have been a little hurt by Williams's initial intention to walk the batter, the veteran reliever would probably challenge Gibson with this best pitch. Gibson decided to wait on a fastball. Gossage threw it, and Gibson hit it in the upper deck at Tiger Stadium for a three-run homer and an 8-4 lead. Detroit won the series four games to one.

By understanding the game situation and the pitcher he was facing, Gibson was able to make an educated guess about the type of pitch he was going to see. He used his head as much as he used his bat and the results were nothing short of spectacular.

Baseball is a thinking man's game. Much like a game of chess, there are attacks, counterattacks, and moves that are made to set something else up. This is what separates baseball from other sports. A pitcher may "throw away" a pitch to set up the hitter for something later, but do you ever see a quarterback throw away a pass to set up a free safety? A team up at bat might sacrifice an out to advance a runner, but have you ever seen a basketball team purposely turn the ball over as part of the strategy for the next time down the floor? The mind games on the diamond are a large part of what gives our nation's favorite pastime its allure.

Ted Williams watches one sail over the fence at Yankee Stadium. Williams will always be remembered for his sweet swing, but he was also one of the *smartest* hitters the game has ever known.

There's no one confrontation that requires good *baseball sense* more than the duel between the pitcher and the batter. It's a confrontation of two egos, both in command of their team's destiny for that at-bat. Neither side wants to lose the fight, and conflicting goals often boil over into flaring tempers.

DO YOUR HOMEWORK BEFORE CLASS BEGINS

Before you even step up to the plate, you need to know your pitcher inside and out, not the information the fans want to know—size, record, and hometown—but how and why he throws his pitches. If you pay attention to the game and study your opponent closely, it's possible to make an educated guess of the pitch every time.

The first thing you should notice about the pitcher is whether he is left- or right-handed. If the pitcher is throwing from the same side as you (righty vs. righty, lefty vs. lefty), you need to start thinking about a fastball that will appear to start at your front shoulder and then come slightly across the strike zone. A breaking ball is going to move away from you, and any pitch that tails is going to have movement toward you. Here are three good tips for same-side pitching:

- Step directly back at the pitcher; don't step into the bucket.

- Drive your front shoulder down into the pitch.

- Don't commit too soon (keep your hands back as long as possible) on the breaking pitch.

When you face a pitcher from the opposite side (righty vs. lefty, lefty vs. righty), the reverse is true. Most everything is coming in toward you, rather than away. This is an easier situation to handle because you see the ball a bit longer. The only pitches that would move away from you are ones that tail or screwballs. These are rarely thrown by young pitchers because of the risk of arm injury.

I was facing Russ "Monk" Moyer one time and I'm fouling off pitch after pitch. The bases are loaded up, so it was a big at-bat. All of a sudden, he looks at me and yells, "Foul this one off, you little s.o.b." He hit me right between the shoulderblades. He did it on purpose, too, even though the bases were loaded.

— *Richie Ashburn*

Always be watchful and observing. You will be surprised at how much you can learn that will be helpful. As the subject is hitting, the observations I suggest are to center on the pitcher, mainly, then the catcher and fielders. Close and constant observation will enable you to know in frequent cases what is coming.

— *Ty Cobb*

Start your game preparation by watching the pitcher warm up in the bullpen. Look for helpful hints such as the sidearm delivery shown here by pitcher Brad Clontz.

> Hitting is a lot more than just picking up a bat and swinging. You've got to be observant, evaluate the situation, know the pitcher and his tendencies, and know yourself. If you want to be successful, you have to become a student.
>
> *— Paul O'Neill*

Northern white ash is particularly desirable for the making of baseball bats because it is strong, stiff, and has high resistance to shock.

The main thing you have to worry about when you're facing an opposite-side pitcher is pulling off the ball too soon with your upper body. Because the pitch is coming in, many hitters tend to open up with their shoulders early and pull the bat through the zone. If you find that this is your problem, a good way to fix it is to plan on hitting the ball up the middle or to the opposite field.

Now that you know what arm your opponent throws from, it's time to monitor how and what he throws. Watch him warm up in the bullpen. Check out his windup. Is it quick or does he take his time? Is it a fluid motion or is it herky-jerky? Does he hide the ball or delay his release? You want to know all these things so that you can time his pitches when you're up to bat.

Once he gets loose, he'll begin to work on locating his fastball. Observe the velocity. Take note of the release point of his fastball. Is it a pitch that comes from straight over the top, three-quarter, or sidearm? Point of release not only dictates where your eyes need to go before he delivers the pitch, but it also may have an effect on whether his fastball has any movement. Three-quarter and sidearm deliveries tend to make the ball tail toward the pitcher's throwing side, and if you're like most hitters, you'd probably prefer a fastball with more velocity than one with more movement.

After the fastball, the pitcher will start to showcase his other pitches, breaking ball, slider, change-up, knuckler, splitter, etc. Notice what each pitch does (How does it break? Is it thrown hard or is it a slow curve?) and whether or not the pitcher changes his windup or release points for any of them. These can be valuable clues.

You also want to look at the pitcher's control. Is he throwing mostly strikes or does he appear to be wild? If he's having trouble getting the ball over the plate, take a few. Be patient. Force him to come at you with a good strike.

Look at each individual pitch. Are his fastballs working while his breaking balls can't seem to find the plate? If this is the case, you can assume that he'll go to the fastball when he's deep in the count. And vice versa.

Finally, watch him again once he gets on the mound. Quite often in the amateur levels, the mound in the bullpen will be inconsistent with the one on the field. It might be a little higher or lower, the distance might be a little off,

John Smoltz, the 1996 National League Cy Young Award winner, displays a power-pitcher's motion. When a hitter faces him, he can expect to see an above-average fastball and a hard slider.

or the wind might be coming in from a different direction. Any one of these factors can have an impact on the pitches. Watch the pitcher on the mound to see if he's having trouble adjusting, and if he is, take advantage of it.

LAST-MINUTE PREPARATIONS

The game is under way and your teammates are at the plate fighting their own personal battles with the pitcher. It's time to do some last-minute cramming. Take note of what pitch the pitcher is starting out each batter with, what pitch he uses when he gets ahead, and what he goes to when he falls behind.

Monitor the time he takes between pitches. A lot of pitchers like to work very fast. This allows them to get in a groove, and before you know it, the at-bat is over. Step out of the box and break up his rhythm. Remember the at-bat belongs to you, not him.

Finally, you're up next. Remember, the on-deck circle is the closest you're going to get to the pitcher before you're actually in the batter's box, so use this opportunity to time pitches. Think about when you're hitting on a batting machine. You wouldn't want to hop in there without first seeing how fast the pitches were traveling. If you did, you'd probably look at the first couple of pitches to get your timing. Unfortunately, you don't have this luxury when you're up to bat in a game. Use your time wisely when you're on deck.

PRE-SWING THOUGHTS AND PREPARATION

It's the big moment. Your turn at the plate. As you walk toward the batter's box, what's going through your mind? If you're a Little Leaguer, your thoughts might be "I hope my sister isn't playing with my Power Rangers right now," but if you're competing on a more advanced level, you're most likely to be thinking about the situation at hand. Mild thoughts might be "What is the pitcher going to start me off with?" or "Should I look to hit the ball to the right side of the infield or find something to pull?" Other thoughts might put

I've always felt a hitter can make important use of the waiting time in the on-deck circle. You are close enough to gauge the full velocity of the pitcher's fastball, and how much his curveball breaks. . . . I like to form an imaginary 12-inch square closing in on the pitcher, to help me visualize where he will release the pitch. When another left-handed batter is in front of me, I try to study the pitcher's pattern. If he starts the first left-handed hitter out with a curveball, it's possible I will get the same pitch. This way you are ready for it.

— Billy Williams

Lenny Dykstra concentrates on the pitcher while he awaits his at bat.

Some hitters get extremely tense during their at bat. Others are more relaxed, such as former Minnesota Twins star Kirby Puckett, who flashes a smile to break the tension.

Fear is your best friend or your worst enemy. It's like fire. If you can control it, it can cook for you; it can heat your house. If you can't control it, it will burn everything around you and destroy you. If you can control fear, it makes you alert.

— *Cus D'Amato trainer of Mike Tyson, Floyd Patterson, and José Torres*

A relaxed player is a confident player. Confidence and a positive attitude result in the lowering of anxiety, thus lessening interference due to antagonistic muscle tension or the loss of ability to direct or control attention.

— *H.A. Dorfman and Karl Kuehl authors of "The Mental Game of Baseball"*

pressure on you. "It would be good if I could drive in an insurance run here because our pitcher is getting tired," or even, "If I don't get a hit, the game is over and we've lost." And there are times when outside influences will creep into your thoughts. "My Dad's here for the first time ever. I've got to show him I can hit," or "If I don't get a hit now, I'm back on the bench for the rest of the season."

To make matters worse, as you step in the box, you hear coaches, fans, and teammates yelling "Get a hit!" and "Relax up there!" which makes you even more worried and tense.

While all of these thoughts may seem unavoidable, they can make you extremely nervous before you even see a pitch. It should be clear that this can't possibly be good for your performance at the plate. Hitting is a complicated process, and you want to be ready physically, mentally, and emotionally when that ball comes across the plate.

LEARNING TO RELAX

In the heat of competition, emotions, whether positive or negative, can run high. Even veteran players will find their hearts racing a little faster in certain situations. Whether you're feeling excited or anxious, you need to take a moment to relax. If you don't, your emotions might start to affect your body in the form of sweaty hands, clenched teeth, or an uneasy stomach. Your muscles will begin to tense up. Failing to take a step back to relax will have a negative effect on your coordination, rhythm, speed, and power.

There are a number of ways to relax before you hit. A number of players simply like to step out of the box and take their time before they begin to bat. Reggie Jackson, one of the premier clutch hitters of all time, used to take an extended period of time before he got into the box when the game was on the line. The extra time can be used to rethink the situation or merely just to calm yourself so you don't rush through the at-bat.

Some hitters talk out loud. If you try this, your tone and your speech should be relaxed. You might want to remind yourself of something you should be trying to do. "Just take the ball back through the middle." What you don't want to say is "I've got to get a hit, right here, right now!" Comments like this

The Inner Game

The inner game of hitting begins the morning of the game. Thoughts of "Who are we playing?" "How well do I play against them?" "Who will I hit against?" and "How will I hit him?" start the competitive adrenaline flowing. I frequently apply past knowledge of the team and pitcher in laying an "inner game plan" for that day. The experience I've acquired may answer questions like these: "Can I bunt against him?" "How do they play me in the field?" "Do they pitch me in or out?"

The answers to these questions may serve only to start the mental preparations for the game, but they also begin the positive approach to that game's performance. The idea of going "four for four" and driving in the winning run is the very least I can hope for.

The drills and batting practice before the game afford us the opportunity to telegraph our "game plan" from the brain to the body in the form of repetition in hitting technique. If today's pitcher is a hard thrower who has tried to pitch me inside, I will consciously work on bringing my hands in toward my body so that the head of my bat will cover the inside part of the plate and strike zone. I will make my stride short and in turn let my hands speed up the acceleration of my bat. This ability to adjust comes from my hours of practice in spring training and other games, and stems from repeated muscle stimulus to hit a pitch in this area.

After working on what will probably be the main area of hitting for the game, I will work on pitches in each area with one or two swings. This may be a pitch low and outside, low and inside, and up and in or high and away. I will try to go with the pitch depending on the area. For example: I will try to pull the inside pitch and the pitch up the middle or outside I will go with to center or to right. The idea of hitting strikes is very important during this period of pregame batting, because a habit formed at this time has a good chance to carry over to the game.

Our "inner game plan" is formed and our preparation is over. The few minutes before the game will be a good time to start your total concentration on the task ahead. Imagine each thrown ball hit squarely and solidly to an open field.

The game has begun and you're at the on-deck circle for your first at-bat. You watch the pitcher and check for these points: What kind of deception does the pitcher use? Where does he release the ball from? Is he working fast or slow? What pitch is he using for his "outpitch?" After this quick analysis the final preparation comes from the on-deck circle to the plate. This 30-foot walk may be as vital to the team as any action during the game. This is where we decide what our offensive job will be. We check with our third-base coach for a sign. If there is none and the "hit" sign is on, we must judge the game situation and apply our abilities to accomplish our offensive goal.

For example, if there is a man on third and one or none out, I will try to hit a fly ball at least deep enough to the outfield to score the runner to the plate. Again, if there is a runner at second base and none out, I will try to advance him to third by hitting a ground ball to the right side of the infield. These are examples of what we must do to win. The execution is done at the plate, but our preparation is done on the way up there, so that we are clear to react to the pitch that is thrown.

Once we reach the plate and take our stance the preparation and game plan are fixed clearly in our minds. The sole act of hitting now depends on concentration; on the ball, body control, and reaction to the pitch. Concentration for me is the total blockage of negative thoughts. These negative thoughts can be, "I can't hit this pitcher" or "I'm slumping and I'll strike out for sure." Thus the control of mind over body will keep us from overstriding, swinging at bad pitches, and the attempt to hit a ball out of the strike zone. This control is subconscious, because once the ball is thrown our bodies automatically react from the many hours of repetition.

Finally, the reaction to the pitch is the split-second recall from the conscious brain that says, "If the ball is inside we will react with intent to pull the pitch and likewise react to pitches in other areas with the proper swing."

With each at-bat the batter faces a new situation and one that is crucial to the success of his team. The batter who has prepared mentally both before and during the game is the man who will be successful in the long run. He will be able to control his mind and body to the point of skillfully hitting a baseball and truly being a master of the "inner game of hitting."

— Steve Garvey

David Justice didn't let the pressure get to him in Game 6 of the 1995 World Series. He belted a sixth inning home run to give the Braves a 1-0 victory and the world championship.

I just try to clear my mind, rethink the situation at hand, and concentrate on hitting the ball where it's pitched. A lot of guys go through a big, long process, but I just try to keep things as simple as possible.

— *David Justice*

One important aspect of relaxation is in your breathing. Most guys stop breathing, especially in tight situations. Then they get light-headed and start hyperventilating. The next thing you know, they're swinging at anything because they're panicky. Breathe deeply and slowly, inhaling through your nose and exhaling through your mouth. That way you get proper oxygen to your brain and your heart, and you can think clearly.

— *Dusty Baker*

just add stress. If you can't think of a baseball-related comment, you could just say something that makes you laugh. If it relaxes you and keeps you from tensing up, then it's good for you as long as you still can concentrate on what you need to do at the plate.

New York Yankee Hall of Famer Yogi Berra used to talk to the umpire during his at bats to stay relaxed. He said that most of the time he didn't pay attention to what he was saying or even to what was being said back to him. But meaningless conversation was the mechanism he used to stay relaxed and focused.

Some hitters stretch before they get into the box. Rolling the neck and shoulders and stretching out the back and arms can keep a batter loose. Visualizing a peaceful place or a favorite spot such as the ocean and the beach or a quiet setting in the woods can also work as a relaxant. Tensing up your muscles for a few seconds and then letting go is another way to keep your body limber.

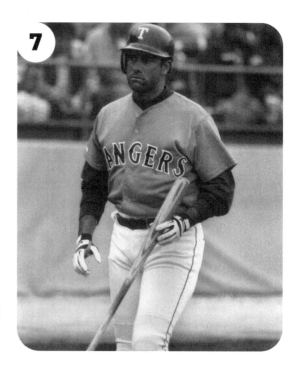

Though some hitters struggle because they try too hard, Will Clark is an example of a hitter who thrives on intensity.

At times, something as simple as breathing can help a hitter regain his form and composure. Even in medical emergencies, you often hear "Just take a deep breath" or "Step back and let him breathe." Think about how many times you've seen a hitter or pitcher pause and take a deep breath at a critical point in the game. In addition to the fact that regular deep breathing will physically help to calm you, just the mere act of paying attention to it will take your mind off what was making you tense to begin with.

VISUALIZATION

Some players like to ensure that their thoughts at the plate will be positive ones, and visualization is the method they often choose. To visualize is to form a mental image, and for the hitter that image should be of hitting the baseball. This shouldn't be difficult, and in fact, it's probably something most people have already done during a boring class or lying awake at night. Now just apply it to the game.

What a hitter visualizes can vary, but it should always be positive: hitting a line drive up the middle, lacing a ball to the opposite field, turning on the inside strike, and so on.

These visualizations can happen anywhere, depending on your personal preference. You can do them the night before the game or when you're in the on-deck circle. Just make sure you give yourself enough time to go through the entire visualization process.

Even if you're not actually visualizing, positive thinking can really make a difference at the plate. You should never go up saying, "I hope I don't strike out," or "If I don't get a hit here I'll be 0 for 4." Think of good things. If you do this with regularity and confidence, then good things will start to happen. You should remember that the game of baseball is supposed to be fun.

Confidence is the foundation of mental strength for the hitter. You should firmly believe that every time you're up at the plate, you're going to hit the ball hard somewhere. Now is the time to let your natural reactions and muscle memory take over, because there is no margin for doubt in hitting.

There is a difference between being confident and cocky, however. Confidence is something that's shown in your performance and kept to

I like to tell hitters to try to listen to the pitcher's heartbeat. That way their minds are relaxed and not thinking about other worries or distractions.

— *Tom Petroff*

When I want to turn it on, I have a routine I go through. I get away from the plate. I stretch, control my breathing, and slow up my heart rate. I slow up.

I start toward the plate, and I imagine myself putting the "sweet spot" in the hitting area just as the ball is getting there. I see a line drive going to center field. It's important to me to see myself putting that bat there and not swinging it. When I visualize, I feel my approach and the contact.

I remind myself to see the release and the spin on the ball. Then I "see it" the way I'm going to see it. I don't want to try too hard or tense up. As I step into the batter's box, I mumble, "All right, Reggie, just let it happen, just let it flow.... Now let it happen." Then I am quiet.

— *Reggie Jackson*

I did my preparation in the afternoon. I liked to lie down for an hour before I went to the park. That's when I went over the pitchers in my mind. We didn't call it visualizing then, but I sure used my imagination.

— *Duke Snider*

Reggie Jackson was nicknamed "Mr. October" for his clutch hitting in post-season play. Here he's seen watching his seventh-inning home run in Game 6 of the 1978 World Series which clinched the world championship for the Yankees.

Roberto Clemente hits an opposite-field home run off Jim Palmer in Game 6 of the 1971 World Series. Clemente is standing way off the plate, possibly coaxing Palmer into throwing a pitch on the outside corner. The catcher appears as if he was set up on the inside corner, but Palmer missed allowing Clemente **to get his arms extended and drive the ball over the fence.**

9

I have a philosophy about hitting that has helped me over the years. It is simply this: I go up to the plate with the confidence that I can hit the pitcher. From then on, it is a matter of intense concentration.

— *Al Kaline*

You have to have a lot of confidence at the plate and you need to be aggressive. There can't be any doubts in your mind. If you're passive at the plate, then the pitcher takes the action to you when it should be vice versa.

— *Will Clark*

yourself. Taunting the opposing team or dancing in celebration is immature and has no place in this game. If you're good people will know it by the way you play the game, not by the way you gloat as you round the bases.

THE FIRST AT-BAT

The golden rule for a first at-bat is to see as many pitches as possible. Work the count deep, so that you become as familiar with the pitcher as you can. Take a pitch and you'll see a minimum of two pitches. You might be able to see five or six. By then, you'll get to know the rhythm of his windup and his release points. It's an up-close opportunity for you to see what he throws and, where, how, and when he throws it. If you're smart and pay attention, the information you get in your first at-bat will simplify your at-bats for the rest of the game.

Watch the pitches all the way in to the catcher's glove. Knowing that you're going to take a ball allows you to really analyze everything about the pitch. The best way to defeat a pitch is to get to know it.

There are two notable times when you may want to swing at the first pitch of your first at-bat. The first is when you're given the hit-and-run sign. You'll have to sacrifice your observation time for the good of the team. The other is when you are hitting late in the lineup and have noticed that the pitcher has started off the previous six or seven hitters with a fastball down the middle. In that case, jump on it. There's no reason to keep giving the pitcher a free strike. Just make sure you have his fastball timed before you get up to the plate. Take advantage and rip a line drive.

Figures 10 and 11: To be a successful hitter, you have to be able to make adjustments, sometimes right in the middle of an at-bat. In Figure 10, Will Clark is fooled badly on the pitch. But he made the proper adjustment and sent the next pitch into the outfield gap.

FUTURE AT-BATS

By the time you come up to the plate for your second and third at-bats, there are a few more developments you might want to factor into your analysis. How have the hitters been treating the pitcher? Is he getting hit hard, and if so, what pitch have they been hitting? If a certain pitch is getting battered, the pitcher might start to shy away from it. Conversely, if a pitch seems to be working well, the pitcher may go to it more often than usual. And it will probably be the "go to" pitch if the pitcher needs an out or has the batter on the ropes.

Also take note of how the pitcher has reacted when there have been runners on base. Perhaps he loses control or velocity when he throws from the stretch. Runners are a distraction and can often take away from a pitcher's performance.

Your previous performances at the plate also make a difference in the type of pitches you'll be receiving. They act as a measuring stick for the pitcher. If something worked for him the first time, he'll more than likely try it again. On the other hand, if you tattooed a certain pitch, chances are good that you won't see it again. Don't let the pitcher be the only one who is using that information. Try to predict what you'll be getting.

Don't forget that you have three strikes to play with. If your strikeout the first time up told the pitcher you're having trouble with his breaking ball, he's going to come at you with that right out of the gate. Take it. Maybe it will miss for a ball. Even if it's a strike, you still have two more to play with. Always remember that because you are given three strikes. You don't have to swing at pitches you don't like. If the pitcher misses and gets behind in the count, all of a sudden the at-bat is less personal. The pitcher will revert back to his customary pitch patterns, and you might get something you like better. When the pitcher is giving you trouble, the more pitches you see, the better. Work the count deep on a tough pitcher.

Most pitchers have a set pattern they will use depending on the situation: pitching with men on base or pitching with the bases empty or any clutch situation demanding a big out.

— *Ted Williams*

If I'm up against a pitcher I've never faced, I watch him warm up . . . try to get an idea of what he throws . . . how he delivers a pitch. A lot of times when I face a pitcher for the first time, I'll take a couple of pitches . . . give him a good look.

— *Pete Rose*

With guys like Ken Griffey, Jr., Edgar Martinez, and Jay Buhner hitting behind me, I know pitchers can't really pitch around me. If they get behind on me in the count, I know they have to come in with a strike so I try to take advantage and swing away.

— *Alex Rodriguez*

The two most important fundamentals a hitter should know if he hopes to reach the majors and stay there are to learn as much as possible about the pitcher, and be aware of the game situation when going to the plate.

— *Frank Robinson*

When I played for the Cards I was watching the Dodgers play Montreal from the comfort of a hotel room somewhere. Steve Bahnsen was pitching for the Expos. Steve Garvey was batting. I forget the inning but I remember what happened quite clearly. Exactly when Bahnsen checked the runner on first base, Garvey took one quick step away from the plate. Amazing. I sat straight up. I'd never seen anyone do this after the pitcher had taken his stretch, and the timing was so perfect that Bahnsen didn't see Garvey do it, either. This step away from the plate could mean only one thing. Garvey was looking fastball inside, and the step away would bring that inside pitch right into his power zone. He got that pitch and pounded a two-run homer.

— *Keith Hernandez*

Believe it or not, the strategy is often the same even if you're having some success with the pitcher. Because you've ripped line drives earlier, the pitcher is not going to want to give you much. If you sit back and wait, you'll probably earn a walk or that nice fat pitch you love to jump on.

Take note of what's happening to the pitcher. Sometimes pitchers just lose their timing; they get out of a groove and can't pitch the way they normally do. Take advantage of this, and let him walk you. The last thing you want to do is help a slumping pitcher out of a jam by swinging at a bad pitch.

In the 1977 National League Championship Series, Dodger pitcher Burt Hooton experienced a performance he would probably rather forget about. Hooton was a pitcher who was known for having good control throughout his career. In fact, he walked only 60 batters in 226.2 innings pitched during that 1977 season. But in the second inning of Game 3 against the Philadelphia Phillies, Hooton totally lost his concentration and control. Holding a 2-0 lead, Hooton allowed a pair of hits and then walked a batter to load the bases. He then walked the next three batters including the pitcher. Hooton was lifted as the Phils took a 3-2 lead.

Who knows what factor shook Hooton up, but the Phils were astute enough to take advantage of it and scratch out some runs. Runs from walks aren't quite as exciting for the fans but they count the same as runs from hits.

Assuming the same pitcher is in the game for the remainder of your at-bats, repeat the same steps after each time at the plate. The more times you face the same pitcher, the better your results should be. Keep in mind, too, that as the game progresses the pitcher will begin to tire, especially if you and your teammates are running deep counts. The velocity on his fastball may decrease, as will the sharpness of his breaking ball. With fatigue comes carelessness. With carelessness come hittable pitches. It's a good time to attack.

FACING A RELIEF PITCHER

In 1879, Will White of the Cincinnati Reds led the National League with 75 complete games. Very impressive, especially considering he also started 75

Always acknowledge the situation when facing a relief pitcher. Is he going to try to get you to hit a ground ball, hit a high pop fly, or strike you out? In most cases, the best pitch you'll see from a reliever is his first.

games that year. A century later, that would never happen. Consider that in 1993 the entire San Francisco Giants staff combined could only muster up four complete games. More and more, relief pitchers have become part of the major league baseball game. In fact, the seventh inning stretch has almost become a cue for the pitchers to begin warming up in the bullpen. So just when you've gotten a starting pitcher figured out, you have to face someone else.

Don't panic. Just look for the same things you looked for at the start of the game. Watch his warm-ups. Check for release points, velocity, and control. If he's coming in during the middle of the inning, you also have to examine the circumstances that resulted in this change in pitching. The game is probably close. The previous pitcher probably gave up some hits or walks, so there are men on base. You are an important out. The relief pitcher isn't going to want to walk you. Nine times out of ten, the first pitch you're going to see will be a strike. Sit back and look for that fastball in the strike zone. If it's there, rip it. If not, then you can safely let it go.

THE FEAR FACTOR

Despite doing all this analysis, some players completely negate it by approaching the plate with fear. It can be fear of a number of things, but a common fear is the very basic one of getting hit by a pitch. While quite a natural reaction, this fear can hinder a batter's success at the plate as much as lack of preparation. Players who are afraid of the pitch tend to step away from it. They're going to have trouble with any pitch from the middle to the outside part of the plate. They'll also completely lose it when a curveball heads toward them initially and then breaks over the plate for a strike.

If you're afraid of the ball, you need to overcome this fear if you want any success as a hitter. Accept the fact that you will get hit. It's part of the game. A pitcher might be wild, the ball might slip out of his hand, or he might just come too far inside. It's going to happen.

Concentrate on the ball and what you're going to do to it, not what it's going to do to you. Turn your fear into determination and let it work for you at the plate. Besides, getting hit isn't a worst case scenario—it really doesn't hurt that much and you automatically go to first base.

Brady Anderson turns his head and front shoulder in to avoid being hit by this pitch.

One of the scariest things I ever did was when I got my first hit off Nolan Ryan. He can be a very intimidating figure because besides throwing so hard, he'll put one right in your ear. The one hit that I can remember was a curveball with two strikes. I had a 1-2 count, and he threw one right at my head, purposely up and in to get me off the plate. And I said to myself okay, he's setting me up for the curveball. He's going to throw that one where he starts it off at my head and it just breaks right over the plate, and he wants me to flinch. It was not an easy thing to do because if I read the pitch wrong, I'd have a hard time getting out of the way. But I saw the pitch and stayed with it and lined a base hit to left field.

— Dave Gallagher

Some experts believe that every ballplayer has a subconscious fear of getting hit, but that makes no sense to me at all. If you're afraid of being hit, you might as well not bother going up to the plate at all. You can't hit the ball if you're afraid it will hit you.

— Carl Yastrzemski

Everybody who's reached the 3000 hit plateau remembers the at-bat, but I remember mine especially because of the circumstances. Dennis Lamp was pitching and he knocked me down with a pitch. After that, I was so determined to hit the ball through the middle that on the next pitch I hit a line drive off his hand. It did damage to his hand and caromed away for hit number 3,000.

— Lou Brock

The best way to eliminate the fear of getting hit is to learn how to defend yourself against getting hit. This should not be done with the stride. You are already stepping toward the pitcher when he releases the ball and this should continue. If you want to get out of the way, turn your upper body. Roll your front shoulder and head in so that your back faces the pitcher. Most of the time, the pitch will miss, but if it does hit you it will be off the arm or the back, rather than the face or the ribs if you bail out in the other direction.

Former major leaguer Don Baylor was hit by more pitches than anyone else in the history of baseball. His stance was relatively close for a big man and he refused to flinch when a pitch came at him. He scored the winning run in Game 5 of the 1986 League Championship Series and the reason he was on base in the first place was because he took one for the team. "I scored the game-winner, having reached base at the start of the inning when Donnie Moore hit me with a pitch," says Baylor. "He wasn't wild. I had just been crowding the plate in my continual refusal to concede the inside part of the plate to pitchers. They believe it's theirs. I believe it's mine. So I've been hit by more pitches than any player in history, more than 260 times. Only Nolan Ryan ever hurt me."

FEAR OF FAILURE

Sometimes a player's fear is more abstract. Negative thoughts, such as the fear of not getting a hit, the fear of not being in the lineup anymore if you fail here, the fear of disappointing your coach or parent, can plague you to the point where you almost guarantee the negative outcome you fear. It's perfectly natural not to want bad things to happen. Nobody wants to be booed as they make the last out of the game with the bases loaded. But you can't let those thoughts consume you or you'll drown in them. Try to channel them into positive energy. Fear of failure can be just as immobilizing as the fear of being hit by a pitch, and therefore fear has no place at the plate.

Fear can hit for a number of reasons. A pitcher with a daunting reputation can often strike fear into an inexperienced batter in a heartbeat. Maybe it's

When things aren't going your way and you begin to doubt your abilities, talk with a coach, friend, or a hitting instructor. Here, Yankee hitting coach Chris Chambliss gives advice to young prospect Matt Luke.

just his reputation, or maybe you've faced him before and you were helpless against him. You can react in one of two ways. You can worry and be convinced that he's going to do this to you again (bad choice), or you can look at this game as a challenge, an opportunity to redeem yourself.

Recall the last game, and try to pinpoint how he got you out. If he was getting you out with the breaking ball, lay off it until you have two strikes against you. Maybe you'll see something else before it gets to that point. If he's always getting ahead in the count, go after a strike early in the count. If you feel you get jammed on his pitches, back off the plate. Choke up on the bat if you think it might help. The idea is to try something different.

Fear often appears during a slump. You've been hitting poorly the last couple of games and you start to question your abilities. You have to remind yourself that slumps happen to hitters all the time. Even the very best hitters in the major leagues have times when they are struggling at the plate. Largely, your slumps will be due to mechanical reasons, which can be adjusted with some hard work, but if you let a slump affect your mental focus and self-confidence, it can snowball into something more complicated. Now, in addition to competing against the pitchers and fielders, you're competing against yourself.

During his rookie season in 1982, Cal Ripken, Jr. was lodged in an offensive slump early in the season. Because he was trying to prove himself as an every-day player, Ripken worsened his disappointing start by worrying about what would happen if he didn't start hitting. Luckily, he pulled things together and went on to win the Rookie of the Year award.

Practice is the best way to overcome fear. You will become better, which will give you more success at the plate, and therefore give you more confidence. You will also be training your body to react automatically, cutting down on the thoughts that fill your head at the plate. Remember, it's virtually impossible to get a hit every time you're up to bat. If you're succeeding only once out of every three at-bats, your batting average will be .333. Pretty darn good. But, of course, getting a hit under your belt doesn't mean you can ease up the rest of the game. You should go to the plate every time thinking this is the day you're going to bat 1,000.

In my rookie season, I was hitting defensively, not wanting to look bad. I was putting so much pressure on myself, that I wasn't thinking clearly. I was down and all I could think about was that I might be sent back to Rochester (the Orioles Triple-A team). I would be OK when I first got to the ballpark, but gradually I would get depressed. And when I went hitless again, I just couldn't wait to get out of there as quickly as I could.

— *Cal Ripken, Jr.*

Be a hungry hitter. If you're one-for-one, go for two-for-two. Never be satisfied with anything less than a perfect day. Baseball is a game of averages.

— *Pete Rose*

Even Paul Molitor, a member of the 3,000 hit club, can gain some helpful tips from Twins batting instructor Terry Crowley.

In 1996, Paul Molitor became the twentieth major leaguer to reach the 3,000 hit mark. Molitor owns some pretty impressive post-season statistics too, including a .418 World Series average (tied for best all-time) and the first five-hit game in World Series history (Game 1 of the 1982 Series vs. the Cardinals).

The only way to pitch him is inside,
so you force him to pull the ball.
That way the line drives won't hit you.

— A pitcher said of George Brett

■ Don Drysdale was the only member of the 1965 World Champion Los Angeles Dodgers who batted .300 that season. Drysdale hit .300 on the nose and also hit seven homers that year.

■ Yankee Stadium is known as the "House that Ruth Built" because great crowds would come out to see the Yankee slugger play at the Polo Grounds (owned by the Giants), thus providing an incentive for Yankee ownership to build their own new stadium. So few were surprised on April 18, 1923 when the great Bambino slammed the first home run in Yankee Stadium history.

■ Carlos Baerga set a major league record on April 8, 1993 when he hit a home run from both sides of the plate in the same inning.

■ Nate Colbert and Stan Musial share the record for most home runs hit in a double header— five. Colbert enjoyed his memorable day as a member of the San Diego Padres against the Atlanta Braves (1972) and Stan the Man had his big day in 1954 playing for the St. Louis Cardinals against the New York Giants.

■ In 1973, Pete Rose went the entire season (680 at bats) without hitting one sacrifice fly. Pretty amazing for a guy who knew how to handle the bat.

■ In 1967, the San Francisco Giants stole only 22 bases as a team. Nine years later, the Oakland A's set the modern day record for most stolen bases by a team in one season when they swiped 341 of them.

■ In 8,147 career at bats, Harmon Killebrew was never once credited with a sacrifice bunt. Eddie Collins, on the other hand, holds the record for most sacrifice bunts with 511.

■ In 1987, Vince Coleman stole successfully 19 consecutive times on *pitchouts*.

HITTING A BASEBALL . . . IT'S ALL
IN THE PHYSICS!

The following interview is with George Manning, vice president of technical services for Hillerich & Bradsby Co., which makes the Louisville Slug-ger. He is in charge of research and development and quality control for the sporting goods manufacturer. Prior to joining Hillerich & Bradsby Co., Mr. Manning was with the Battelle Memorial Institute and the True Temper Corporation, where he served in both research and management capacities.

While at Battelle and True Temper, the largest manufacturer of golf shafts in the world, he developed and coordinated tests on the famous "True Temper Swing Machine." Manning's machine has become the industry standard for performance evaluation.

Along with his golf expertise, Manning is now heavily involved in baseball and softball. He insists that baseball and softball, like golf, is a proving example of the result of the interaction between matter and motion, that is, physics.

Some say that our entire life is ruled by physics. This sounds pretty logical when you realize that physics, in its most specific sense, is a science of matter and motion. Perhaps physics does cover just about everything. But we will leave that debate to the scientists and concentrate on one specific area that *definitely* depends on physics: hitting a baseball with a bat.

Understanding what happens when a bat strikes a baseball can be tremendously helpful in developing hitting skills. So get ready for some basic high school physics and some interesting facts you probably never knew about the very simple action of hitting a thrown ball with a bat.

Q. What actually happens when a thrown ball meets a swinging bat?

A. Very basically, when an impact occurs we have to take into account several factors, including the mass of the bat, the velocity of the bat, the mass of the ball, and the velocity of the ball. We also have to be concerned with what is called the "coefficient of restitution" (which is a fancy phrase for velocities of objects *before* and *after* they make contact) between the bat and the ball.

Q. Does the ball really flatten at impact?

A. Yes, it flattens, but it only stays on the bat for a couple of centimeters of travel of the bat. So the ball and bat would be in contact only over that very short period of time.

Q. At that point where the ball is in contact with the bat, does the *bat* flatten?

A. A solid wood bat does change its shape slightly, but very little in comparison to the ball. Some of the new metal bats change shape and flatten considerably in comparison to the ball. Both the ball and bat come back to their original shape. Obviously, if an aluminum bat is not heat treated properly, for example, it flattens and does not come back to its original shape. This causes the bat to absorb a lot of the ball's energy, and you end up not hitting the ball as far.

Yes, the Speed of the Pitch Does Add Distance When the Ball Is Hit

Q. What factors influence how far a ball travels when hit with a bat?

A. The factors are the speed of the bat, the speed of the ball, the mass of the ball, the location of the hit of the ball and the bat, the angle of the hit, the weather conditions, the coefficient of restitution between the bat and the ball, the ball's surface condition, the direction of the bat at impact, the direction of the ball at impact, and the spin on the ball. There are probably a dozen other less significant factors that are also going to determine how far a ball will be hit. For example, let me expand on something I brought up earlier. The coefficient of restitution that I mentioned is the relationship of the ratio of the velocities *before* things contact to the ratio *after* they contact. For example, if you are dropping a ball against the floor, the coefficient of restitution is determined by the height from which you drop the ball and how far back up it comes. The higher you hold the ball, the higher the ball will bounce. You can look at the coefficient of restitution on a number scale. Assume that the number 1 is the maximum capability that you could possibly achieve. If you drop the ball from head height, and it bounces back up to that exact same height, then you have achieved the maximum capability, which is 1. There would be no losses of energy in the ball at all. You might call it the "perfect rebound," which is the coefficient of 1. However, it never really comes up to 1! A most usual coefficient would be somewhere around 0.5. But even if you could achieve the perfect rebound of 1, it would *never* come higher than the height from which you dropped it, assuming it was a free-fall drop. If you had putty and dropped it on the ground, it would just stop as a glob on the ground, and you would have a coefficient of restitution that would be 0. If you had something *perfectly* elastic, it would be 1. So there are the two extremes. Now, if you put any additional energy whatsoever on that ball, then you have changed the whole picture. For example, if you *throw* the ball against the ground instead of just dropping it, it will bounce higher. Likewise, a ball can come off the bat faster than it came *onto* the bat because you are putting energy in from the bat itself. You added something—the speed of the swing—to it. It is no longer a simple "rebound."

Q. What would the middle range be?

A. The middle would be 0.5. Basically, the coefficient of restitution is a measure of the velocity that occurred in the impact. It's like the internal energy. If you don't use any of it up, you don't lose anything in the coefficient of restitution.

Q. Could there be different reasons for low or high coefficient? For example, if the ball is wet, or wound tightly, or wound loosely?

A. That's correct. And remember that the coefficient of restitution is affected by *both* the ball and material that it is striking. So if you had a very soft ball and used something that would absorb the energy in the bat, you end up with a very low coefficient of restitution. So anything that absorbs energy will result in that ball coming off the bat slower.

Q. What is the "sweet spot" or the center of percussion on a baseball bat?

A. The center of percussion is a single point on a bat. That is the point where you want to strike the ball because it gives you the most energy exchange *into* the ball. If you hit anyplace else on the bat, you are actually wasting energy by absorbing too much of it. This cuts down on distance, and you also wind up with a sensation known as "stinging" of the hands. It is interesting to note that the center of percussion of the bat can be affected by *how* the bat is used. If I just have a bat standing in the corner, the center of percussion of that bat is different at the point than it would be if a man picked it up to swing it. Anytime you hold the bat with your hands in a slightly different location on the bat, you have changed the center of percussion. So, keep in mind that the center of percussion *does* change (or move) depending on the way you hold the bat. So you have to decide how you are going to hold it *before* you can decide where the sweet spot is.

Finding the Sweet Spot. Hold onto a bat about three inches up from the knob with your index finger and thumb. Take another bat and tap the barrel of the bat you are holding. Begin tapping at the mid point of the bat working your way towards the barrel end. As you tap the barrel you will feel the vibrations of the tapping in your fingers holding the handle. As you move down the barrel, the vibrations will become less and less until you reach a point on your bat where no vibration occurs. That is the sweet spot.

Q. In other words, a person who chokes up on the bat and a person who holds it right down on the knob may have different sweet spots, even though they are using the exact same bat?

A. That's right. Now, they wouldn't be very far apart, but they would be different. Also a sweet spot *is* a spot. It is *not* an area. One of things that they want to do in making bats is to make the effects of hitting *off* that spot less meaningful, so that it turns out being an effective *area*. Since hitting on the exact center of percussion every time is extremely difficult, we try to manufacture our aluminum bats so that they are "more forgiving" when hit slightly off the sweet spot. We feel this is a great aid to the average hitter. The really good hitters hit on the sweet spot more consistently than bad hitters. And that's one of the reasons we have bad hitters.

"I Didn't Even Feel Like I Hit It."

Q. Can a person tell when he has hit the ball on the sweet spot?

A. Theoretically, you should feel little or no reaction with your hands. When a bat strikes a ball there is a slowing down of the bat from the energy exchange, but when you hit the ball on the ideal spot, you feel like saying, "I didn't even feel like I hit it!"

The Customer's Always Right. When selecting a bat, most players go by feel. "Whether or not a bat is scientifically right doesn't matter," says Chuck Schupp, coordinator and sales representative for bats provided to major league players by Hillerich & Bradsby Co., maker of the Louisville Slugger. "If the player thinks he hits better with one kind of a bat, he does," says Schupp. "For instance, a lot of these guys say they want the widest possible grain, and that is not necessarily the best piece of wood."

Q. What happens to the ball and the bat if you hit the ball in either direction *off* the sweet spot?

A. Basically, if you hit the bat on the sweet spot, the bat would move straight back. But, if you hit it to the right of the sweet spot, that barrel end wants to come around in that direction. This, in effect, is what causes a loss of the exchange of energy because the effect of the velocity of the bat transferred to the ball is much less. In other words, you are once again wasting energy.

Q. Now, what about the direction of the ball?

A. If you hit the ball on the sweet spot, it's going to go straight off the bat. You can swing a little earlier, still hit the sweet spot, but hit it to left field (if you are a right handed batter). Likewise, you can hit it on the sweet spot, but swing a little late, and you will hit the ball to right field. The direction the bat is traveling at the time it hits the ball is going to have a big effect on how you are going to hit it. Even though you hit the ball on the sweet spot, you can still hit it in the air, on a line, or into the ground—it depends on the path of the bat.

Q. Then a ball hit on the sweet spot in not always a line drive?

A. No, it's not. It is a straight line that is the result of the direction that the bat is traveling and the direction that the ball is traveling when they meet. If you have a good level swing and you hit the ball in the sweet spot, you are certainly going to be in line with the direction the ball is coming from more closely. Now please keep in mind that we are really talking about baseball in this particular instance. Slow pitch softball would be a different matter since the ball and bat usually do not travel in straight lines. But the line of action of the ball and the line of action of the bat should be in *direct* opposition to each other.

Crazy Idea? Or Is a Better Mousetrap About to Be Built?
One physicist has an idea how to reduce the weight of wood bats and still get optimum performance. Peter J. Brancazio theorizes that since there is nothing in the rules of baseball that says you can't taper the bat at both ends, you could configure a bat that would have a thick section where the sweet spot is but tapered drastically toward the end. This would give a fat barrel where one needs it for contact, and take weight off the end. Says Brancazio, "You need the long bat to protect the plate but usually when you hit the ball off the end you're just fouling it off." So if you sometime soon see a batter step up to the plate with a stick that looks like it's been sharpened at both ends, don't be astonished. You read it here first!

Q. Can you move a sweet spot?

A. Well, as we have mentioned earlier, you can theoretically move a sweet spot. Since it is the center of percussion of a bat, the batter can move it depending on how he holds the bat. But the bat manufacturer can also move the sweet spot depending on how he designs the bat. This opens up a whole new world of possibilities in the future design of bats. If you are a singles hitter, you may well want a truly different bat than a home run hitter would want. And we might want to design a different bat for those two types of hitters.

Q. Theoretically, let's say that the sweet spot (for the purpose of this question) is located exactly six inches form the end of the barrel. Now, if I choke up on that bat, is the sweet spot going to move out closer to the barrel of the bat or more towards me?

A. The sweet spot of the bat won't change locations on the bat much, but in relation to your hands as you choke up, it will get closer.

Q. Is the batter, in essence, shortening the bat?

A. Yes, he is indeed shortening the bat. But the effect on the sweet spot is not the same as using a shorter bat. You might say that the player at the plate, whether he wants to or not, is changing the performance of his bat by the way he holds it. If he chokes up with the same weight bat, it is much easier to get the bat up to speed.

Q. Is a person who chokes up on a bat less likely to be a power hitter?

A. Yes, potentially he is.

Q. And he doesn't hit it as far?

A. As a general statement, that is correct. One of the things that certainly would qualify would be if he is using a very, very heavy bat and that is one of the reasons he's choking up. He may well generate just as much power by choking the bat up as he would by taking a shorter bat that's lighter weight and holding it on the end.

Q. So what we are talking about is bat swing speed?

A. Yes, and this is terribly important. It's really more important to get bat speed than it is to get bat mass.

Q. Can we enlarge a sweet spot?

A. You can't enlarge a sweet spot because by definition it is a point. You can reduce the drop off of performance as you move away from the sweet spot. Golf clubs have done this, and you can do it effectively in a baseball or softball bat. In fact, that's what we have done with the aluminum bat, and it is one of the reasons it performs differently than a wood bat. You haven't made the sweet spot bigger, but you have made the effect of hitting off the sweet spot less punishing. In other words, you have not necessarily enlarged the sweet spot, but you have made the effect of hitting one inch off the sweet spot a lot less significant. We can do this more easily with an aluminum bat than we can with a wood bat.

Q. How can a player find the sweet spot, or center of percussion, of the bat, and how could he utilize such knowledge to help his hitting?

A. Well, you can get a pretty good estimate of it. You can grab a bat at the knob and hold it fairly loosely

Ideally Weighted Bat? Probably Not Yet Made. Most players use a bat that is too heavy. The low swing speed of a heavy bat reduces the distance a ball travels and the speed with which a ball rebounds from the bat. Bats around 25 or 26 ounces may be the best; however, these are lighter than almost anything now offered in aluminum models. And 30 to 33 ounces is the lowest weight range of the bats made of white ash.

and then tap it with another bat. The point where you get a totally different sound and no vibration in your fingers is generally very close to the sweet spot of the bat. Then you could mark it with a piece of tape or something, and you could stress that "this is where this bat wants to be struck." This might be one training aid in helping players hit closer to the center of percussion.

Q. Is the balance point of a bat important?

A. Yes, the reason that the balance point is important is that the center of percussion is affected by the way the material is distributed in the bat, and the center of balance represents one factor in how that material is distributed. But I must stress that this is not as important as the center of percussion.

Heavy Bat + Fast Swing = Long Balls

Q. In a previous question, we touched upon mass and velocity. Will a heavier bat hit a ball farther than a light bat?

A. The answer is yes, *if* it is swung at the same velocity as the light bat and they are both hit on the center of percussion. However, most people can't swing a heavier bat as fast. There is a limitation to each batter's ability to generate energy. The range of weights is not terribly broad. I don't know of anybody who has done this with baseball bats or softball bats, but it has been done with golf.

Golf clubs have been taken and intentionally made very light and intentionally made very heavy. We have a good golfer swing through light beams to measure the club and velocity. We do discover

that you can get to a point with light clubs where they just don't go any faster. You can also get so heavy that they really slow down, but between a fairly wide range the slow down in velocity and the increase in mass is almost compensation, so that the end result of your hit is pretty close to being the same.

Now one of the things that's different in golf than in baseball is that a golfer is hitting a stationary ball. He can wait for his swing with that heavy club. But you just can't wait for the ball with a heavy bat, so I suspect it is more sensitive in baseball, but we can say almost certainly that a heavier bat would be more difficult to swing. The formula I discussed earlier shows that because the mass of the bat is so much greater than the mass of the ball, the velocity is a much more significant factor than the mass of the bat. So you really want a lighter bat that you can swing faster, because an increase in velocity is a bigger factor in how far you will hit the ball than an increase in the mass. Actually, the more you increase the velocity, you actually increase the effect of the mass. An object that weighs 30 ounces and is swung at 50 miles per hour is going to be more potent than if it is swung at 40 miles per hour.

Q. So most people who get a big healthy piece of timber or aluminum should be striving for more bat speed. Is that right?

A. That's right. The one question that I think might not exist though, and certainly the factors are still correct, would be in slow pitch softball. The ball is so slow in relationship to everything else that you really have time to apply a large energy input. You are not nearly as affected by the changes in the directions of the ball. It isn't going to make wild curves, breaks, and this sort of thing. You can probably handle a heavier bat and still get good velocity out of it. You can stand back and wait for the ball and build up a lot of energy to put into the heavier bat, and probably obtain the same velocity that you could with a lighter bat in baseball. So a heavier bat *could* be an advantage in slow pitch softball.

Q. But the big key is that normally you cannot obtain the velocity with a larger bat?

A. That's right. At least with the bat control that is necessary.

Q. If you are an extremely strong player, it is still very unlikely that you can swing a 42-ounce bat as fast as you can swing a 33-ounce bat.

A. I don't think there is any question about that, but you might be able to swing a 36-ounce bat *nearly* as fast as you can swing a 33-ounce bat. Or you may be able to swing a 42-ounce bat faster than anyone *else* can swing a 33-ounce bat.

Q. How important is "wrist snap" at the moment of impact? Does that increase bat speed?

A. Yes, in baseball, golf, or any kind of activity where you are trying to get maximum velocity, but have a limitation in how much time and how much energy you can put into it, the advantage of a wrist snap is paramount. You can keep the mass tucked in close to the center that you are rotating around until the last instant. Say, for instance, you are swinging a simple broom. If you hold it by the handle and swing it way out, it is terribly difficult. But, if you turn the bristles around toward you and swing the handle, it becomes very easy. This is an example of the fact that the closer you keep the mass to the center of rotation, the easier it is to accelerate the speed. So, the reason a golfer does it, and the reason a baseball player wants to use wrist snap is to get a lot of energy stored into his body and available for exchange into the bat while it's tucked in close. Remember, it takes a lot less energy to get up to a faster speed this way. Then, when he wants

to flick it out, he wants to do it at the last second and get the mass away from the center of rotation. One of the things you have done in the course of getting your body movement is that you have stored a lot of energy in your body, and you get to *exchange* that energy through your hips, shoulders, arms and wrists *into* the bat. So you have stored the energy for release in a way that is extremely efficient.

Aluminum vs Wood: Off-the-Sweet-Spot Hits Go Farther with Aluminum

Q. Let's look at a basic question that is a center of controversy in both baseball and softball. Does an aluminum bat hit a ball farther than a wood bat?

A. Yes. There are many reasons, not the least of which is that the construction is different. It is easier to make a lightweight aluminum bat than it is a lightweight solid wood bat. Larger barrels have been shown to hit the ball farther than smaller barrels. Again, it's easier to make a certain weight specification with aluminum to a full barrel diameter than it is with wood. Off-the-sweet-spot hits will go much better with aluminum than with wood, so an aluminum bat is more forgiving to a hitter. Tests in college baseball and local amateur leagues shows that home run production is more than doubled with aluminum bats as compared to wooden bats.

Q. Can we get more bat speed out of an aluminum bat that weighs exactly the same in overall weight as an equivalent wood bat?

A. Yes, because the swing weight of an equal weight aluminum bat (resistance to acceleration) will generally be less. You would expect that accompanying these characteristics would be a change in the location of the center of percussion. It may well be that one of the reasons a lot of people can hit farther with aluminum is that the point of the bat they have been hitting has not been the center of percussion with a wood bat, and they can get closer to hitting the center of percussion when they go to an aluminum bat. You simply have more

Hit the Ball, Willie . . . If You Can! A major league bat must be a single piece of solid wood, no more than 42 inches long or more than 2.75 inches in diameter. There are no weight limitations. Baseballs are 2.9 inches across, making this one of the few hit-the-ball sports in which the area of the striking implement is smaller than the ball.

area to work with in aluminum bats without losing as much of the exchange of energy between the bat and the ball. The trampoline effect of aluminum bats results in less energy loss at impact and greater velocity off of the bat. Greater velocity means more hits and more home runs.

Q. The trend in bat weights today seems to be three to four ounces less than it use to be. Is this the name of the game?

A. Perhaps, but there is some lower limit that you wouldn't want to go below. The feel will be important, and you will lose some of that if you go too light.

Q. If you "construct" a good solid base hit, what would it look like?

A. Well, at least theoretically, if you want the maximum distance, that ball is going to have to leave that bat at a 45-degree angle. There would be a lot of conditions that wouldn't allow you to hit it at a 45-degree angle and get maximum velocity. In slow pitch softball, that's pretty easy to do.

Q. How significant is ball speed? Is the old adage, "The harder they come in, the harder they go out," a valid statement?

A. Absolutely. In fact, one of the things I have calculated with our bat machine, which utilizes a *stationary* ball, is how much faster we have to swing to get the effect of a pitched ball. If you would take the 90-mile-per-hour fastball as being the standard of a major leaguer, we have to hit 50 percent faster with the bat on our machine (hitting a stationary ball) in order to get the same distance as we would if that ball were coming in at 90 miles per hour.

Q. So, if the pitcher throws a slow curve that's, say, 45 miles per hour, you are going to have to swing the bat faster to hit the same distance you would with a ball that's coming in at 90 miles per hour?

A. That's right, you have to supply most of the energy on a curve ball. Factors that determine how far the ball is going to travel include the initial velocity when it comes off the bat and the angle at which it comes off, plus other factors such as the weather conditions. So, if a fast ball is really fired into the batter, it is going to come back faster than if it was served up nice and easy. Granted, it is harder to hit a fast ball, but when you hit it where you are supposed to, it will go farther.

Q. What should a hitter strive to do when at the plate?

A. He should strive for maximum bat velocity and control. You want to get the maximum speed that you can and still hit the ball on the sweet spot.

Q. But what if I want to place the ball? Do physics come into play here?

A. Yes, we probably are not looking for maximum distance, but are more interested in controlling and being able to pick the spot on the field where we are going to hit the ball. So we might well want to use a different type of bat. In other words, we may be dealing with a different shape of bat, a different weight bat, and a different center of percussion. If I want to control the ball when it strikes the bat I may want to locate the center of percussion and distribute much of the weight more towards the handle.

Q. Is there any way that a coach can determine if his players are achieving a maximum swing speed with a certain weight bat? Does it take a lot of money and special equipment?

A. Well, you have to have some special equipment, but I don't think we are talking about a lot of money. There have been a number of devices made for golf that have been the promotional type of gimmick where you come in and just swing your club through light sensors. They let you try different clubs and you get to pick the one that you get the maximum velocity out of. The same kind of thing could be done with bats; you could swing them and determine which bat gives you maximum velocity. I suspect that is what most players do anyway, by trial and error.

Bat Speed Is Not the Only Thing

Q. Would it behoove a college or high school coach to discuss the actual hitting of a baseball with a physics professor?

A. Yes, this would be worthwhile. Primarily because there are some things that you need to understand so that you can at least try to guide players in the right direction. One of the things that I think would be *best* to understand is that the effect of hitting on the center of percussion is so much more significant than a small change in bat velocity. The guys going up there swinging from their heels probably could get much longer hits by swinging more in control. I think that's pretty common sense, but I sure see people, even in the major leagues, look as if they are swinging totally out of control, especially in the late innings when a home run will make the difference. Everyone seems to suddenly decide they are going to go up there and kill it. And when they are *trying* to kill it, they not only spoil everything but they don't let the physics of hitting a baseball work for them.

Q. Is the trend toward lighter bats today a sure fire answer to distance?

A. I surely believe it is in the right direction. All things being equal, it's the most likely course of action to yield benefits. It should contribute to the bat speed, and bat speed is most important in determining how far you hit the ball.

Q. What about the seemingly large number of broken bats seen in today's major league games? What causes this?

A. One very significant reason for an apparent increase in breakage is the bat that batters are stepping up to the plate with is the lightest bat they can use. And the wood properties are such that when you go to light bats, they get weaker. In some instances where you get jammed, the bat is going to break.

Q. What should an individual look for in the bat he uses?

A. Well, the only qualification I'd make is what does he want in performance? If he is looking for distance, he should use a bat with the biggest barrel, yet lightest weight bat he could comfortably swing.

Q. Is there the possibility that players might be sacrificing durability for performance?

A. That's right, but I think I would do what they do. If they hit that ball right on the sweet spot, it probably won't break. But if they hit it where they are not supposed to, it stands a strong chance of breaking. But the lightweight bat will give them greater distance if they get their swing speed up tremendously. Therefore, it's probably worth the risk.

Wrist strength, bat speed, and a fluent swing are all important factors in hitting. But batters experience their best results when they hit the ball off the "sweet spot" of the bat.

TAKING THE
COLLAR

10

"All hitters go through slumps, but good hitters contain them to a short period of time."

— *Paul O'Neill*

Hitting is the best and worst of baseball. There's nothing sweeter than getting a hit right off the fat part of the bat, but there's nothing worse than having twenty at-bats without feeling that sensation once. It's called a slump and some players will do anything to get out of it. "I've seen guys pour gasoline on their bats and burn them right in the dugout," says Hall of Famer Richie Ashburn. "I took mine to bed, to get to know it a little better. I know that sounds weird, but in a slump a player will do anything."

Slumps are as much a part of the game of baseball as the National Anthem and the seventh inning stretch. They happen to hitters on every level and for every reason, both physical and psychological. But even though slumps are unavoidable, that doesn't mean they have to continue forever.

RECOGNIZING THE SLUMP

Because hitting a baseball is such a precise maneuver, it's hard to do it exactly right every time. A fraction of a second early or late means an out, just as a fraction of an inch too high or low means an out. Even though it's ridiculous to assume that anyone can do this right time after time, an out can still be infuriating. Bo Jackson, a phenomenal athlete, once was so angry after a strikeout that he broke his bat over his head.

But missing the ball once or twice or even three times in a row means nothing. In fact, since the statistical standard for a great hitter is .300, you can strike out, fly out, or ground out seven out of ten times and still be pleased with your batting average.

The time to worry is when your performance gradually declines from one game to the next. If you go quite a few at-bats with only a few or no hits, then you're probably in a slump.

There are a number of other indications that you might be in a slump. Does the ball seem faster as it flies toward you at the plate? Are you having trouble getting the bat into the hitting zone on time? Are you ending up off balance after your swing? When you see "your pitch," the one that you usually hit hard, are you fouling it off?

If you feel uncomfortable in any way when you swing the bat, chances are that you are doing something different and that is the reason you're in a

I think a slump is any time you go about 15 times at bat without a hit, and you find that you're not hitting the ball on the fat part of the bat. You're not driving the ball. You can be hitting the ball hard and have tough luck and be hitting it right at someone. But when pitchers are getting you out with pitches you should be hitting, somewhere along the line, you have to make a correction in your mechanics.

— Andre Dawson

1

Even the best players in the game, such as three-time National League MVP Barry Bonds, can look bad at the plate. The secret is to recognize what you're doing wrong, and correct it as quickly as possible.

2

Hitting slumps can be mentally grueling. Sometimes they may even cause hitters to glare at their bats.

slump. Your swing might not feel as smooth or you may feel off balance when you swing. If this is the case, you should take immediate steps to analyze and change your hitting approach.

SOLVING THE PROBLEM

The majority of slumps are mechanical rather than mental, so taking care of the glitch in your swing is the only way to get yourself out. When you make an out, don't get angry; it will just get in the way of your analysis. Rather than putting more and more pressure on yourself with each ensuing at-bat, you should ask for advice and work hard in batting practice to change.

Try to figure out what went wrong. Look for patterns. Are you making all your outs in the same place? Are you pulling all your fastballs? Are you late on pitches? Do you feel awkward when you swing? Some hitters are their own best coaches and can almost feel what they are doing wrong, but if you can't pinpoint the flaw in your swing right away, ask for advice from your coach, a teammate, or anyone who knows what a good swing should look like.

If possible, you may want to videotape your swing. A videotape is helpful because you can play it over and over again, each time looking at a different aspect of your swing. There are five especially common problems—overswinging, overstriding, stepping out, dropping the back shoulder, and judging the strike zone poorly—and they should be the first things you look for on tape.

OVERSWINGING

Overswinging is one of the most common faults among players of all ages, skills, and styles. Weak hitters frequently feel that if they swing harder the ball will go farther. Power hitters sometimes go to the plate thinking anything short of a home run is unacceptable, and swing away. Some hitters tense up in a

Let me repeat—and even repeat it again and again. Don't try to kill the ball. All well-hit balls, especially the long ones, come from balanced, well-timed swings. It's the same with the swing of a champion golfer. The theory is absolutely the same. The good ones don't press.

— Mickey Mantle

Don't overswing for a long hit. This weakness causes slumps. After hitting a long and hard ball, the thought will come to mind that you did not swing hard. Actually, it was timing. And the next time up, you will be tempted to take an unnatural cut, trying for a still longer ball. Watch that, for as a rule the results are not good.

— Ty Cobb

Every hitter on every level is going to struggle. The most important thing is not to panic. You have to have the confidence that eventually you will come out of it. If you lose confidence a minor slump can become a major slump.

If it's a mechanical problem you're having at the plate, figure out what it is and work on correcting it in practice. If it becomes mental, you're probably pressing too much. Just focus on seeing the ball and hitting it hard and eventually things will turn around.

— *Tony Gwynn*

I found that most slumps come from overswinging and overstriding. If you swing too hard you upset your sense of timing, and if your stride is too long you are able to apply but little of your power. So when you find yourself in a slump, shorten your stride and cut down also on your swing.

— *Tris Speaker*

Hitters who slide forward, taking a long stride, lock their hips and fail to turn. This locks their arms. The bat, instead of swinging in an arc, is actually sliding forward. There is little wrist snap and the sliding bat goes under the ball and produces a pop-up. They brace against their front leg but otherwise their power is completely locked up.

— *Lefty O'Doul*

tight situation and instead of swinging the bat like they normally do, they try to put extra power behind it and overswing. And when some players get into slumps, they try to kill the ball, hoping to force their way out. All these responses are completely wrong.

When you swing too hard, you create tension, and tension is the enemy of the hitter. If you aren't relaxed and loose, your hands will have trouble bringing the barrel of the bat to the ball in time. You'll get jammed. On top of that, trying to swing harder means you'll be jerking your head and shoulders rather than using your normal smooth swing. This will probably pull your head off the pitch.

OVERSTRIDING

Overstriding can spell death to your success at the plate because that one step affects your entire swing. By stepping too far with your front foot, you throw off your timing and lose power and balance. When you overstride, your hips automatically become practically useless. They get very little thrust from the legs. Now you're relying solely on your upper body and arms to swing the bat. With your legs farther apart, you also lose leverage. On top of that, stepping too far can coax you into committing yourself too early and shifting your weight too soon.

Some people may argue that Yankee Hall of Famer Joe DiMaggio took a big stride and had great success, hitting 369 home runs. But it was actually his stance, not his stride, that caused his legs to be so far apart. He started with them that way. His stride actually consisted of picking his foot straight up and putting it back down in the same spot. Although he didn't go anywhere with that stride, he still needed to pick the front foot up in order to recoil and then transfer his upper and lower body into the swing.

When the hitter strides too far, he loses the rotational power that is generated from the lower half of his body. B.J. Surhoff is forced to swing weakly at this pitch using only his upper body.

STEPPING OUT

You might be keeping your stride short, but where are you striding to? If you're stepping away from the plate, this might be the source of your problems. If you step away, your head and swing inevitably follow, making you extremely susceptible to any pitch that isn't on the inside part of the plate.

Fear of being hit is one reason that players, especially young ones, move away like this. When a right-handed hitter faces a right-handed pitcher (or lefty faces lefty), the release point is on the same side of the plate as the batter. Because the hitter steps as the ball is released, he often reacts to the location of the pitcher's hand and not to where the ball is thrown.

If this is your problem, there's a good drill to overcome it. Have a coach or friend pitch tennis balls at you at a light pace. Have the thrower aim inside or right at you. This will teach you how to get out of the way, and show you that you're able to get out of the way a lot more often than you thought. Even if you do get hit, it won't hurt, and you can practice turning into a pitch with your front shoulder.

DROPPING THE BACK SHOULDER

High pop-ups, long fly balls, and increased strikeouts are all symptoms of a hitter who is dropping his back shoulder. Once you drop your back shoulder, the barrel of your bat immediately goes below your hands. This forces you to drag the bat on an upward angle through the hitting zone. With the swing arc already having a natural upward swing to it, this extra uppercut will have you hitting the bottom of the ball or swinging underneath the pitch.

Some players only have to worry about this swinging glitch when they're given a low strike. If this is your problem, remember that your entire body should go down to get the pitch. Don't just drop the bat head.

KNOW THE STRIKE ZONE

Too many times hitters don't even give themselves a chance at the plate because they don't wait for a good pitch to hit. Even though the pitcher is your opponent, you might be your own worst enemy if you're overanxious and swing at anything, strikes or not. Once pitchers notice that you'll chase bad pitches, they won't give you anything you can hit.

Although you want to be aggressive and swing the bat when you're up at the plate, you still want the pitcher to come to you. If he sees he can't bait you with bad pitches, he'll be forced to come in with strikes. You even can wait for one you really like. Just as the pitcher has four balls to work with, you have three strikes. If you can't handle inside pitches well, wait for something else. By waiting, you're more likely to get something right in your hitting zone. That does a lot for getting a hitter out of a slump.

That said, you still don't want to be too tentative or too picky. Being selective doesn't mean waiting for the perfect pitch through three called strikes. Just remember, your main goal is merely to avoid the bad pitches.

The greatest single difference between a major-league and minor-league batsman is the difference in his judgment of the strike zone. The major leaguer knows better the difference between a ball and a strike. He knows better whether to swing or take a pitch.

— Branch Rickey

Roger Maris rolls his top hand over too soon, and beats the ball into the ground.

4

OTHER POSSIBLE PROBLEMS

There are some other reasons for slumps, especially among young players. When a player is starting out, all he wants to do is make contact with the ball. Unfortunately, a lot of young players view this contact as meaning they're doing it right and so they don't look to improve.

Many coaches will preach to their young players to simply see the ball, step, and swing. Where's the *recoil* in this sequence? It's like shooting an arrow without pulling the bow all the way back. And where's the *follow-through*? Often the young batter thinks his job is done when bat meets ball. If he treats his rear foot as if it were glued to the ground, he won't rotate. This means he's only swinging with his arms which will kill any power the player might have.

Once hitters reach a level where pitchers throw with higher velocity (high school or American Legion), they often begin to use too much bottom hand and develop an inside-out swing for every pitch. Because the pitch gets in on their hands more quickly, the batter reacts by pulling the bottom hand of the bat to the ball instead of snapping the top hand through the hitting zone. If you notice you're hitting even inside pitches to the opposite field, this might be the source of your slump.

Hickory wood was first used along with ash in making baseball bats. However, it was eventually dropped because its excessive weight could not meet the demands and preferences of today's players.

BACK TO THE BASICS

If things are going so badly that you can't even pinpoint the root of your problems, go back to the basics and start working from square one. Write down a list of everything you think is important for a good swing and then go through it, checking against every detail of your swing. Make sure you're using the right size bat, and check your grip and stance to make sure they're comfortable. Measure your stride to see if it's the correct length. Notice if you're getting your hips open and timing it with the swing. Pay attention to your launching position and what your bat angle is. Observe your swing arc and see if your head stays down throughout the entire swing.

Like a car that isn't running well, maybe all you need is a tune-up. Work on each area to make sure your parts are all in sync. You need to be patient and practice simple repetitive drills from the tee or soft tosses. Once you begin to

Hitting is fun, but it can be extremely frustrating. The difference between hitting a home run and flying out to the outfield can be a fraction of an inch. Brady Anderson puts a good swing on this pitch. However, the barrel of the bat is a split-second too late, and catches the bottom half of the ball. Even though his approach is mechanically sound, Anderson flies out to left field.

feel confidence in your swing again, then move on to regular batting practice. Take things gradually and have a positive attitude. Negative thinking will produce negative results.

Breaking out of a slump can be like coming back from a cold or flu. Recovery isn't instantaneous. It's a slow process, and you can't rush it or you might have a relapse or worse. Don't think you can stop focusing on your problem just because you get a hit. Focusing is what got you that hit. One lucky swing of the bat won't change things, other than giving you back some of your confidence. Slumps take a lot of effort to overcome. You have to train yourself out of the bad habit you've developed. Slumps are unavoidable, but if you stay on top of your game, chances are good that yours will be infrequent and short.

WHEN IT'S NOT A SLUMP

Sometimes the statistics may be screaming "slump" and you can't figure out what's wrong. It could be nothing but a string of bad luck. If your bullet-like line drives are all of sudden getting caught by the fielders, don't worry.

A slump is when you're not making good contact with the ball. I go back to the basics. Check my mechanics—stride, hands. I go into batting practice and try to hit the ball up the middle.

— *Ryne Sandberg*

Considering everything, I still feel positive thinking is the best and fastest cure for a slump. This way you are thinking of just one thing: making contact with the pitch.

— *Billy Williams*

Baseball is frustrating that way. You can hit a ball 400 feet to dead center for an out, but the guy batting after you mishits a bloop that drops between the second baseman and the right fielder, and he gets on base. Believe it or not, your hitting is in better shape than his because you hit the ball solidly. Your biggest problem is trying not to dwell on it, because that will cause you real problems.

However much you train and practice, you can never create the exact circumstances for the upcoming at-bats. Other sports you can perfect. The well-placed chip shot in golf or the perfectly executed field goal in football are rewards for hours of practice. In baseball, you can do everything correctly at the plate and still end up with an out. This is not slumping.

Outs don't necessarily mean you're slumping. If you make solid contact, you've done well. What happens after that is pretty much out of your hands. Going 0 for 4 with three line-drive outs isn't slumping; it's bad luck. Just keep concentrating on hitting the ball hard, and *don't worry about your statistics.* Baseball is a game of averages. Sometimes you hit at a better clip than your overall average; sometimes you hit worse. Sometimes your line drives will be caught; other times your bloops will fall in. As long as you pay attention to why you're having your ups and downs, you'll be fine.

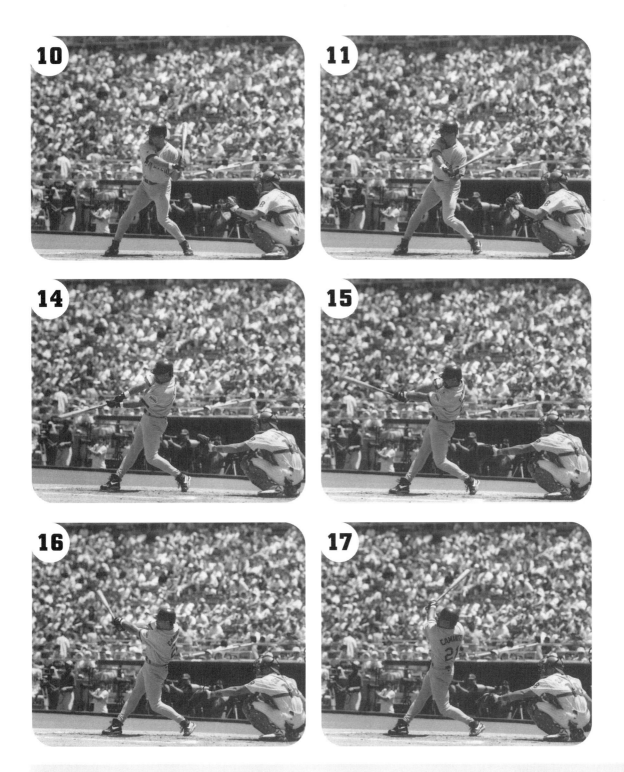

A great way to avoid slumps is to swing at pitches you know you can handle. Ken Caminiti is a low-ball hitter from the left-hand side of the plate, and gets a good pitch to hit. Ken's hips begin to open as soon as he recognizes that it is an inside pitch (Figure 12). Though he drops the barrel of the bat slightly (Figure 13), he keeps his front shoulder in. Caminiti has a rigid front leg at the point of contact, and his wrists are still unbroken. Using a swing that travels with an upward arc, Caminiti finishes off with a high follow through.

On September 7, 1993 "Hard hittin'" Mark Whiten, an outfielder for the St. Louis Cardinals, lit up Cincinnati Reds pitching for 4 home runs and 12 RBIs. Whiten is the latest major league player to hit four homers in a game.

I just go up there with the intention of knocking the ball out of the ballpark and swing.

— Hack Wilson

- Despite having only average running speed, Will Clark tied a National League record by grounding into just two double plays during the 1987 season; the fewest by a player with at least 500 at bats.

- The 1969 world champion New York Mets won despite a regular season team batting average of .242, the lowest ever for a pennant winner.

- Yankee pitching coach Mel Stottlemyre can give his pitchers some pointers on hitting, too. As a pitcher for the 1964 Yankees, Stottlemyre tied a major league record by recording five hits in a game. Mel helped his own cause with 4 singles and a double.

- In 1947, St. Louis Cardinal Red Schoendienst defined the term *0-for* when he set the National League record for futility by going 0 for 12 in a doubleheader.

- Ted Williams is perhaps the greatest hitter in baseball history. Among others, Williams holds the record for the most consecutive times reaching base (16), which he set in 1957 with two singles, four home runs, 9 walks and a hit by pitch.

- George Brett holds the major league record for most consecutive games with three or more hits. Brett did it in six straight games during the 1976 season.

- Power hitters aren't the only guys who draw intentional walks. Wade Boggs, a player known primarily as a singles hitter, led the American League in intentional free passes a record six straight times between 1987 and 1992.

- In a 1987 game against the San Francisco Giants, San Diego Padres Marvell Wynne, Tony Gwynn and John Kruk opened the game with back-to-back-to-back home runs. That's a major league record.

PRACTICE AS YOU PLAY

11

"When I was a kid, I'd practice swinging at anything that could be rolled into the shape of a ball . . . a rag, paper, anything. And if I didn't have a bat, I'd use a broomstick."

— *Pete Rose*

Pete Rose is a prime example of a ballplayer who maximized his potential through hard work and vigorous training. Though many players had more natural talent than Rose, he made up for that with his desire and commitment to improve.

I saw him play when he was seventeen in 1958. We had to grade the players as to how high we thought they would go. I put down, "No higher than A ball." He actually made himself into a ballplayer. It's great to see how wrong a scout can be if a boy really puts effort into it.

— Scout Lenny Merrllo on Pete Rose

Once January rolls around, I hit every day. I hit at least 50 balls off the tee to work on mechanics. Once I start hitting live, the first month I'll hit every ball to left field. I don't even try to pull the ball because that's a natural reaction. I don't worry about turning on the ball until spring training.

— Tony Gwynn

The game of baseball has changed constantly throughout its history, but there is one thing that will never change. *Becoming a good hitter doesn't happen overnight.* It takes thousands and thousands of hours of practice. There are no shortcuts or magical words that will accelerate the process. It demands a lot of patience, repetition, learning, and conditioning to progress and to raise the caliber of your abilities. And it never stops. You can *always* improve.

If you're a .265 hitter, you should strive to hit .285. If you end your season batting .350, you should aim to hit .375 next season. It's inconceivable for a hitter to stroke a base hit 100 times out of every 100 at-bats, but ultimately that's what you should be aiming for. No good hitter, no matter how incredible his stats were, has ever said, "Well, I think I finally have this hitting thing mastered, so I don't have to practice anymore."

You need practice for two reasons. You need it in order to get better, and you need it in order not to get worse. If you rest on the success of your hitting today, you can be sure your teammates and opponents will be better than you tomorrow.

"SPRING TRAINING"

No matter how good your season was last year, you still have to go through the rigors of spring training. It would be nice if your past season's credentials earned you a free pass through reviewing the fundamentals of hitting, but it just doesn't work that way. Hitting is a complex act that requires good balance, timing, and muscle memory. Whether it's been a couple of weeks or a few months since you last swung, you need to start from square one and gradually work your way back to live batting practice. Breaking down the stance, stride, and swing are essential to ensure that you're practicing proper mechanics.

For the first few days of spring training, you should run through a checklist of points to make sure your basic movements are correct.

The Boston Red Sox work out at their spring training facility in Fort Myers, Florida. Even the major league players need time to sharpen their skills and work on improving before the season begins.

In the batter's box:
- Is your grip appropriately comfortable?
- Is the width of your stance all right?
- Do you have proper balance?
- Is your head turned with both eyes facing the pitcher?

As you stride:
- Are you stepping straight toward the pitcher?
- Is it a short, soft stride?
- Is your weight still on your back leg?
- Are your hands and front foot going in opposite directions?

As you swing:
- Are your hips rotating as your hands are coming through?
- Is your swing level?
- Is the barrel of the bat in the hitting zone at the point of contact?

DRY SWINGING

Dry swinging is a good way to make sure you're doing all of these things correctly. Because you're not concerned about making contact with the ball or how far it goes, you can pay full attention to the course of your swing from start to finish. You can discover the flaws in your swing much more easily if you don't have to worry about pitch identification, situational hitting, and timing.

Aside from allowing you to analyze your swing, dry swinging will help train your muscle memory. Every time you swing the bat, with a ball involved or not, you're helping muscle memory. The better it is, the less thinking you have to do at the plate. Given that you're going to have to analyze the pitch as it comes in, you don't want to tie up your brain with swing details. Let your muscle memory take over.

This can be even more beneficial if you visualize a pitch coming in when you're dry swinging. An inside strike has to be hit out in front of the plate with full hip rotation. A ball over the outside corner has to be met farther back and

DiMaggio certainly knew the value of practice. During the 1939 World Series between the Yankees and the Reds, the Yanks were at Crosley Field, taking a brief drill to accustom themselves to the infield and its surroundings. Finally, all the Yanks left the park, all but DiMaggio. He stood at the plate waiting and suddenly coach Johnny Schulte reappeared with a couple of outfielders. They went into left and center and Schulte went to the mound.

For 20 minutes, DiMaggio stood there and swung until his arms were tired. He kept hitting and hitting without a stop. Now DiMaggio had led the American League that year with a .381 average—he wasn't a busher. But in the first two games of the series he'd gotten only a couple of infield hits. His timing was bad, and he was swinging off stride. So what did he do? He took time to practice.

The next afternoon DiMaggio stepped into a ball and drove it beyond the center field fence. Two runs scored. The Yankees won. Why? Because not even as great a player as DiMaggio was too proud or too busy to practice his hitting.

— *Rogers Hornsby*

I spend a lot of time watching videotapes of myself hitting. I've got one tape of myself getting base hits and another of me hitting balls hard whether they went in for hits or not. I'll watch them between drills in the off-season to keep the pictures in my mind.

— *Tony Gwynn*

To build lower arm strength, I'd recommend hitting at least 100 balls a day with a weighted bat. You can hit a ball on a batting tee or into a net in the backyard or basement. This will lead to quicker, faster hands and give you the confidence to wait as long as possible before committing your hands to the swing.

— *Harry Walker*

The good hitters have the desire to work and practice. Sometimes we tend to work on the things we do well and forget to work on our faults. Practice in the batting cage on the things that are giving you trouble is the prime key to good hitting.

— *Harmon Killebrew*

the hips don't open quite so much. Because your swing changes with different pitches, you have to train your muscles to react correctly to all the situations.

As you practice dry swinging, imagine the course of a pitch in flight. Call the pitch out and take your cut. "Strike down the middle," or "low and inside strike," or "high strike on the outside corner" are some examples. Sometimes you might want to throw in a pitch that's out of the strike zone and remind your body what it feels like to take a pitch. Stride and then follow the "ball" all the way to the "catcher's glove."

Dry swinging in front of the mirror is a good way to monitor your swing. Videotapes work, too. Sometimes your swing may feel good but look bad. An obvious mistake can be picked up with a little visual aid.

TEE WORK AND SOFT TOSS

The next step is to begin tee work and soft tosses. These are the best ways to work on form and mechanics. The most successful major league players in the game use basic drill work to prepare themselves for an upcoming season. Even though they know they'll be facing 90-mile-an-hour fastballs once the games start, they first use the tee or soft toss to make sure they're executing proper swing mechanics. There's no point in worrying about the opponent when the problem might lie with them.

Drill work is a good place to work on pitches you don't like to hit. It's more gratifying to go out and practice the pitches you hit well, but if you want to improve, you also have to practice the ones that give you trouble.

If you're like many hitters, the way you handle pitches that give you trouble is by merely avoiding them. That may work fairly well at lower levels, but if you want to move up, you're going to have to learn to hit that difficult pitch, or at least handle it with some success.

Pitchers can often discover your weaknesses, and they'll feed off that area in the strike zone when they find it. Take a lot time to work on what gives you trouble. It will make you a better hitter and a tougher one to get out.

Figure 4: Hitting off the tee is one of the best ways to work on your form at the plate. It teaches the hitter how to deliver the barrel of the bat directly to the ball, and keep the head down throughout the swing. Figure 5: To practice hitting the ball to the opposite field off of a tee, move the tee back and away from you so it's even with your back leg. Take a full cut, but don't fully rotate your hips. This may feel awkward at first, but keep practicing.

Roberto Alomar, the all-star second baseman who signed a three-year deal in 1996 with the Baltimore Orioles for $18 million, got where he is today through hard work and dedication. He's always kept a central focus on what it takes to be a consistent and dangerous hitter. Writing in *Sports Illustrated* (January 29, 1996), Tim Kurkijian noted, "In his first spring training, Alomar immediately impressed the Padres all-star right fielder Tony Gwynn when he hauled a big bag of baseballs to a back diamond and hit off a tee for an hour—a commitment to hard work that hasn't diminished over the last 11 years."

Instead of worrying about fastballs and breaking pitches right off the bat, you should try working off the tee like Alomar. But don't hit just for the sake of hitting. The last thing you want is to hit 100 balls a day with a bad swing. Concentrate on what you are doing right and wrong with your swing. Eventually, you will perfect your swing, and it won't matter what pitches you're given. Instead of your worrying about the pitcher you'll be facing, he'll be worrying about you.

BATTING PRACTICE

All hitters, whether they're 13 or 30, look forward to their turn at the plate during batting practice. Players shag balls in the field for 15 or 20 teammates just so they, too, can get their cuts at the plate. But batting practice isn't just about the fun and excitement of finally getting to bat. Every time you swing the bat in BP, you should have a purpose in mind. This is the one opportunity you have to work on putting everything together: vision, timing, balance, recoil, stride, rotation, swing, and follow-through. Batting practice gives you the opportunity to work with a pitcher and with fielders, to ensure that at game time you are bringing a finished product to your at-bat.

Hitting with a purpose doesn't require a whole lot of thought. It just means that you pay attention to what you're doing. Instead of going up and whacking every pitch as far as you can, you go up and make decisions. Hit the ball where it's pitched. Look to hit line drives. If every ball you hit is sailing down the

You have to repeat the movements to establish the "muscle memory." That is, you have to train your muscles to react in the proper way. You can't simply go down to the batting cage, take a hundred whacks at the ball, and pat yourself on the back, thinking, "I've done my work for today." Because if you practice incorrectly, you'll be teaching your body bad habits, and you'll have to work doubly hard to correct them when you get older.

— *Dusty Baker*

Ted Williams was notorious for taking hours of batting practice. During the off-season, Williams would often carry a bat around wherever he went.

The drills and batting practice before the game afford us the opportunity to telegraph our "game plan" from the brain to the body in the form of repetitive hitting. If the pitcher is a hard thrower who has tried to pitch me inside, I will consciously work on bringing my hands toward my body so that the head of my bat will cover the inside part of the plate and strike zone.

— Steve Garvey

When I was pitching, I could look at how a guy was standing at the plate and try to throw to the off spot. I can see if you move up in the box, if you crowd the plate. The guy who steps away from the plate will be weak outside. The stance just gives me an idea of where I might throw. I try to get you to bite on your weaknesses.

*— Bill Castro
Milwaukee Brewers
bullpen coach and
major league pitcher for
10 years*

left-field line, you're not working on anything. The key to having quality batting practice is concentrating on every pitch just as you would if you were up at the plate during a game.

Create situations for yourself. Assuming you're given nine swings, get yourself swinging by starting off with a hit-and-run. This will get you to put the bat on the ball and put it on the ground somewhere. Hit the next two balls to the opposite field so you can see the ball a long way and time your swing. On the fourth swing, move the runner on second base to third by hitting the ball to the right side of the shortstop. Then hit the next good pitch in the air to the outfield to score the runner from third base. On the last four pitches, swing away. *This does not mean you should try to kill the last four pitches.* Drive the ball where it's pitched. Always swing the bat with authority, but do it in a controlled and relaxed manner.

Batting practice can also come in handy when you're looking to repair your swing. Because you are hitting a bunch of pitches all at once, batting practice is a good place to look for problematic patterns. For example, if you're pulling everything foul, maybe you're pulling your front shoulder off the ball too early. If everything you hit goes to the opposite field, the barrel of your bat could be dragging and you need to use your top hand more. A lot of fly balls could indicate you're uppercutting, whereas weakly hit balls might mean you're hitting off your front foot. By distinguishing exactly what your fault is, you can isolate that region and begin to work on correcting it. If you're still not sure, it's time to go back to the tee and soft toss again.

PRE-GAME BATTING PRACTICE

It's imperative to get some practice swings in before each game to make sure you're ready to perform. It gets you loose and acts as one final checkpoint for proper mechanics. Often at the high school, American Legion, collegiate, and professional levels, teams take live batting practice during their pre-game warmups. If you're given this opportunity, use it to spray solid line drives around the field. It won't help you in the least if you try to launch the balls over the fence. Just hit the ball hard and hit it where it's pitched.

Exercise good balance and timing. On your final hit, practice running the bases. Pay attention to where the next batter is hitting the ball and run the bases exactly as you would if it were a game situation.

If your team doesn't take batting practice before the game, try to meet early with a friend or teammate and take some swings on your own. It only takes about 10 or 15 minutes and can be of great assistance come game time. At the very least, do some soft toss drills, hit off a tee, or dry swing. Going into an at-bat cold is extremely difficult and can have a negative effect on a hitter's success.

BATTING DRILLS

We have already mentioned that hitting off a tee and doing soft toss are two of the best drills to practice form and proper mechanics. However, there are several variations to both that can help you isolate and work on specific swing problems.

If you've found that your swing has an uppercut to it, this first drill is a good one for you. Set up two tees, one about four to six inches higher then the other, with a ball on each. The high one should be in the back about a foot behind the front tee. Now try to hit the ball off the front tee without disturbing the ball on the back tee.

If you have an inside-out swing, you need to work on emphasizing your top hand. A good way to do this is to remove the bottom hand from the bat entirely. Get down on one knee and choke way up with the top hand (Figures 7 and 8). Have someone soft-toss the ball to you and swing the bat one-handed. The burden of getting the barrel of the bat on the ball is now entirely on your top hand. If your bottom hand is the one having trouble, simply switch knees, let go with the top hand, and choke up with the bottom hand.

To help your bat speed and exercise your peripheral vision, have your partner soft-toss from the catcher's position. The flight of the ball will now be

D on't waste a single swing of batting practice. It isn't a time for fooling around; it is a time for practice, practice, and more practice. Learn to use the bat skillfully while you are taking batting practice. Play mental games, set up different situations, and try to execute what you think the situation would require.

— Charley Lau

These drills will isolate the top and bottom hand in your swing. First work on the top hand. Kneel down on your front leg and choke up about a third of the way on the bat. Work on firing the barrel of the bat at the ball.

Figures 9 and 10: Repeat the same drill now using only the bottom hand. This exercise is a little more difficult because your bottom hand is usually weaker than the top hand. Choke up a little higher, and snap the barrel at the ball. Both of these drills work on improving your wrist action. Figures 11 and 12: Another form of a soft toss is to have the feeder set up behind you. This drill promotes peripheral vision and improves bat speed. Look straight down at home plate. Once you see the ball come into your field of vision, attack the ball. This drill is not easy and takes a lot of practice. Don't become concerned with how well you hit the ball; just work on catching up to the ball with the barrel.

going the opposite way from a pitch. As you're waiting to hit, look directly down at home plate. Once you see the ball pass the plate, explode to the ball to make contact. It will feel like you're trying to catch up to the ball. Don't worry about how well you hit it; just make contact. This is purely a speed and peripheral vision exercise. It's a difficult one, however, so it may take a few rounds before you make contact.

Pepper is always a good game for your hand-eye coordination. It will also help you if you tend to drop your back shoulder when you swing. Because it's played at a short distance, it requires place hitting. It forces you to watch the ball into the bat, and it makes you aim for the top half of the ball to keep it out of the air.

WEIGHT TRAINING

Baseball training includes more than just working on swing mechanics. You have to train your entire body as well. Look at it as upgrading the tools you've been given. Unfortunately, getting that upgrade requires long-term dedication. Just as learning to hit is a long slow process, so is getting in shape and building muscle. It takes a lot of hard work and dedication, but it pays off in the long run. Muscular training and body conditioning can enhance your skills in a number of crucial areas:

- power—the ability of the muscles to contract repeatedly and explosively

- quickness—the ability to accelerate, to move fast from a standing start

- flexibility—the ability of a joint to twist and turn through a full range of movement

- balance—the stability achieved through the equality of opposing forces

- endurance—the ability to withstand stress and stay strong

Strength and conditioning has become very important in the game of baseball, and there's a demand for it, especially because the players have seen the benefits of staying in shape. The longer you don't work out and get out of shape, the longer it takes to get back in shape. Look at a guy like John Kruk. He always joked about being a ballplayer, not an athlete, and it ended up costing him a few years off his career. The guy was a great hitter, but his body broke down. When you say a guy lost a few years off his career in the big leagues, that translates into millions of dollars.

— Tim Bishop strength and conditioning coach for the Baltimore Orioles

13

In 1988, Jose Canseco became the first player in baseball history to ever hit 40 home runs and steal 40 bases in the same season. His speed and power epitomizes the prototypical player of the 1990s.

The Growth of Gonzalez

When Juan Gonzalez was signed in 1986 as a 17-year-old outfielder from Puerto Rico he weighed 175 pounds. During his first professional season in the Gulf Coast League, he hit .240 with no home runs. In 1988, he struggled in the Florida State League, batting .256 with only eight home runs. In 1989, he began to experience the benefits of weight training. He put on 40 pounds of muscle to bring his weight to 215 pounds. In 1992, with the Texas Rangers, he led the American League in home runs with 43, and did it again in 1993, when he slugged 46. Gonzalez is an excellent example of a player who maximized his potential by working hard in the weight room.

Weight training has played a major role in my career. It's allowed me to stay strong throughout the entire season. I do a lot of work in the off-season with weights to build strength and to rehabilitate injuries. During the season, it's more of a maintenance program. Getting stronger has made me more of a well-rounded player, especially at the plate.

— Lenny Dykstra

Adding size, strength, and durability doesn't make a ballplayer, but it can certainly improve the ability of someone who already has ballplaying skills. The emphasis on building strength and muscle has spread throughout every major league organization and is also practiced at collegiate and high school levels. In the mid-1980s, only a few major league organizations had strength and conditioning coaches. Today, every big league team has one and many also carry assistants.

If you're a young player, you should look to build up your entire body, not just a few areas. Once your whole body is strong, you can concentrate on your "baseball muscles." These would be the legs, the trunk, your upper back, your forearms, triceps, and hands. Your chest and biceps also need to be developed, but not too much because excessive buildup in these areas can make you stiff at the plate.

When you're building strength in your entire body, you don't have to work all of it every workout. Break each muscle region down into groups, and do multiple exercises for each area. Isolating specific body parts is beneficial for two reasons:

1. It allows you to work that specific region harder. Concentrating on one area gives that muscle group the special attention it needs to maximize its development. When you work all areas in one session, you may not be spending enough time with certain areas.

2. Working some regions one day and others the next allows time for muscles to rest and recuperate. When you lift weights, you're breaking down muscles and muscle tissue. Those muscles need time to rebuild themselves before they are worked again. If you don't work them alternately, you can burn out and your progress in the weight room will begin to suffer.

A good sample of the grouping you can do is to do chest and legs one day, shoulders and triceps the next day, and back and biceps the third day. You can work abdominals and forearms at the end of every day. After a few weeks, switch up the pairs to give yourself a little variety. How often you work out should be dictated by your body. Some athletes like to work out for three days and then take a day off, others go only two with a day off, and still others will work out for five days during the week and take the weekend off. Try a few routines and see how your body responds. For example, if you go three days but find your body doesn't have enough strength to get a good workout on the third day, reduce it to two.

Once you've developed a strong, muscular frame, you can begin to use drills that will isolate the muscles most important to hitting. Hand, wrist, and forearm strength are vital to a player's power and bat speed at the plate. Upper and lower back muscles play a role in the swing. Finally, the trunk and legs, an area overlooked by many young players, need to be worked on because they are a tremendous source of power.

When you work the muscles, you should incorporate three to five different exercises for each body part. How many sets you do will vary depending on the amount of weight and the number of repetitions.

The off-season is the best time to build and condition your body to elevate your game to a higher level. Pre-season and regular season is too late. At this point your time should be devoted to working on fundamentals and improving your skills in the field. A rigorous muscle workout while you're also doing baseball workouts can cause muscle fatigue, tightness, and soreness. It's fine to maintain during the season, but don't try to add mass.

Maintaining the strength you've built up can be very difficult during the season. You obviously want to reserve your energy for the field, not the weight room. And the higher your level of play, the more time the game takes up. A professional ballplayer's work day can last up to eight hours between the white lines. When you add travel to those numbers, it can become both mentally and physically grueling. Spending a lot of time hitting the weights after a game is almost impossible.

There are ways to do it, however. Instead of working out almost every day, curtail your sessions to a few times a week. Also, rather than doing the one- to two-hour sessions that you did in the off-season, work out for just half an hour. The key to this shortened workout is to raise the intensity level. Push heavier weights fewer times.

Cardiovascular training keeps the body fit and agile. Because there's a lot of standing around during a game, training off the field is necessary to stay in shape and keep extra weight off. Distance running is a good method of improving endurance, as are bicycling, swimming, and other aerobic activities.

Getting your wind and legs into game shape during the off-season should consist of a lot of short sprints and agility exercises. Running in baseball, whether it's in the field, on the basepaths, or out of the batter's box, requires quick explosive movements. Full-court basketball and racquetball are two sports that are excellent conditioning for baseball players.

Cross-training can only help a young athlete. It works different muscle groups and keeps weight down. Competing in a lot of different sports teaches younger players how to train and how to stay in a routine. So play as many sports as you want, but once you decide that baseball is the one you want to focus on, then develop your specific weight training program.

During the off-season, we like to address all aspects of conditioning—flexibility, strength, speed, power, endurance, and agility. We do a lot of cross-training to make the baseball player a better overall athlete.

—B.J. Baker
strength and conditioning
coach for the
Boston Red Sox

Before you begin any weight program, however, be sure you get advice from a professional or a coach. Too much weight or incorrectly performed exercises can cause irreparable damage. When training with heavy weights, especially free weights, it's very easy to put too much strain on a muscle. Even the best athletes in the world have professional coaches who guide and advise them through their training.

AVOIDING INJURY

On September 6, 1995, Baltimore Orioles shortstop Cal Ripken surpassed the record set by Yankee great Lou Gehrig when he played in his 2,131st straight game. Gehrig's streak of 2,130 games, amazing in itself, was considered unbeatable until Ripken defied logic by extending the all-time mark.

The fact that these ballplayers carried such incredible streaks isn't coincidence. Both Ripken and Gehrig had a relentless desire to play every day, and both were dedicated to getting in shape mentally and physically. They were just as intense working out after the game as they were before and during it. Their mental and physical training was extraordinarily vigorous and concentrated. According to Tim Bishop, the Orioles' strength and conditioning coach, "Cal trains as hard as anyone I've ever seen. He also exhibits incredible mental toughness, and the combination of the two makes him an extraordinary athlete. He has the ability to block out any pain or nagging injuries that would force the average player out of the lineup for a couple of games. He gets his treatment, and then once it's game time, he forgets about what's bothering him and is totally focused on the game."

Dedication to a training program and concern and care for your body will help you turn out performances like Ripken and Gehrig. You can have all the talent in the world, but if you're injured, you're not much use to your team. You want to do everything you can to stay healthy, and staying in shape is a large part of that. There are no guarantees, but if you take good care of your body, you'll be less likely to have an injury. Never discount the importance of constancy.

Legs are so very important to the hitter. If you took the legs competely out of the swing, the hitter might hit the ball to the outfield if he's lucky. The legs are the foundation of your swing. If you have a weak lower body, it's going to affect your power all the way up.

— Tim Bishop

A season's bats uses 40,000 Northern white ash trees.

Staying physically fit can help decrease the chance of injury. Hall of Famer Lou Gehrig was one of the strongest men in baseball during his time. Gehrig played in 2,130 straight games, and never missed a day's work due to injury.

Becoming More Flexible

Flexibility is the range of motion throughout which a joint can move. The best way to develop a joint's range of motion is to stretch the surrounding muscles.

Developing flexibility serves several purposes for an aspiring batter. First, it prevents injuries. Secondly, it enables you to exert strength over a greater range of motion. Finally, stretching the muscles relieves general soreness.

Here are five guidelines for safe and effective stretches, as described by Matt Brzycki, coordinator of strength and conditioning programs at Princeton University. Remember, this work should be done on a daily basis.

- Relax during your stretching to allow a greater range of motion. Inhale and exhale without holding your breath.
- Each stretch should be pain-free. Pain indicates that you may be exceeding your limits which could results in a muscle strain or pull.
- Stretch under control without bobbing or bouncing. Any type of jerking movements can promote tissue damage.
- Hold each stretch for 30–60 seconds. Increase the duration of your stretch as your flexibility progresses.
- Attempt to stretch a little farther each time. Although you don't want to go too far, you have to push it a little to improve.

Brzycki recommends several flexibility exercises: 1) neck forward, backward, and to the side, 2) scratch back, 3) handcuffs, 4) standing calf, 5) V-sit, 6) butterfly, 7) spinal twist, 8) quad stretch, 9) knee pull. The stretching program may be individualized to meet personal preferences.

1 Neck Forward, Backward, and to the Side
Interlock the fingers behind the head and slowly pull the chin to the chest. Place the hands underneath the chin and slowly push the head backward. Place the right hand on the left side of the head and slowly pull the head to the right shoulder. Repeat the stretch for the right side of the neck.

2 Scratch Back
Place the left hand on the upper part of the back (behind head), grab the left elbow with the right hand and slowly pull the upper torso to the right. Repeat the stretch for the right side of the body.

3 Handcuffs
Place the hands behind the back, interlock the fingers and slowly lift the hands up as high as possible.

4 Standing Calf
While standing upright, step forward with the right foot. Bend the right leg at the knee but keep the left leg straight and the left foot flat on the ground. Repeat the stretch for the right leg.

5 V-Sit
Straighten the legs, spread them apart as far as possible and point the toes upward. Slowly reach forward as far as possible without bending the legs.

6 Butterfly
Place the soles of the feet together, draw the heels as close to the buttocks as possible and place the elbows on the insides of the knees. Bend the torso forward while slowly pushing down with the elbows against the knees.

7 Spinal Twist
Keep the right leg straight, place the left foot on the outside of the right knee, place the right elbow against the outside of the left knee and look to the left as far as possible. Repeat the stretch for the other side of the body.

8 Quad Stretch
Lay on the right side, grab the left instep with the left hand and pull the heel toward the buttocks. Repeat the stretch for the right side of the body.

9 Knee Pull
Lay flat on your back on the ground with the legs extended. Grasp the left leg behind the knee and pull it toward the chest. Keep the right leg straight and the toes pointed upward. Repeat the stretch for the right side of the body.

Barry Bonds has won three National League Most Valuable Player awards. In the process, he became the only NL player ever to hit 40 home runs and steal 40 bases in a season in 1996, and is also one of four players to compile 300 home runs and 300 stolen bases in their career. He is joined by Willie Mays, Andre Dawson, and his father, Bobby Bonds.

I never worried about the fastball.
They couldn't throw it past me. None of them.

— Hank Aaron

- Cal Ripken is known for his longevity, his good fielding and his power hitting. Speed, however, is not one of Cal's most impressive traits. In 1989, Ripken set a major league record for the most at-bats in a season (646) without hitting a triple.

- The 1996 Baltimore Orioles set an all-time record by having seven players hit 20 or more home runs.

- The New York Yankees set an all-time record for most home runs in a season against one club when they pounded 48 homers off the Kansas City Athletics in 1956.

- Joel Youngblood is the only major leaguer to ever collect hits for two different teams on the same day. On August 4, 1982 Youngblood played for the New York Mets in an afternoon game against Chicago and managed a two-run single off Cubs starter Ferguson Jenkins. Youngblood was then traded to the Montreal Expos who were playing a night game in Philadelphia against the Phillies. Youngblood left Chicago and traveled to Philadelphia in time to appear for the Expos and get a single off Phillies starting pitcher Steve Carlton. So Youngblood played for two teams in two cities in two time zones and hit safely in each game.

- During an April, 1953 game against the Washington Senators in Griffith Stadium Mickey Mantle hit the longest measured home run in baseball history—565 feet! The pitcher was Chuck Stobbs.

- On April 15, 1994 Fred McGriff, Terry Pendleton, and Tony Tarasco hit back-to-back-to-back home runs in the first inning. Three days later, McGriff accomplished the same feat in the opening frame, this time teaming with Ryan Klesko and David Justice.

- Joe DiMaggio may have been a little hotter with the stick than you think during his record 56-game hitting streak. During that span, he rapped out 91 hits including 15 homers and 55 RBIs for a scalding .408 batting average.

- Reggie Jackson not only tied a record by hitting three home runs in a World Series game. He hit them in three consecutive at-bats on three consecutive pitches.

a history of slugging in baseball

1900s to 1920s — Dead Ball Era

1911
Outfield fences are added to many ballparks. This allows outfielders to move in because the fence will stop the ball. It also paves the way for home run hitters.

1912
Ty Cobb hits .420.

Frank "Home Run" Baker leads the league with 10 home runs.

1919
The end of World War I sparks a burst of interest in baseball, and fans flood the parks in record numbers.

Babe Ruth breaks home run record of 24 by hitting 29.

1920
Babe Ruth is sold by the Red Sox to the Yankees for a record amount of money. That year he shatters the home run record with 54. He will lead the Yanks to seven World Series appearances (they win four). The Red Sox have never won a World Series since Ruth left.

Ray Chapman dies after being beaned in the head by Carl Mays.

Average major leaguer hits .290. Total home runs for year: 937.

1921
Owners rule that the game will be played with a new white ball at all times. Any ball that became too dark or scuffed would be replaced.

Spitball is banned.

1922
George Sisler hits .420.

1924
Rogers Hornsby hits .424, the highest average ever in the twentieth century.

1925

Ty Cobb announces that he is going to hit home runs to prove he is a place hitter by choice. In his first game, he hits three home runs, two singles, and a double. The next day he singles and hits two more dingers. Satisfied, he returns to slapping the ball past infielders.

1927

Ruth hits 60 home runs as New York Yankees' Murderers Row rules the game.

1930

Ruth (49) and Lou Gehrig (41) combine to hit 90 home runs. Hack Wilson clouts 46 home runs for the Chicago Cubs and drives in 190 runs, an all-time record.

1933

Jimmie Foxx wins the Triple Crown: .356 BA, 45 HRs, and 163 RBIs.

1936

Joe DiMaggio debuts as a Yankee.

1939

Ted Williams arrives in the major leagues.

1941

World War II takes its toll on offensive baseball. Major league batting average drops from .278 during the 1930s to .260 in the 1940s.

Ted Williams hits .406. It's the last time a player hits over .400. Joe DiMaggio sets record with 56-game hitting streak.

1947

Ted Williams wins the Triple-Crown for the second time, and for the second time he is not chosen as the American League's Most Valuable Player.

1950

Major league batting averages continue to slip, but for the first time, over 2,000 home runs are hit in a single season.

1959

All professional fields built after June 1, 1958 must have a minimum distance of 325 feet down the lines and 400 feet to center-field.

1960s and 1970s

Stadiums expand and Astroturf is introduced, increasing the importance of speed and contact hitting.

1961

New York Yankee Roger Maris socks 61 homers. Mickey Mantle hits 54 out of the yard making them the only teammates to ever hit more than 50 home runs in the same season.

1962

National League expands to 10 teams as the New York Mets and Houston Colt 45s join the league. The California Angels join the American League.

Maury Wills breaks Ty Cobb's single-season stolen base record by swiping 104.

1963

Strike zone is expanded from the top of the shoulder to the bottom of the knee. This has an immediate impact as the average major league hitter bats only .246.

1968

The year of the pitcher. Carl Yastrzemski wins the American League batting crown with a .301 average. Bob Gibson posts a 1.12 earned run average in the National League.

1969

In an effort to help hitters, the mound is lowered from 15 inches to 10 inches above the rest of the playing field.

1975

American League adopts the designated hitter as a permanent official rule.

1976

The Cincinnati Reds win their second straight World Series title. Led by Pete Rose, Joe Morgan, Johnny Bench, and Tony Perez the "Big Red Machine" dominates the National League in the mid-1970s.

1977

Toronto and Seattle join the American League.

1980s and 1990s

Players become bigger and stronger than ever through weight training programs. Diluted pitching, due to expansion and newly built, hitter-friendly ballparks combine to put power in offensive baseball.

1980

George Brett hits .390, the closest anyone has come to .400. Brett, a student of Charley Lau's weight shift system, displays rotational style as well.

1982

Rollie Fingers becomes the first player in major league baseball history to collect 300 saves. Gaylord Perry is ejected from a game for throwing a spitball. Dave Kingman of the New York Mets leads the National League with 37 home runs, but has the lowest batting average (.204) by a first baseman since 1901.

1985

Pete Rose becomes the all-time hits leader by breaking Ty Cobb's career record of 4,191. New York Yankee Don Mattingly drives in 145 runs. Wade Boggs racks up 240 hits, the most by any player since 1930.

1986

Mike Schmidt wins his third MVP Award.

1988

Wrigley Field becomes the final stadium to fall victim to night baseball. Tony Gwynn wins the National League batting title with a .313 average, the lowest mark in National League history. A hobbled Kirk Gibson wins Game 1 of the World Series with a dramatic, pinch-hit two-run home run in the bottom of the ninth inning.

1990

Chicago White Sox reliever Bobby Thigpen sets the major league record with 54 saves.

1993

Batting average for major league hitters is .264. Season home run total reaches 4,030. Florida Marlins and Colorado Rockies join the National League through expansion.

1994

The players' strike halts Tony Gwynn's bid to hit .400—he finishes shortened season at .394.

1995

Mark McGwire amasses the greatest home run ratio ever, hitting 39 home runs in just 317 at-bats. Albert Belle hits 50 home runs and 52 doubles. Tony Gwynn (.368) wins his sixth batting title.

1996

The year of the home run. A record 4,962 homers are hit with several offensive records falling in the process: 27 players hit 40 or more home runs (previous record was 8), 43 players hit 30 or more home runs (previous record was 28), 50 players drive in 100 or more runs (previous record was 32), and the Orioles break the club record for homers, socking 257.

Barry Bonds joins his father, Bobby Bonds, Andre Dawson, and Willie Mays as the only four players in major league history to hit 300 home runs and steal 300 bases.

individual lifetime batting records

Highest Career Batting Average

	Dates	Player	Avg.
1.	1905–28	Ty Cobb	.367
2.	1915–37	Rogers Hornsby	.358
3.	1908–20	Joe Jackson	.356
4.	1888–1903	Ed Delehanty	.346
5.	1907–28	Tris Speaker	.345
6.	1888–1901	Billy Hamilton	.344
7.	1939–60	Ted Williams	.344
8.	1892–1910	Willie Keeler	.343
9.	1879–1904	Dan Brouthers	.342
10.	1914–35	Babe Ruth	.342
11.	1914–32	Harry Heilmann	.342
12.	1882–94	Pete Browning	.341
13.	1923–36	Bill Terry	.341
14.	1915–30	George Sisler	.340
15.	1923–39	Lou Gehrig	.340
16.	1890–1905	Jesse Burkett	.339
17.	1896–1915	Nap Lajoie	.338
18.	1982–	Tony Gwynn	.337

Most Career Hits

	Dates	Player	Hits
1.	1963–86	Pete Rose	4256
2.	1905–28	Ty Cobb	4191
3.	1954–76	Hank Aaron	3771
4.	1941–63	Stan Musial	3630
5.	1907–28	Tris Speaker	3514
6.	1961–83	Carl Yastrzemski	3419
7.	1897–1917	Honus Wagner	3418
8.	1906–30	Eddie Collins	3313
9.	1951–73	Willie Mays	3283
10.	1896–1915	Nap Lajoie	3244
11.	1977–	Eddie Murray	3218
12.	1973–93	George Brett	3154
13.	1926–45	Paul Waner	3152
14.	1974–93	Robin Yount	3142
15.	1973–95	Dave Winfield	3110
16.	1967–85	Rod Carew	3053
17.	1961–79	Lou Brock	3023
18.	1978–	Paul Molitor	3014
19.	1953–74	Al Kaline	3007
20.	1876–1897	Cap Anson	3000
21.	1955–72	Roberto Clemente	3000

Most Career Home Runs

	Dates	Player	HRs
1.	1954–76	Hank Aaron	755
2.	1914–35	Babe Ruth	714
3.	1951–73	Willie Mays	660
4.	1956–76	Frank Robinson	586
5.	1954–75	Harmon Killebrew	573
6.	1967–87	Reggie Jackson	563
7.	1972–89	Mike Schmidt	548
8.	1951–68	Mickey Mantle	536
9.	1925–45	Jimmie Foxx	534
10.	1939–60	Ted Williams	521
11.	1959–80	Willie McCovey	521
12.	1953–71	Ernie Banks	512
13.	1952–68	Eddie Mathews	512
14.	1926–47	Mel Ott	511
15.	1977–	Eddie Murray	501

Most Career Runs Batted In

	Dates	Player	RBIs
1.	1954–76	Hank Aaron	2297
2.	1914–35	Babe Ruth	2211
3.	1923–39	Lou Gehrig	1990
4.	1905–28	Ty Cobb	1961
5.	1941–63	Stan Musial	1951
6.	1925–45	Jimmie Foxx	1921
7.	1951–73	Willie Mays	1903
8.	1977–	Eddie Murray	1899
9.	1926–47	Mel Ott	1861
10.	1961–83	Carl Yastrzemski	1844
11.	1939–60	Ted Williams	1839
12.	1973–95	Dave Winfield	1833
13.	1924–44	Al Simmons	1827
14.	1956–76	Frank Robinson	1812
15.	1897–1917	Honus Wagner	1732
16.	1876–97	Cap Anson	1715
17.	1967–87	Reggie Jackson	1702

Most Career Extra Base Hits

	Dates	Player	Hits
1.	1954–76	Hank Aaron	1477
2.	1941–63	Stan Musial	1377
3.	1914–35	Babe Ruth	1356
4.	1951–73	Willie Mays	1323
5.	1923–39	Lou Gehrig	1190
6.	1956–71	Frank Robinson	1186
7.	1961–83	Carl Yastrzemski	1157
8.	1905–28	Ty Cobb	1139
9.	1907–28	Tris Speaker	1132
10.	1973–93	George Brett	1119
11.	1925–45	Jimmie Foxx	1117
12.	1939–60	Ted Williams	1117
13.	1973–95	Dave Winfield	1093
14.	1977–	Eddie Murray	1089
15.	1926–47	Reggie Jackson	1075
16.	1926–47	Mel Ott	1071
17.	1963–86	Pete Rose	1041
18.	1976–96	Andre Dawson	1039
19.	1972–89	Mike Schmidt	1015

Most Career Pinch Hits

	Dates	Player	Hits
1.	1962–82	Manny Mota	150
2.	1949–67	Smoky Burgess	145
3.	1973–89	Greg Gross	143
4.	1973–84	Jose Morales	123
5.	1954–66	Jerry Lynch	116
6.	1923–37	Red Lucas	114
7.	1971–85	Steve Braun	113
8.	1969–83	Terry Crowley	108
9.	1975–92	Denny Walling	108
10.	1963–75	Gates Brown	107

Most Career Strikeouts

	Dates	Player	Ks
1.	1967–87	Reggie Jackson	2597
2.	1962–82	Willie Stargell	1936
3.	1972–89	Mike Schmidt	1883
4.	1964–86	Tony Perez	1867
5.	1971–86	Dave Kingman	1816
6.	1968–81	Bobby Bonds	1757
7.	1976–83	Dale Murphy	1748
8.	1961–79	Lou Brock	1730
9.	1951–68	Mickey Mantle	1710
10.	1954–75	Harmon Killebrew	1699
11.	1972–91	Dwight Evans	1697
12.	1973–95	Dave Winfield	1686
13.	1965–82	Lee May	1570
14.	1963–77	Dick Allen	1556
15.	1959–80	Willie McCovey	1550
16.	1973–91	Dave Parker	1537
17.	1956–76	Frank Robinson	1532
18.	1977–95	Lance Parrish	1527
19.	1951–73	Willie Mays	1526
20.	1966–84	Rick Monday	1513

Most Career Stolen Bases

	Dates	Player	SBs
1.	1979–	Rickey Henderson	1186
2.	1961–79	Lou Brock	938
3.	1905–28	Ty Cobb	892
4.	1979–	Tim Raines	787
5.	1985–	Vince Coleman	752
6.	1906–30	Eddie Collins	743
7.	1910–29	Max Carey	738
8.	1897–1917	Honus Wagner	703
9.	1963–84	Joe Morgan	689
10.	1976–94	Willie Wilson	668

individual batting records

Batting Average

	Dates	Player	Avg.
1.	1924	Rogers Hornsby	.424
2.	1901	Nap Lajoie	.422
3.	1922	George Sisler	.420
4.	1911	Ty Cobb	.411
5.	1912	Ty Cobb	.410
6.	1911	Joe Jackson	.408
7.	1920	George Sisler	.407
8.	1941	Ted Williams	.406

Hits

	Dates	Player	Hits
1.	1920	George Sisler	257
2.	1930	Bill Terry	254
3.	1929	Lefty O'Doul	254
4.	1925	Al Simmons	253
5.	1930	Chuck Klein	250
6.	1922	Rogers Hornsby	250
7.	1911	Ty Cobb	248
8.	1922	George Sisler	246
9.	1930	Babe Herman	241
10.	1928	Heinie Manush	241
11.	1985	Wade Boggs	240
12.	1977	Rod Carew	239
13.	1927	Paul Waner	237
14.	1937	Joe Medwick	237
15.	1921	Harry Heilmann	237

Extra Base Hits

	Dates	Player	Hits
1.	1921	Babe Ruth	119
2.	1927	Lou Gehrig	117
3.	1930	Chuck Klein	107
4.	1932	Chuck Klein	103
5.	1948	Stan Musial	103
6.	1995	Albert Belle	103
7.	1937	Hank Greenberg	103
8.	1922	Rogers Hornsby	102
9.	1930	Lou Gehrig	100
10.	1932	Jimmie Foxx	100
11.	1920	Babe Ruth	99
12.	1923	Babe Ruth	99
13.	1940	Hank Greenberg	99
14.	1935	Hank Greenberg	98
15.	1927	Babe Ruth	97
16.	1937	Joe Medwick	97
17.	1930	Hack Wilson	97

Most Runs Batted In

	Dates	Player	RBIs
1.	1930	Hack Wilson	190
2.	1931	Lou Gehrig	184
3.	1937	Hank Greenberg	183
4.	1927	Lou Gehrig	175
5.	1938	Jimmie Foxx	175
6.	1930	Lou Gehrig	174
7.	1921	Babe Ruth	171
8.	1930	Chuck Klein	170
9.	1935	Hank Greenberg	170
10.	1932	Jimmie Foxx	169
11.	1937	Joe DiMaggio	167
12.	1934	Lou Gehrig	165
13.	1930	Al Simmons	163
14.	1927	Babe Ruth	163
15.	1933	Jimmie Foxx	163

Strikeouts

	Dates	Player	Ks
1.	1970	Bobby Bonds	189
2.	1969	Bobby Bonds	187
3.	1987	Rob Deer	186
4.	1986	Pete Incaviglia	185
5.	1990	Cecil Fielder	182
6.	1975	Mike Schmidt	180
7.	1986	Rob Deer	179
8.	1991	Rob Deer	175
9.	1986	Jose Canseco	175
10.	1979	Gorman Thomas	175
11.	1963	Dave Nicholson	175
12.	1989	Bo Jackson	172
13.	1986	Jim Presley	172
14.	1968	Reggie Jackson	171
15.	1980	Gorman Thomas	170
16.	1993	Rob Deer	169
17.	1990	Andres Galarraga	169
18.	1984	Juan Samuel	168
19.	1987	Pete Incaviglia	168

Most Home Runs

	Dates	Player	HRs
1.	1961	Roger Maris	61
2.	1927	Babe Ruth	60
3.	1921	Babe Ruth	59
4.	1932	Jimmie Foxx	58
5.	1938	Hank Greenberg	58
6.	1930	Hack Wilson	56
7.	1920	Babe Ruth	54
8.	1928	Babe Ruth	54
9.	1949	Ralph Kiner	54
10.	1961	Mickey Mantle	54
11.	1965	Willie Mays	52
12.	1977	George Foster	52
13.	1956	Mickey Mantle	52
14.	1996	Mark McGwire	52
15.	1947	Ralph Kiner	51
16.	1955	Willie Mays	51
17.	1947	Johnny Mize	51
18.	1990	Cecil Fielder	51
19.	1938	Jimmie Foxx	50
20.	1995	Albert Belle	50
21.	1996	Brady Anderson	50

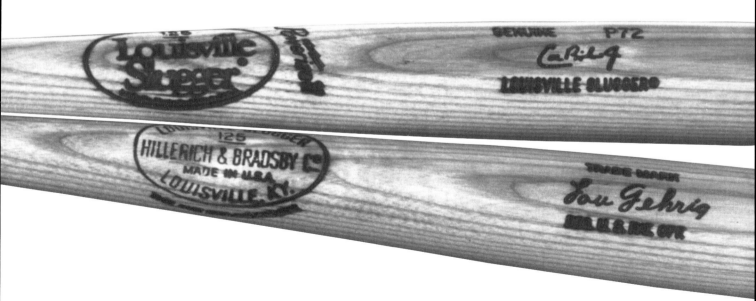

the heart of the game

Located on 8th and Main Street in downtown Louisville's historic district the Louisville Slugger Museum is easy to find. Just look for the world's tallest bat—a Babe Ruth model, number R43—which is painted on the knob that reaches several stories high.

The museum is a tribute to baseball's greatest hits and hitters. Upon entering, visitors are treated to a film, "The Heart of the Game," which relives some the greatest hits in baseball and gives hitting tips and anecdotes from top players such as Tony Gwynn and Johnny Bench. The main attractions include a plant tour, which demonstrates the wood bat production process that transforms a bulky block of wood into a meticulously crafted Louisville Slugger; a replica of Bud Hillerich's original workshop, and a recreation of what it's like to face big league pitchers such as Roger Clemens and Dwight Gooden.

FOR MORE INFORMATION
Groups, call (502) 588-7227
Other, call (502) 588-7228
or fax (502) 585-1179

HOURS: 9 A.M. – 5 P.M. (EST)
Monday – Saturday
Closed Sundays and Holidays

LOUISVILLE SLUGGER MUSEUM
800 West Main Street
Louisville, Kentucky 40202
http//:www.slugger.com/museum

HITTING GLOSSARY

aluminum bat
A metal bat used by amateur players at every level, but not in professional baseball where it is prohibited. The bats first became popular in the early 1970s. Scientific studies have proven that balls hit with aluminum bats travel farther and faster than those hit with wooden bats.

athletic position
A "stance" which athletes from a variety of different sports use as a solid base or foundation. The feet are shoulder-width apart, knees flexed, and there is a slight bend at the waist. Think of a guard playing defense in basketball, a goalie in soccer, or a tennis player preparing to receive a serve.

barrel
The top part of the bat, where the diameter is greatest. You want to hit the ball with the barrel of the bat.

base on balls
Also known as a *walk*, a base on balls is awarded to a batter who takes four pitches outside the strike zone without swinging.

baseball sense
An instinct for making the right move on the baseball diamond. Baseball sense is generally not something that can be taught to a player. Instead, it is accumulated by playing many games.

bat speed
The velocity with which a hitter swings the bat. The greater the bat speed the farther the ball will travel when hit.

batter's box
A six-foot by four-foot rectangular area, marked with white lime or paint, adjacent to home plate where the batter stands as he waits for the pitch to be thrown. There is a batter's box for right-handed hitters and a batter's box for left-handed hitters. Hitters must keep both feet inside the box while waiting for the pitch and while hitting the ball.

batting average
A statistic that measures a player's ability as a hitter. It is expressed in thousandths and is calculated by dividing the number of hits by the number of at-bats. In professional baseball, the standard of excellence is a batting average of .300, which means the player got 3 hits in 10 at-bats. Hitting a baseball is so difficult that succeeding 3 out of 10 times means you are an excellent batsman.

batting practice
The period before each game when players from both teams are given an opportunity to practice their hitting. The idea is for each hitter to loosen his muscles, work on his timing, and adjust to the surroundings of the ballpark. Batting practice is called *BP* for short.

choking up
The act of gripping the bat above the knob at the end of the handle. Batters choke up to gain greater control of the bat.

clean-up hitter
The name for the fourth hitter in the batting order. This position is always occupied by one of the best hitters in the lineup. It is assumed that this batter has the ability to *clean* the bases of runners with his hits. One of the most famous clean-up hitters in history was Lou Gehrig, who batted directly behind Babe Ruth in the lineup. Those runners the Babe didn't drive home were cleaned up by Gehrig.

clutch hitter   A batter known for his ability to get a hit with runners on base and in key situations. Clutch hitters come through when it counts.

Dead Ball Era   The time before 1920, when the game was played with a much less lively ball—a *dead ball*—and bunting, baserunning, and tactical play were emphasized. The *dead ball* era came to an end when Babe Ruth popularized the home run. Fans preferred the home run to lower-scoring tactical games.

drag bunt   A surprise move where the batter bunts the ball away from the pitcher in an attempt to get a hit. This is different from a *sacrifice bunt* where the batter's main purpose is to advance a runner.

follow-through   The continuation of the swing by the batter after the ball has been hit or missed. The follow-through is essential: To gain maximum hitting power you must hit *through* the ball.

grip   The manner in which the batter holds the bat. Some batters grip the bat down near the end at the handle, others choke up. Ty Cobb, one of the greatest hitters of all time, gripped the bat with a space between his hands for greater control.

guess hitter   A batter who tries to anticipate which type of pitch is coming. Hitters who guess what pitch a pitcher is going to throw do so based upon the game situation (count, score, men on base, etc.). They also take into account their past experience against the pitcher and any pitching pattern they have observed during the game.

hit-and-run   A play run by the team at bat where the runner on first base takes off for second as soon as the pitcher releases the ball. The batter then tries to hit the ball into the spot vacated by the shortstop or second baseman, who is covering second in an attempt to retire the runner. The play is high risk, high reward. If the batter misses the ball, the runner will most likely be thrown out at second; if the batter hits a line drive to an infielder, the runner will be doubled off first. But if the batter is successful at hitting the ball through the infield, the runner will probably make it to third. Even if the defensive players field a ground ball they cannot make a double play because the baserunner is already in motion.

home run   A four-base hit where the ball is driven out of the playing area in fair territory. A four-base hit that does not leave the playing area is called an *inside-the-park home run*. Home runs are also called *round-trippers*, *circuit clouts*, *bombs*, *dingers, get-outs, taters,* and many other colorful names.

hybrid hitter   A hitter who has the ability to hit for average and power. Mo Vaughn is an example of this type of hitter. A hybrid hitter may also vary between weight shift and rotational hitting.

inside-out swing   A swing when the batter's hands are ahead of the bat barrel as the ball is contacted. Most inside-out swings result in the ball being hit to the opposite field.

launch position   The position the batter is in just before he swings the bat. His front foot is planted on the ground after the stride, and the batter's hands and bat are cocked behind his back shoulder.

leadoff hitter   The first player in the batting order. This position is usually occupied by a good hitter who is also a fast runner. The first batter in an inning is also called a leadoff hitter.

overstriding   A stride when you take too long a step toward the pitcher. This causes the head and upper body to drop, making it hard for the eyes to properly track the ball. Also known as *lunging*.

pepper   A practice drill involving one batter and several fielders. The ball is pitched to the batter who chops the ball on the ground to the fielders. Whoever fields the ball throws it back to the batter again and the sequence is repeated. Players use pepper as a way of loosening up for the game and as a means of improving hand-eye coordination.

power hitter   A player who has the power to hit the ball a long way. A power hitter is a player known for hitting home runs and other extra-base hits consistently.

protecting the plate   The action of a batter who swings at a pitch with the idea of fouling it off. Batters do this with two strikes when a pitch is close enough to swing at but not good enough to hit solidly. They hope to foul off the pitch and get something better to hit on the next pitch.

push bunt   A bunt where the batter tries to *push* the ball past the pitcher while keeping it short of the infielders.

release point   The spot in his delivery where the pitcher lets go of the ball. Smart hitters focus their eyes on the release point to get the best and longest possible look at an incoming pitch.

run-and-hit   An offensive play where the runner takes off with the pitch and the batter swings at the pitch if it is a hittable ball. This play differs from the *hit-and-run* in that the batter has the option of swinging at the pitch or taking it.

run batted in (RBI)   A run that is caused by a particular batter as a result of either a hit, a sacrifice, a hit by pitch, or a walk. When Player A scores from third base on a single by Player B, Player B is credited with a run batted in (RBI).

run scored   When a player reaches home plate without being put out, and before three outs have been recorded, he and his team are credited with a run scored.

sacrifice bunt   A bunt where the batter bunts the ball with the sole purpose of advancing a runner. The hitter is not charged with a time at bat for a sacrifice.

sacrifice fly   A fly ball caught in the field of play that allows a baserunner to score without an error being committed. The batter is credited with a run batted in (RBI) but is not charged with an at-bat.

slash   The act of hitting the ball sharply, often to the opposite field. Also, if the batter bluffs a bunt and then hits away with a chopping, abbreviated swing, that's a slash, too.

slugging percentage   A statistic that measures a player's ability to hit for power with extra-base hits. The number is represented in thousandths and is calculated by dividing at-bats into total bases. Babe Ruth holds the record for the highest single-season slugging percentage with .847 in 1920.

slump   When a batter has an extended period of poor hitting performance he's experiencing a slump.

spray hitter   A batter who hits the ball to all parts of the field but without much power.

spring training   A period of several weeks in duration (February and March) when professional players practice, condition themselves, and play in exhibition games. Spring training camps are located in Florida and Arizona.

squeeze bunt   A bunt that is executed as a runner from third is advancing toward home. The play is often called the *suicide squeeze* because if the batter fails to execute the bunt properly the runner will be "dead" at home plate.

stance   The position assumed by the batter in the batter's box as he awaits the next pitch. When the batter's front foot is farther from home plate than his back foot the stance is *open*; when the front foot is closer to home plate the stance is *closed*; when both feet are parallel to the closest edge of home plate the stance is *square*.

step in the bucket   When the batter's front foot moves away from home plate during the stride he has stepped in the bucket. This often occurs when a batter is fooled by a curve ball that appeared to be coming toward him but instead curved over the plate. It is very difficult to hit the ball successfully if you step in the bucket. Your front foot should go *toward* the pitcher during your stride.

stride   A batter's step toward the pitcher when swinging. Many of the game's greatest hitters, including Joe DiMaggio and Paul Molitor, have had very short strides. A long stride is not recommended.

strike zone   An imaginary area over home plate between the batter's knees and his armpits. Any pitch thrown in this area will be called a strike if it is not swung at.

strikeout   When a batter swings and misses with two strikes or does not swing at a pitch in the strike zone with two strikes, a strikeout is recorded. A strikeout is also recorded if a batter attempts to bunt with two strikes and bunts the ball into foul ground.

sweet spot   The place located on the barrel of the bat that is most ideal for hitting the ball. A ball that hits the sweet spot makes a *sweet* sound and receives the maximum transfer of energy from the bat.

swing   When you move the bat in an attempt to hit a pitched ball you have created a *swing*. It's also called a *cut* or a *rip*.

timing   The ability of a hitter to gauge the speed and path of a pitched ball and then to swing his bat so that it hits the ball.

uppercutting   When you swing the bat on an upward arc you are uppercutting the ball, and you will most likely hit a fly ball.

INDEX

BIBLIOGRAPHY

Alexander, Charles. *Rogers Hornsby—A Biography*, New York: Henry Holt and Company Inc., 1995.

Bak, Richard. *Lou Gehrig—An American Classic*, Dallas, TX: Taylor Publishing Company, 1995.

Baker, Dusty, Mercer, Jeff and Bittinger, Marv. *You Can Teach Hitting*, Indianapolis, IN: Carmel, IN and Msters Press, 1993.

———, *The Baseball Encyclopedia* (Tenth Edition), New York: Macmillan, 1996.

Baylor, Don with Smith, Claire. *Don Baylor—Nothing But the Truth A Baseball Life*, New York, St. Martin's Press, 1989.

Bichard Bak. *Ty Cobb—His Life and Tumultuous Times*, Dallas, TX: Taylor Publishing Company, 1994.

Burns, Ken and Ward, Geoffrey C. *Baseball—An Illustrated History*, New York: Alfred A. Knopf, Inc., 1994.

Carew, Rod with Pace, Frank and Keteyian, Armen. *Rod Carew's Art and Science of Hitting*, New York: Viking Penguin Inc., 1986.

Cohen, Richard. *The World Series*, New York: The Dial Press, 1964.

Creamer, Robert. *Babe—The Legend Comes to Life*, New York: Simon and Schuster, 1974.

Dorfman, H.A. and Kueho, Karl. *The Mental Game of Baseball* (Second Edition), South Bend, IN: Diamond Communications, Inc., 1995.

Feldman, Jay, *Hitting*, New York: Little Simon, 1991.

Frommer, Harvey. *Shoeless Joe Jackson and Ragtime Baseball*, Dallas, TX: Taylor Publishing Company, 1992.

Gillette, Gary. *The Great American Stat Book 1994*, New York: Harper Perennial, 1994.

Gwynn, Tony with Rosenthal, Jim. *Tony Gwynn's Total Baseball Player*, New York: St. Martin's Press, 1992.

Hart, Stan. *Scouting Reports—The Original Reviews of Some of Baseball's Greatest Stars*, New York: 1995.

Kernandez, Keith and Bryan, Mike. *Pure Baseball*, New York: HarperCollins Publishers Inc., 1994.

Lau, Charley and Glossbrenner, Alfred. *The Art of Hitting .300—Revised and Updated by Tony Larussa*, New York: Penguin Books, 1986.

Lau, Charley with Glossbrenner, Alfred. *The Winning Hitter*, New York: Hearst Books, 1984.

Monteleone, John. *Branch Rickey's Little Blue Book*, New York: Macmillan, 1995.

Nemac, David (updated and edited). *Great Baseball Feats, Facts and Firsts*, New York: Penguin Books, 1990.

Nemac, David. *The 20th Century Baseball Chronicle*, Lincolnwood, IL: Publications International, LTD, 1992.

Nemac, David. *The Players of Cooperstown*, Lincolnwood, IL: Publications International, LTD, 1994.

———. *Newton At the Bat—The Science in Sports*, New York: Charles Scribner's Sons, 1984.

Reidenbaugh, Lowell. *The Sporting News Cooperstown—Where Baseball's Legends Live Forever*, St. Louis, MO: The Sporting News Publishing Co., 1983.

Ryan, Nolan and Terre, Joe with Cohen, Joel. *Pitching and Hitting*, Englewood Cliffs, NJ: 1977.

Schmidt, Mike and Ellis, Rob. *The Mike Schmidt Study*, Atlanta, GA: McGriff and Bell, Inc., 1994.

Seaver, Tom with Lowenfish, Lee. *The Art of Pitching*, New York: Hearst Books, 1984.

Seiderman, Arthur and Steven, Schneider. *The Athletic Eye*, New York: Hearst Books, 1983.

———. *The Sporting News Complete Bseball Record Book—1996 Edition*, St. Louis, MO: The Sporting News Publishing Co., 1995.

———. *Sports Illustrated's 1996 Sports Almanac*, New York, Little, Brown and Company, 1996.

Will, George. *Men at Work*. New York: Macmillan Publishing Co., 1990.

Williams, Ted with Underwood, John. *The Science of Hitting*, New York: Simon and Schuster, 1971.

Winfield, Dave with Swenson, Eric.*The Complete Baseball Player*, New York: Avon Books, 1990.

Articles from Louisville Slugger Archives

Allen, Dick. *Hitting*

Bench, Johnny. *Power Hitting*

Carew, Rod. *I Can't Teach You To Hit*

Cobb, Ty. *The Science of Batting*

Fonseca, Lou. *some Real Batting Tips*

Garvey, Steve. *The Inner Game of Hitting*

Hornsby, Rogers. *Hornsby Hitting Hints*

Killebrew, Harmon. *Help Yourself to Better Hitting*

Mantle, Mickey. *Hitting Helps*

Reese, Pee Wee. *My Advice to Young Hitters*

Rose, Pete. *More Hits*

Sisler, George. *How to Hit*

Sisler, George. *How to Raise Your Batting Average*

Snider, Duke. *Let's All Hit*

Speaker, Tris. *Thoughts on Batting*

Williams, Billy. *Determination Plus Practice Equals Better Hitting*

Williams, Ted. *How to Be a Better Hitter*

Yaztrzemski, Carl. *Hitting Styles of the Greats*

O'Doul, Lefty. *How to Bat*

Kiner, Ralph. *Power Hitting and Place Hitting*

Walker, Harry. *So You Want to Hit*

John J. Monteleone is author and editor of several sports books, including *The Baseball Scouting Report* (HarperCollins), *The Encyclopedia of Sports in America* (Scholastic), *Branch Rickey's Little Blue Book—Wit and Strategy from Baseball's Last Wise Man* (Macmillan), *What Makes a Boomerang Come Back—The Science of Sports* (Longmeadow), *The Game and the Glory* (Prentice-Hall), and *A Day in the Life of a Major League Baseball Player* (Troll). He has reported sports and general news for the *New York Times* and *Washington Post*. Mr. Monteleone is a former minor league baseball player and in 1964 *The Sporting News* collegiate All-America baseball team selection at Seton Hall University. He plays in an over-30 baseball league in Montgomery County, PA and lives near Princeton, NJ in Hopewell Township.

Mark Gola is a sports reporter for the *Princeton Packet* newspaper chain, high school and American Legion baseball coach, and hitting clinician; he is currently writing an instructional book on baseball for children. He was a 1994 all-conference and northeast regional All-America selection at Rider University, where he compiled a lifetime .316 batting average. He plays in a Collegiate Baseball of America (CBA) league in Mercer County, NJ and lives near Princeton, NJ in Hopewell Township.